# AIN'T NOTHING LIKE FREEDOM

To my father and mother,
Billy and Leola,
who taught me the power of DIGNITY
and to speak without fear,
and who set the best example, by doing!

And to my son, Coy,
who surprises me every day
with his deep understanding
of the challenges confronting humankind
and their solutions.
By his actions,
Coy will be a part of the solution
and that makes me proud.

Billy, Leola, and Coy
show me the power
that resides within all of us
when we are loved!

# AIN'T NOTHING LIKE FREEDOM

BY

## CYNTHIA McKINNEY

CLARITY PRESS, INC.

ISBN:      0-9853353-1-9
               978-0-9853353-1-1
E-book:  978-0-9860362-1-7

In-house editor:  Diana G. Collier
Cover:  R. Jordan P. Santos
Cover photo: americantechnologies.net
Cartoons: StudioBendib / www.bendib.com

Clarity Press, Inc.
Ste. 469, 3277 Roswell Rd. NE
Atlanta, GA. 30305 , USA
http://www.claritypress.com

# TABLE OF CONTENTS

**FOR THE RECORD**

# FOREWORD

You may only know former Congresswoman Cynthia McKinney as she has been portrayed in the press: as "controversial," "angry," or acting as if she is "above the law." As someone who knows Cynthia and has worked with her, I want to explain how what you have heard is either false, or true in a different way than the media spin claims. If all you know of Green Party 2008 Presidential Candidate Cynthia McKinney is what you've heard from FOX News, Cox Communications, or the Atlanta Journal Constitution, you don't really know her at all.

Sadly, much of what passes as news or political commentary in today's media is little more than an extension of productions like the Jerry Springer or Maury Povich shows onto the political leaders that want social change. The media have become fight promoters, adding to the division of our country on issues that don't matter, when we need to have reasoned, rational discussions to work together to address the issues that do matter.

Is Cynthia McKinney "controversial"? Of course, but not as part of her personality. George Orwell noted that, "In a time of universal deceit, telling the truth is a revolutionary act." When Cynthia speaks truth to power, the corporate controlled media try to make her the issue or to belittle her, without addressing either the facts or what she actually says.

When so few people actually stand up and speak out in Congress on the issues of war, poverty and social justice, she stood out as its conscience. And in their embarrassment, the powers and politicians she challenged and exposed responded by attacking; and those who knew what she says was right but were afraid to bear the political cost of saying it themselves, retreated. In that isolation, she was sometimes be singled out as "controversial."

She refused to shy away from the hard issues, like the wars in Afghanistan and Iraq that were planned long before September 11, 2001 (9/11), or the lies and lack of accountability of those who failed to defend us on 9/11, and then used this tragedy to take us into a nightmare of endless, fruitless and costly wars.

She was the lone non-Gulf state Democratic voice on the House Committee investigating the federal government's lack of response to the devastation of Hurricane Katrina.

She held the only Congressional briefing critical of the 9/11 Commission's flawed conclusions and faulty recommendations, introducing the analysis of scholars, investigators, and former intelligence agents who joined the 9/11 victims' family members in questioning the premises and findings of that official inquiry.

As a member of the House Armed Services Committee, she questioned Secretary of Defense Rumsfeld on malfeasance by military contractors and missing billions in the Pentagon's budget, as well as the reasons for the failure of NORAD air defenses on 9/11--questions that further revelations have legitimized, but that he has to date refused to answer.

As a Congresswoman, McKinney held fast to the principles of accountability and transparency in government, which are the cornerstones of democracy. She called for a full release of thousands of government records still buried on the life and assassination of Dr. Martin Luther King, Jr. and the murder of Hip Hop artist Tupac Shakur.

She consistently tried to get Congress to continue its examination of the intelligence and police agency abuses of the past, under COINTELPRO, CHAOS, GARDEN PLOT and other unconstitutional and illegal programs, aimed primarily at African Americans, Native Americans, other people of color and all those who dissent and organize to address injustice and war. These programs did not end with the revelations of the Senate's Church Committee investigation in the 1970s; they have been renewed and expanded by the Department of Justice, Federal Bureau of Investigation, National Security Agency, Central Intelligence Agency, Pentagon, Defense Intelligence Agency, and the new Department of Homeland Security since September 11, 2001.

McKinney introduced legislation to renew Congressional hearings and to suggest renaming the J. Edgar Hoover Building, which houses the FBI that he led into such infamy during his long reign of control, after Senator Frank F. Church instead, whose passion for civil rights and liberties and the balance of government powers is shared so strongly by Cynthia McKinney herself.

While in Congress, McKinney was the voice for the voiceless constituencies that find no representation in the halls of power. Cynthia was a voice, and sometimes the only voice, for the special concerns of African-American youth of the Hip Hop generation, for those who question authority and want Congress to play that critical role in a democracy, and for those who want an end to war and injustice.

Having worked closely with Cynthia McKinney, I know she is neither a racist nor an anti-Semite, as some have claimed. Quite the opposite, she is a person who stands strong against prejudice and racism and any injustice based on gender, race, or nationality. Her opposition to some of the policies and military actions of the state of Israel, and the conservative Zionists who support them in Israel and in lobbying efforts in the United States, is not based on a prejudice against all Jewish people. Nor is her sometime strong criticism of the ongoing racism and continued prejudice that have eroded the gains of the civil rights movement of half a century ago based on a hatred of all white people. Her criticism is based upon a zero tolerance for racism.

Her opposition to policies and actions is not prejudice, it is critical judgment, based on the standard of what people and governments should do to promote justice and peace. Racism is prejudice plus power; the power to exploit, deny due process and liberty, and disfranchise a whole people over time by those who control decision making, either through dictatorship, deception, the tyranny of a majority, or a privileged minority. Racism is more than an attitude or a personal hatred.

Dr. Martin Luther King, Jr. longed for a world where individuals were judged by the "content of their character." In my experience, that is the way Cynthia McKinney makes her assessments, and no single group, nationality or color can claim either perfection or lack of character as a whole.

Systems of privilege set in once racism or sexism or greed has attained the power to make prejudice count. These systems usually favor one group over another, and that is the injustice Cynthia opposes; and those who maintain its benefits, and conceal or carry out its abuses are the individuals she challenges and critiques. That is what makes Cynthia "angry" – injustice. In her daily life, and in the communities she represents, she is sweet, funny, and friendly. But when she confronts the arrogance and falsehoods of power with the outrage of the afflicted, that is an anger that can make a difference.

As a Congresswoman, McKinney actively tried to be a "representative" of the people that elected her to Congress six times. She spoke for the concerns of African-Americans that are not reflected elsewhere. She worked closely with the Congressional Black Caucus on key issues and supported establishment of a Tri-Caucus of Black, Hispanic, and

Asian representatives on the Hill. She responded to the calls for help from her constituents, and assisted enlisted people and veterans by proposing legislation to change the rules of the systems that are violating their rights or failing to help them. She put on the historical record the questions that many are afraid to pose to systems and people of unjust privilege and power.

Cynthia also has a unique relationship with the white community. She reaches out to all segments of the community, including those who do not agree with her. Her opinions and assistance are sought by Independents, Progressives, Leftists, Democrats, Libertarians, Republicans, and the non-political. She demonstrates a readiness to work with people who represent the entire political spectrum if that will get her to her next goal. In fact, she has often said that there is much more that unites us than divides us. She attributes her ability to cross what have been used by some as barriers to her Southern heritage—where she saw and benefited from the willingness of a critical number of individuals to work with each other in order to reach a common goal. When she hears a plea for help, Cynthia will respond.

I also know that former Congresswoman McKinney did not feel herself to be "above the law" or beneath the truth. She constantly held herself and the people in power to the Constitutional principles and laws that should govern them without the need for intervention, since they all take an oath to defend them. She called for full accountability when structures were out of control or failing the people they are meant to serve. She held the U.S. government to its international treaty agreements, United Nations conventions, and principles of international law.

She applied those rules to herself as well. When a Capitol police officer failed to recognize her as she entered the Longworth House Office Building and put his hands on her and demanded she show identification it was not the first time that such discourtesy was shown to McKinney while a Congresswoman—during her six terms in Congress, there were many times when officers claimed not to recognize her. Days later, the media made a resolved matter into a national issue. But a grand jury heard the facts and dropped all charges. Cynthia had the strength of character to apologize on the floor of Congress, something the Capitol Police officer and his supporters in the Fraternal Order of Police have never done in any forum. This is despite violating both their responsibility to recognize those they have sworn to protect and the historical principle that no Member of Congress can be impeded or arrested on their way to a vote or in the conduct of their official duties. Even after a grand jury dropped all charges, the media continued to make the issue a national matter. A Capitol police officer failed to do his duty to recognize and protect a Member of Congress, touching her inappropriately. Yet Congresswoman McKinney was vilified in the media as if she were the culprit.

Cynthia McKinney's father was a police officer, and she has good relationships with police and the public alike. In many of the earlier instances when the Capitol Police failed to recognize her, they have visited her office afterwards with respects, apologies, and even flowers. The teenage pages that work for Congress have to recognize all the Members of Congress to keep their jobs. Professional Capitol Police officers are trained in facial recognition methods that have nothing to do with pins or hairdos. So the question remains, who was acting "above the law" in these circumstances? And even, why?

If you knew her through any direct experiences besides the distorted lens and spin of the press and media, you would know Cynthia McKinney is a delight to be around. She is caring, humorous, outgoing, and empathetic to a wide range of people. She carries herself with decorum and professional conduct in serious situations as well. She is polite and often overwhelmed by the love and respect that she is shown by so many others.

It is only when confronted with injustice, arrogance, falsehood or gratuitous power that Cynthia McKinney shows her sense of moral outrage, her personal strength, and her abiding commitment to truth and justice. As an admirer and student of Dr. King's work and words, she is a "drum major for justice" and a woman who speaks truth to power. She is a strong and principled African-American woman, and a heroine to the powerless whom she speaks to and for, and to those who defend them.

Having known Cynthia and worked with her for more than a decade she is one of the finest role models I have ever known. I have continued on because I saw her refuse to give up. She has suffered great indignities and unfounded attacks with a grace and demeanor that sets her head and shoulders above some of the "toughest" men I have ever known. You will meet her in this book, perhaps for the first time. This woman tells the truth, no matter the cost. And in doing so, she will make you think and at times make you smile and even have a good belly laugh. She is a giant and her integrity and honesty are among the rarest commodities left in the world of politics today.

**Mike Ruppert**

INTRODUCTION

# THE THIRD TIME MUST BE THE CHARM!

For some strange reason, the contents of this book were stolen not once, but twice. So I have vowed to sit down and not get back up until this book is done. I almost kept that vow. However, the fact that you're reading this right now means that I succeeded at least in getting it completed. But what in the world could I possibly write that would cause my manuscripts to be stolen TWICE? What in the world could I possibly write that would upset people?

The truth.

And that is what you will find in these pages.

*At least now I'm writing!*

As you will read, my story really started while I was in the Georgia Legislature where I took my first "stand" for the people. And so while this book will be brutally honest, it will also be as raw as the truth sometimes is.

**What in the world could I possibly write that would upset people? The truth.**

So, in a way, I'm happy to be writing this book. Well, let me take that back. Because the tough realization is that what I write now is in the public domain, but what I write now ought to be on an official public record, like the Congressional Record. We'll get into that a little bit more, a little bit later. However, with that having been said, now I can honestly state that I'm happy to be writing this book.

I should be happy to write any book. I've been writing so

long--speeches, press releases, Floor Statements, everything except my dissertation. My mother has never relented on the fact that I still have a dissertation to write. And so, with the FREEDOM that I've found, I'm in the process of writing my dissertation, too! FREEDOM does have its advantages. As for the book, however, it seems that the people around me have always clamored for me to write a book. Guerrilla News Network and Ian Inaba showed me that I really do have a book to write, because they did an entire feature documentary, American Blackout, on just a few of the issues I've championed. So, if I were to put all of my issues together, I think it would be quite a tome.

This isn't a tome, but it is a beginning. Funny thing, when you're busy doing the work, it takes a special kind of discipline to record the work that you do. I haven't had that discipline. So, for this work, I've had to rely on the historical record through media accounts, original documents that I or others have retained, and the memories of those who were involved with me at the time of trying to make the world a better place for humankind and for Mother Nature.

So, OK, now that I'm convinced that I really do have several books worthy of others reading, I might just begin my writing career in earnest and say a big thank you to all of you who have at one time or other told me, whispered to me, or those of you like my mother who browbeat me into writing and completing this book. Because as soon as this one is done, another one has already been contracted to follow it!

Many Thank Yous!

I do want to take this opportunity to thank some people who really put their heads and their hearts into this work. First of all, the small circle of Atlanta and New York men who are serving as my readers: Phil Smith and Dr. Don Smith. And the men who know and love me, and I them, like Mike Raffauf, my attorney; Michael Hourigan, who understands me to my core; Mike Ruppert and Mark Donham who were there for me even before I knew them—how could I ever say thank you enough to them; Hugh Esco, who turned down a job with me in 1992 after I won the Congressional seat, to build the Georgia Green Party; Eric Hovdesven, friend, supporter, volunteer; and Bishop Felton Hawkins whose deep Biblical understanding informed me on the special Bible women Esther, Deborah, Naomi and Ruth. Pastor Carolyn Driver whose words inspire me to this day and my "ABC Girls" as we "change vehicles" many times throughout life and chart our course on a new path to the same destination; and Carol Gould who made many of the aforementioned introductions possible and demonstrated true friendship. It was Pastor Driver who coined the phrase for us "changing vehicles" to connote the various "vehicles of life" that take us to on our journey and ultimately to our final destination.

The "ABC Girls" (Adrienne Cole, Brenda Clemons, Carshena Williams) plus Faye Coffield (who was our security) are joined by two very smart guys: Jason Groves and John Judge. Jason, you're the only one I haven't heard from lately! And, My'rna Jenkins, the first voice heard by many people who tried to reach me has been with me through both of my vehicle changes and she, better than just about anyone else, knows what "changing vehicles" really means in my life.

Then, there is Clyde Baccus, known by everyone as "Jocco." Jocco has been a McKinney family fixture since the McKinney family was engaged in politics. So, you know that has been a very long time. Jocco represented the Congressional Office in Georgia's rural areas, that I call "the Heartland." And to this day, for the work that we did, Jocco is loved by the people of Georgia's Heartland who were at one time represented by me.

And wherever you saw Jocco, you knew Mario Chatman was also somewhere around. Even when they were not in the same room, they thought just alike. Eventually, the pair became known as "Frick and Frack!"

I also must mention my long-time family friends, Sherrie and Henry Friedman who stuck with me and my family through thick and thin.

David Josué has been by my side and has advised me since he came to visit his Congressional Representative with French books in tow. I guess he must have heard some of my broken French interviews on the France TV channels. Otherwise, how would he have known to bring those books? His sense of style (à la mode française) has definitely created the BD and AD Cynthia: Before David and After David. In fact, it was David and some young people (led by Charisse at White Diamond Images) who decided in 2006 that I should "let my hair down." They did a fantastic job, I got lots of compliments, but well, the rest is history!

Lucy Grider-Bradley, otherwise just known as Lucy, was my campaign manager. Meticulous, detail oriented, professional, she's the last one who edited this book. In fact, she told me that the first draft of this effort was dull, boring, dry, uninteresting, and sterile—and for those of you who know Lucy, you know that, for her, was nice and gentle! And she was right because I began this effort by saying to myself that I was going to just tell my story and not name any names and protect Members of Congress and others in the course of my dealings with them.

But, then Charles Onana, famed investigative journalist and author in France intervened and became sort of the executive director in this unfolding book drama, not letting a day pass without calling me to check on my progress. He had come to my home and gone through my papers and he learned the facts on many of the initiatives that I had championed while in Congress—despite his limited facility with the

English language! So, with Charles's guidance, I was encouraged to tell all of some of the stories, to name names, and to tell the whole truth and nothing but the truth. Charles added the sauce picante, or hot sauce, to this work's pages.

If I remembered all of the professionals who became whistleblowers or who inspired my work on Capitol Hill and beyond, the list would be so very long. Because from Wayne Madsen to Kelly O'Meara to Mike Ruppert to Sibel Edmonds to Indira Singh to William Pepper to Steve Cokely to Leuren Moret to Remigius Kintu to Greg Palast to Cindy Sheehan, from Michael Hourigan to the countless African patriots who risked their lives and trusted me from Angola to Mozambique, from Tanzania to Congo, from Sierra Leone to Rwanda to provide secrets of U.S. policy in the region. The list would run from Paul Larudee, Nobel Peace Laureate Mairead Maguire, Matthias Chang, Malaysian Prime Minister Tun Dr. Mahathir and his wife Tun Dr. Siti Hasma to Greta Berlin and the Free Gaza Movement; all of these people have played a role in the making of this book. Honestly, I am just the vessel, and they are its true authors.

And then there is the Green Party and its visionary founders who understood that the essence of political practice in this country should not necessitate leaving one's values behind. I would like to take this moment, also, to say a word of thanks to the Black Caucus of the Green Party that has stepped up to the plate and made a striking difference in the politics and the business of the Party.

Don Debar (whose real name is Don DeBerardinis, but who knows him by that name?!) is like my alter ego. Don is smart, witty, and great with a video camera! Much of the video work that you see of me posted on the internet has been touched in one way or another by Don Debar. And Don is who I called when I was under attack by the Israeli military. And just as the Israelis were about to board the boat, he was on the line with one Member of Congress who really didn't have a clue what was about to happen to me, promised to call a press conference on Friday, but of course, I was apprehended by the Israelis in a matter of minutes.

Importantly, nothing that I have ever done or that I am about to do could be possible without the love and guidance of my mother and father, Leola and Billy McKinney. All that I am is because of them. By their example, they are teaching me conscience, values, right and wrong, the importance of relationships including how to disagree and how to love. It is my parents who instilled in me the necessity to educate myself, serve others, and achieve. I continue to do all three only because of their overwhelming support.

Much of what motivates me is not just about today. As a mother, I must be concerned about the future that leaders are creating for our children. I remain hopeful about our ability to create a better tomorrow because, as a mother, I know that we have no other choice. I dedicate all that I do to my son, Coy. So that his world will be a bit better because I was in it.

Let me add here that Coy has been a good son. This will come as news to him because it is coming from me! But I want the public record to reflect what I think. Honestly, my biggest fear was that he would develop into an Uncle Tom, that is, someone satisfied with the status quo of injustice. These people are paraded in front of young people as if they are appropriate role models. Yet, they care little about the common good and do even less for people in need.

Yes, I did try to instill in my son a sense of personal responsibility; yes, I did try to inform him of the secrets that shape U.S. domestic policy and the facts behind the reason the world looks as it does today. Yes, he knew about COINTELPRO when he was 6 years old! But I did not know at all if my talking and sometimes preaching was falling on fertile soil, that is, a brain that would take that information and process it accordingly.

Well, I am proud to say that my son did, indeed, hear those facts. He is now into permaculture and agriculture and he is a graduate from a public interest law school, and his friends and roommates are young people who know what the problems are and who are living a solution. In the end, we all have a choice to be a part of the problem or a part of the solution. Today, my son has chosen to be a part of the solution—just like his mom. And that gives me great pride.

Now, is he perfect? Like any mom, I'd like to think so; but I know that his mom is far from perfect, and I'm sure that he can point out each imperfection. And that's alright because not a single one of us is perfect. I love despite imperfections and I can be loved despite imperfections. That is a big lesson to learn.

I suppose the final, big thank you must go to the people who have entrusted their hopes and aspirations with me as I have tried to serve as a voice for the voiceless, a sojourner for truth, and a champion for peace, justice, human rights, and a better America. They know that every day I served them with love and dedication. I never sold out their dreams for a better America and a more responsible America in the global community. I never compromised on the values that mean so much to all of us, but that some merely profess.

And I know that my supporters have never let me down. In the 2002 Democratic Primary, over 40,000 Republicans "crossed over" and voted in the Democratic Primary to defeat me. The mainstream (Larry Pinkney of BlackCommentator.com coined the phrase "corporate-stream") press lied and reported that there really was no Republican crossover voting: instead, they reported that my loss was due to middle class Blacks no longer needing representation with my kind of civil/human rights orientation.

My 2002 election night line was, "The Republicans wanted to beat me more than the Democrats wanted to keep me."

Instead of sitting down after that election loss, I criss-crossed the country speaking out against Bush's Wars and spoke out in favor of 9/11 Truth.

In 2004, despite careful planning by Democrats and Republicans opposed to my tenure in Congress (and much to their surprise), I prevailed in the Democratic Primary without a runoff. The corporate-stream press never retracted their previous political obituary for me about Democrats in my district not supporting me and also incorrectly reported that polls suggested that I would be in a runoff.

The local Atlanta press, the same press that lied about the Civil Rights Movement and Dr. Martin Luther King, Jr., continued their lies about me. They picked up the "Black folks no longer need civil/human rights activists" theme again. But, they sank to an even lower standard when a 2006 *Atlanta Journal and Constitution* headline blared, "McKinney Indicted" with no indication that the headline was referencing neither me nor my father until one read the entire "news" story to see that the story referenced a different McKinney who lived in Texas. The record will reflect, however, that the dual challenges of an open primary (that allowed Republicans to "cross over" once again and vote in the Democratic Primary), electronic voting machines, and a new district, reconfigured in the Tom DeLay-inspired series of mid-decennial redistrictings that took place throughout the country, were central factors in my having to add that last line to my election night speech wishing the new Fourth District Congressional Representative well. Yes, they threw everything at me including the kitchen sink—and it worked. Despite the redistrcting and the rest, including more money from the pro-Israel Lobby to my opponent, my mother maintains that the electronic voting machines were the real culprit in my second election loss and I agree with her.

My 2006 election night line was "Electronic voting is a threat to our democracy."

After that election, we gathered affidavits collected from voters all over metropolitan Atlanta who voted in my race, but who should not have been able to do so because they didn't live in my district. When my race came up on their Diebold touch screen machine, they had innocently voted the ballot that was on their screen. Only in the runoff election when the Fourth District race was not on their screen and they inquired as to why, were they told that they did not live in the Fourth District.

One county election supervisor told my attorney that reports surfaced that my name was on the ballot even in South Georgia. We are calling these votes "phantom votes" because they appeared anywhere, inside or outside of the district, in the Primary Election and then were "disappeared" in the Runoff Election. My question is: what happened to those votes? Were they counted? And how? Since the precincts were not even in the Fourth District, was there a mechanism to bypass the precinct and county totals and send those phantom votes straight to the Secretary of State's central tabulators under the control of Diebold and Newt Gingrich's former political and teaching base of Kennesaw State University? And what of the voters whose votes had been deflected to me, and then removed? What about their right to vote in the District to which they actually belonged, rather than to have their votes just disappear?

Further, some voters in my own Fourth District complained that my name was not visible to them at all without them having to manipulate the machine to scroll down the screen, which they didn't know how to do. My attorney, Mike Raffauf, and a committed team of computer experts led by Roxanne Jekot investigated the anomalies experienced by voters in my District using Georgia's Diebold touch screen voting machines. Although Georgia Courts ruled that we just have to trust the announced election results, an investigation by Bev Harris of Black Box Voting listed troubling areas in which Georgia's election process lacked security and transparency, especially in my Congressional race. I'm sure that the election data would have been released if it would have shown that there was no electronic tampering with the vote count. In the absence of being able to see the actual election data, the announced election results remain circumspect in my opinion and that of many computer voting activists.

I know that my supporters have never let me down (despite malignant disinformation from the special interest press) and are anticipating what comes next. Every day, I am contacted by people who long for the chance to have real representation, not just go through the motions of voting for a representative. They believe in America and are looking for a new way, a third way, because this way isn't working. They are looking to me to "change vehicles" at least one more time and not leave them behind. Because they know that I will never be untrue to them: that my issues are their issues, vital to our country's survival--today and tomorrow.

So, finally, to those people who have supported me throughout my career and who have given me the opportunity to champion their causes, to the ones who have contacted me with "buyer's remorse" due to their votes (not for me) in the 2008 election, and the ones who have only thought about contacting me, but who have not done it yet, please know that my love goes out to you.

I feel ya! I am receiving those positive vibrations. Keep them coming. I want you to know that I rise because of you. And rise again, we surely shall.

20

Despite the hatemongers.

So . . . I'm happy to be writing this book.  I truly love to write.  And so, what you're about to read is a labor of love for me and I hope you will enjoy it.

CHAPTER 1

# THE LIFE I LIVE

There was a reason why I never bought anything when I moved back into my DC apartment. I can't quantify it, or even qualify it, really.

People have never really known the life I live. I'm what most would call a simple person. I don't have extravagant needs or wants. And so, during my first term in Congress, which lasted for ten years, I accumulated awards, and plaques, and medals, and public papers. But not things for myself.

My parents taught me to not be materialistic and to live within my means. I had a childhood that was ample for me, satisfying all my needs and many of my wants. Maybe that's why I didn't attach too much importance to material things. At any rate, after my first election loss, after those ten years in Congress, I had accumulated much from the public domain for the public archives, but only just enough personally for a Spartan life in my DC apartment.

Besides, I had never really thought of DC as home, either, despite spending on average five days a week there on Capitol Hill. For me, "my home" remained in Georgia and that's where I concentrated my attention.

That's kind of interesting because, honestly, I never really had a home in the political scheme of things, either. I never really enjoyed the support of the "insiders," because in my opinion, the price of their support was far too expensive in terms of my values and my own sense of integrity. Consequently my base was always "the outsiders," in other words, the people. So, it is clear that as long as I remained unapologetic in my unwillingness to compromise key values, I would continue to be an outsider, just like the people I represent.

My father had warned me when he first got me to follow him into politics that I would never be an insider if I held true to my values. His words proved to be true. But what I quickly witnessed was that the material reward goes to those who sell out and rarely to those whose commitment to truth, justice, and peace is unwavering.

The Georgia Democratic Party surely didn't want to have me as its standard-bearer. In going through newspaper articles, I found a real fear openly expressed that the face of the Georgia Democratic Party could be mine and that was anathema for the small coterie of "Good Ol' Boys" in charge of state politics. Surprisingly, I was able to see in retrospect that not only the Good Ol' Boys were wringing their hands about the possibility of Senator Cynthia, but so too was the pro-Israel Lobby. (Remember, the "Good ol' Boys" had redistricted me so many times in an effort to rid Congress of me that I had almost represented the entire state--at least its major media markets--in various iterations of my Congressional District. The boomerang on that was that more people knew me, such that they really did have reason to fear that I might actually attempt a Senate run. After all, I had not signed "the pledge" of loyalty to Israel which made my presence in the U.S. Congress anathema to the pro-Israel Lobby—more on that later.)

Now, Georgia's White Democrats never hesitated to use my popularity around the state with Black Georgians to pump up the Black vote to get themselves elected. Because, of course, without the black vote, the Democratic Party, not just in Georgia, but all over our country, would basically become a permanent second party. For example, during redistricting, Democrats act as if there is no Voting Rights Act on the books and choose to draw districts with just enough Black voters to keep the district Democratic, but not with sufficient Black voters that could wake up and elect a Black Democrat. It's a fine line that is walked and we will see that played out in the reapportionment and redistricting activities just concluded in every state at every level of government. So, the calculation is to give the Black political class just enough to keep things as they are, and to not rock the boat for the Democratic or Republican Parties and more importantly, the powers behind them. This is a behind-the-scenes manipulation of U.S. political possibilities that the public rarely ever sees. The result is that, even with the swinging pendulum, both parties do just enough to prevent a wholesale exodus out of the two-party paradigm, thereby limiting political expression. Political behavior, as long as it remains inside the two-party paradigm, becomes predictable. And predictable political behavior, while good for the existing power configuration, is not good for those of us who want real change. In this kind of framework, real solutions need not be seriously considered and more and more people will lose hope in the power of their vote. Our alienation from the political process and our failure to cast an informed vote helps retard our ability to gain power. Therefore, there is method to the madness of those who currently control political power in the United States. They have, all along, been doing everything they could to reduce the black vote. By what better means than despair?

When erstwhile Democrat Zell Miller called me "loony" for asking about advance warnings coming into the Bush Administration about the tragic events of September 11th, 2001, other Georgia Democrats said nothing while I was vilified. Even Max Cleland, who later quit the 9/11 Commission complaining of a cover-up, conveniently piled on at the time and said that he knew for a fact that I was wrong. But look at it now: over 1,000 architects and engineers have stood up for 9/11 truth; over 100 university professors and other Scholars for Truth questioned the 9/11 Commission report, led by David Ray Griffin, Ph.D., Professor Emeritus of Claremont School of Theology. Veterans for Truth and Pilots for Truth organizations sprang up. Pilots for Truth has a remarkable video. And speaking of videos: numerous documentaries have been published over the internet, by independent researchers and have even aired on national television in several countries. Michael Moore made millions of dollars from his blockbuster "Fahrenheit 9/11" and even Oliver Stone, who popularized the questions surrounding the assassination of President John F. Kennedy for an entirely new generation of Americans, spoke out for transparency and truth about 9/11. Today, there is a global community of truth seekers, average ordinary citizens who stopped what they were doing because the Bush Administration's explanation for what happened in plain sight was so very pathetic. What's surprising, because the official explanation so pitiful and the crime was so blatant, is that there weren't more Members of Congress who spoke up. I guess I was so busy doing my job that I didn't recognize when I was supposed to let the sound of silence prevail.

Incredibly, after I was defeated in the Democratic Primary by Republican "crossover" votes in 2002 while the state and national Democratic Party leaders sat by and did nothing to help me—National Democratic Party leader at the time, Senator Chris Dodd, felt close enough to call me and ask me to stick with the state Party ticket—"for the good of the Party." Then came the barrage of calls from their Black lackeys, including certain "civil rights" icons, asking me to do the same. My response to them all was that I would be as loyal to the Democratic Party as the Democratic Party had been to me. My father openly told our then-Democratic Governor while the Governor was, predictably, campaigning for reelection at a Black church, that he would personally defeat him for what the Governor did to me.

Needless to say, Georgia went Republican for the first time in its history in November 2002 and has lined up solidly behind the Republican Party ever since. Timid Democrats, afraid of supporting a Black woman and of offending the pro-Israel Lobby are the reason Georgia, with a better than 30% Black (and Democratic-voting) population, remains in the Republican column. Due to the Democrats' fear of standing up for me as I had stood up for them, in 2002, I was defeated for the first time in a decade by a Black candidate who was supported by Republicans, had given campaign contributions to Republicans, and to whom Republicans had given campaign contributions. The State Democratic Party, led by our Governor at the time, refused to even question the legitimacy of such a candidate running as a Democrat. Clearly, the Democrats were willing to take any Republican under their wings as long as that Republican had the backing of the pro-Israel Lobby, which proved more important to them than the Black vote without which they cannot win elections. That Republican Democrat running against me (who was also quite popular with the Confederate Flag crowd) eventually became the Democratic Party's nominee. The silence of state and national Democrats can be traced back to the pro-Israel Lobby that recruited and financed my opponent to the extent that she was even able to outspend me!

True to my father's promise, the Governor was defeated even after spending a historic—at that time--$20 million. Can you imagine having $20 million to spend to get RE-elected and still losing? It was unheard of in Georgia and my father was pleased that the gross betrayal by someone who used to be his friend had been corrected. The bankruptcy of the state Democratic Party was further demonstrated when Republicans entrenched their position in the state in 2004, 2006, 2008, and in 2010 won every Constitutional Office in Georgia. And all of this in a state that is almost 45% people of color!

I see Georgia's shift to the Republicans, despite its very large Black population, partially as the result of White Democrats sitting in back rooms and studying which milquetoast Blacks will be useful tools for White Democrats' political aspirations while being sure not to actually work and speak to the aspirations of the Black community. These desperate conditions persist in the Black community because of the complicity of certain Black political actors in the status quo policy arrangements.

> I see Georgia's shift to the Republicans, despite its very large Black population, partially as the result of White Democrats sitting in back rooms and studying which milquetoast Blacks will be useful tools for White Democrats' political aspirations.

It's interesting that even though the Fourth District, as drawn before the 2010 Census, was nominally a Democratic district—drawn to elect a Democrat--Republicans correctly calculated that they could control its politics and thereby control the politics of the state by tactical use of crossover voting. The politics of the state?

Absolutely!

First of all, the Democratic Party's claim on White voters in Georgia has shrunk dramatically. Prior to the Presidency of Barack Obama, the Democratic Party's grip on Black voters was loosening, too. There is a solid reason for that: any investment that doesn't yield dividends will be jettisoned for one that does. However, in Georgia, the Black vote was becoming quite powerful in determining who went to the Statehouse or to the doghouse—to turn Malcolm X's phrase. However, because the Democrats' choice of "back-room approved" Black "leaders" increasingly failed to energize Black voters around the state, Democrats failed to gain the Black turnout needed to ensure statewide victory. Combine that with the Georgia Democrats' failure to appeal to the White vote in any significant numbers, despite alienating their Black voter base and watering down their essence so much that they became unattractive caricatures of the Georgia Republican Party. This was the recipe for a looming Democratic Party disaster.

The largest trove of Democratic voters in Georgia is in the Fourth Congressional District. The calculation is simple: if Black voters in the Fourth District and around the state are energized, Republicans lose; if Black voter turnout is even marginally depressed, Republicans win. I remember reading a study prepared for Zell Miller and the Georgia Democratic Party putting the Black turnout as a percent of the total vote necessary for Democrats to win statewide at just over 40%.

It's not rocket science.

As I see it, the Republicans have figured out what it takes for them to win in Georgia—which really should not be a Republican state; yet, in my opinion, the Democrats are unwilling to do what it takes for them to win—that is, welcome and embrace authentic non-White policy priorities and personalities. In other words, to change the way they do business. Even with a Black man from the Democratic Party in the Presidency, the Black community will tire of such symbolism if it remains unattached to real gains and material change in the community's conditions. What is rocket science, then, is how either of these two special interest political parties can remain in business over the longer term given the U.S.'s changing demographics and the growing White minority's unreadiness in both the special interest parties (Democrats and Republicans) to cede policy priorities to this country's growing non-White (and soon-to-be majority) population.

> Even with a Black man from the Democratic Party in the Presidency, the Black community will tire of such symbolism if it remains unattached to real gains and material change in the community's conditions.

As I see it, the Democratic Party has at least three primary constituents: Black voters (more than 90% of the Black vote goes to the Democratic Party whether it delivers anything of substance or not to the Black community); pro-Israel money (estimated to be as much as $30 million per election cycle); and lastly, union money and votes. The

Democratic Party cannot afford to lose any one of these base constituent groups or else its viability will surely be tested and may be lost. My
venture into 9/11 Truth clearly animated the pro-Israel Lobby that went
on the offensive against me in 2002, thus rendering this as an accurate
description of what happened to me: "The Republicans wanted to defeat
me more than the Democrats wanted to keep me." Sadly, the Democratic
Party remains tightly woven to those three constituent groups with labor
and Blacks continuing to get the shaft. There is always hope that this
policy configuration will change. But I'm not holding my breath. One
thing is for sure, we the people are the only ones who can make any
political party promote the policies that reflect our values.

In fact, ultimately, the Democratic Party will have to accept
authentic Black and Brown leadership, prominently within its ranks and
with real power if it is to stop the erosion of its support among Black,
Brown, and progressive White communities. But even more important
than the right faces in the right places, is the substantive policy changes
that the Democratic Party must make or I believe it will wither on the vine
as a result of its affirmative decision to not deliver policy prescriptions
for problems endemic to its base constituencies. This should be accompanied by increased interest in independent politics as the Democratic
Party increasingly shows its inability to deliver on key priorities set by its
base constituencies.

I focus here on the internal politics of the Democratic Party. The
Republican Party is in even worse shape with a dwindling constituent
base due to its decision to lock into a diminishing demographic, relatively
speaking, and because of its unwillingness to expand its view of acceptable
policy prescriptions.

When I taught political science, well before I entered the political fray as a candidate for office, I understood politics' definition as the
authoritative allocation of values in a society. However, the true practice
is so much more complex and ridden with machinations than that rather
sterile definition. From the dismantling of my district in 1996 and the
malicious primary election crossover voting organized by Republicans
in 2002 and again in 2006, to the targeting by the pro-Israel Lobby and
seeing its tentacles spread across the political spectrum, I have learned
a lot about the practice of politics.

In fact, just after my 2006 primary election, one Republican
Member of Congress told me, "If you can't pick strong friends, pick weak
enemies." Pause for a moment to let that sink in. When it was uttered, it
was a revelation for me. That's been the overriding theory behind the use
of Georgia's open primary and second primary statutes—enacted during
Georgia's moment of "White Resistance" to integration. This theory has
been the motivation for a practice used twice to keep me out of office.
I was viewed by the Republicans (and the Democrats who acquiesced

in that view) as a strong enemy and their choice of replacement for me and for the voters of my district was for them a "weak enemy." So, I was first elected to Congress in 1992, lost my bid for reelection in 2002, was reelected in 2004, and then was defeated again—er, rather, the election was stolen in the primary election of 2006. This Republican theory—practice—of selecting the weakest enemy makes ultimate political good sense, and is working for them even today: I still get requests regularly from the public as if I am still in Congress and I get complaints from people in need from around the State of Georgia about their lack of representation since I left office. Not much I can do about that now, unless . . .

Ironically, one of my first moves as a newly elected Member of the Georgia House of Representatives back in 1989 had been to join a lawsuit with other civil rights leaders against Georgia's second primary (runoff) statute. We lost that battle a few years later due to Democratic Party intransigence on the issue and a conservative court. Had I been successful, Republicans would not have had forcing me into a runoff as a tool to carry out their strategy for my elimination from as well as their subsequent takeover of Georgia's politics.

I was also a plaintiff in a successful lawsuit to force Georgia to change the way its judges were elected to allow Black voters an equitable opportunity to elect judicial candidates of their choice. Then-Governor Zell Miller appointed Denise Majette, my Republican-picked opponent in 2002, to a judgeship as a direct result of the success of that lawsuit. You could say that we "civil rights-ers" shook the tree and the fruit fell into Denise Majette's hands; and she used that fruit, then, to campaign against the need for additional tree shakers! (See what became of that, p. 288-9.) In fact, I was disparagingly labeled an "agitator" by her in that campaign, but I wonder where this country would be now if it had not had agitators well placed throughout its history.

You could say I continue to learn the best political lessons during my massive struggle to make the political process meaningful to the masses of Americans for whom politics is seemingly meaningless because they think it results in little good for them.

Well, it's not supposed to be that way.

Sadly, my experience has been that it's so difficult to do the right thing in politics and it's too darn easy to do the wrong thing. But, as long as it is that way, we all have work to do.

My mark on this great institution—that is, the political infrastructure of our country—I hope, will be that one day all of the people will be served and not just a privileged few.

So, in 2005 when I was reelected to Congress, and found myself on a plane going back to Washington, D.C., I reentered my apartment and it was . . . bare. Just like I'd left it. It had beautiful parquet floors—but there was nothing else, but those beautiful floors! And, in 2006 when I began my exit from Congress for the second time, it was funny that I really didn't have much to pack: a couple of personal grocery carts, which people really don't use very much in Georgia because Metropolitan Atlanta is not yet a walking community; and an inflatable mattress that I bought from Assantewaa Nkrumah-Turé, the receptionist on staff in the D.C. Congressional office. I had cleared out all of my clothes a long time ago, and never really brought a wardrobe of clothes to D.C. anyway. Just enough cleaning things to keep the apartment tidy. Not much else. No jewelry, no toiletries, everything brought to D.C. just for use at the time, and then carried back to Georgia until the next trip.

My "home" was always where my constituents were.

Does that tell you anything? Upon reflection, it tells me a lot. Here's what I think it means . . .

My Father, Billy McKinney, taught me how to read legislation.

My Mother Leola and my Campaign Manager Lucy made sure I got to write some.

Needless to say, pundits were shocked in 2004 when I declared myself a candidate for reelection to the Congress from Georgia's Fourth District after they had pronounced me dead. (Cartoon by Khalil Bendib, www.bendib.com.)

CHAPTER 2

# FROM A DIFFERENT CULTURE

By 2003, after ten years in Congress, I had not become a Washington insider because my focus remained on the needs of the people. There were many times when I was offered the possibility to ingratiate myself with this special interest group or to take advantage of that perk, but I always refused. So, what was it like when I stepped back into Congress in 2005 after a two-year hiatus and a bruising campaign where all the gloves came off?

During that brief interregnum from 2003 to the beginning of the campaign in 2004, I was invited to speak all over the country, and in Spain and India. Most importantly, what the interregnum personally meant to me was that I could open my window blinds and curtains and let the morning light shine in. You see, during my time in Congress, I had been the target of unimaginable hatred coming from all over Georgia and all parts of the country. My hate mail had become legendary. As unfortunate as it might seem, honestly, I had become accustomed to the usual "n-word" this and "n-word" that of the Ku Klux Klan variety. But then, after the targeting by the pro-Israel Lobby, I noticed that the hatred took a particularly different, more "in-your-face' course and more alarmingly, a more ominous tone. For example, one day I was cleaning my son's bedroom and when I began to clean the blinds hanging at his window, I opened them—just by chance--and looked out and lo and behold, what did I see looking back at me! A strange man with a camera! Now, I live smack dab in the middle of a Black neighborhood; White men don't normally stand in front of any house taking pictures. This was a way more aggressive, invasive presence.

Then, there was the other time when I was outside with my son enjoying a moment together that we rarely got to experience, when seemingly out of nowhere, a slow-riding van with the sliding side door open cruised by my house, and it was filled with White people, one of whom was a video cameraman capturing the idyllic setting of me and my son outside washing the car! This time, unlike before, I was prepared and able to get a license plate number. To no avail, whatsoever. Because when the license plates were run, the plates didn't even match the vehicle they were assigned to! I do need to interject right here a word of appreciation to the police of DeKalb County who personally took care of me and looked after me in the midst of these strange goings on. This is when I began to study up on covert and false flag operations. (Covert operations are activities that a government does in secret because it doesn't want anyone to know that it operates that way; false flag operations are actions carried out by one party, but blamed on, and made to look as if done by, another.)

The third straw for me came directly at my Georgia house and I had to call 911 for police help. The perpetrator in that case served time in jail for stalking and got a guilty conviction thanks to the work of two DeKalb County solicitors, including then-DeKalb County Solicitor Robert James whose office remained vigilant and delivered justice.

The hallmarks of the stalking case in particular, and those of other cases, lead me to believe that I must have made it onto an important list of people for somebody to watch—and that these were concrete manifestations of that. As a result of repeated occurrences, I was forced to keep all of my blinds and curtains closed most of the time. Unfortunately for me, there have been many more incidents of strange people, cameras, and goings-on outside my home or round about me. In fact, I just had to rip my wallphone from the wall because it was talking to me. Yes, incredibly, the phone was talking to me. I decided to write a piece about the soft repression I experience on a regular basis. It's one of the things I have learned to live with and understand very well from my reading of the U.S. Government's Counter-Intelligence Program (COINTELPRO) Papers, that this kind of targeting is "par for the course" for those strong enough to act on their beliefs.

Someone's at my door. Let me see what's going on. No car visible. Who could that be? A thin White man. I have cameras. The thud of a slammed car door. No car sound. No one any longer in my vicinity. Amazing. It just happened again! I won't even begin to list all of the strange occurrences I've experienced, like the Verizon-truck-driving telephone repair man sitting outside a home I was visiting and when approached about why he was just sitting outside of the house, he gave another address on the street as the reason he was sitting outside the home I was at. David Josué was with me and we went up and down and up and down the street to verify that the address was non-existent. It was—non-existent.

I would have a lot more photos for this book had my external hard drive not been stolen in a recent burglary of my home! Along with my passport! Things got so bad in 2011 that Wayne Madsen wrote about it and reported on Russia Today TV about these visits and phone calls to my friends. In this regard, Wayne's story on the "Israeli art students" is instructive. And please be sure to read the COINTELPRO Papers to fully appreciate the political environment that exists in this country for some people and for increasingly more people since September 11, 2001 provided a handy excuse for stripping U.S. citizens of the Bill of Rights. Now targeted assassination of U.S. citizens even on U.S. soil has been floated as if it's legal! Alas, if the people only knew the true price of conviction. Sadly, I think if they only knew, far fewer would be willing to pay it. Though respect for those who venture there might rise. When I look at protests I wonder if they really know/are up for what they are getting into. And I wonder whether the publicity we do see about that isn't yet another tool used by the state to ward off more protest. But still, I am convinced, that the majority of people on this planet want to do what is right and want to have that done to others in their name. It's the small cabal of sociopaths that we allow to get away with this type of behavior that must be stopped. And that's our work for right now. Otherwise, the repression that's permitted with the massive power of today's technology will be nothing but a trap inside the matrix for all of us. If the sociopaths can keep us afraid, on edge and divided by any silly measure, then they will continue to win. Our challenge now—indeed our imperative—is to keep them from winning.

The 2012 "death threat" business is in my opinion along the same lines. I had just returned from Cape Town, South Africa in 2011 where I was serving as a juror on the Bertrand Russell Tribunal on Palestine that had found the practices in Israel toward the Palestinians had features equivalent to South Africa's and international definitions of apartheid. Then, immediately upon my return, I received a call from the Federal Bureau of Investigation (FBI) telling me that they wanted to protect me from some "racists" from North Georgia. Immediately, I understood that these poor White people had probably been framed and that somewhere lurking around them was probably an "informant" or an outright FBI agent stoking them to make whatever statements they did make—which then served as a means of intimidation which the FBI wielded against me, in guise of protecting me. This was just one more of many messages sent to me by agents who place Israel's agenda over that of the United States and will do anything for that "passionate attachment."

While I'm on this subject, let me just state right now, in case something should happen to me by way of attack, whether physical or on my character.. I am not a closeted gay, lesbian or transgender. I am not a pedophile. I am not suicidal. I do not have a passionate attachment to the "good life," life in the "fast lane," or to mountains of material things. Therefore, if anything happens to me that is even somewhat suspicious, please know that I have been targeted by people I believe are Israelis or their agents operating covertly with false identities who probably think they are doing good for that country. Nothing could be further from the truth, however, as I am just a peace activist wanting human rights and dignity for all and because Malcolm X, Dr. Martin Luther King, Jr., and my father are my role models and I know their stories well of threats and intimidation, I will not voluntarily stop my pursuit of peace based on justice and truth.

So, how did I become such a perceived pain to whoever this is that orchestrates this kind of thing? I say "perceived" because I'm not really a pain except to people who want war, carnage, injustice, and policies disrespectful of our planet and of basic human rights. I just want my government to tell me the truth, respect human and environmental rights, and to pursue peace. And I dare to speak out about it. So, to answer that question, I guess I should start at what I believe is the beginning. Gil Scott-Heron wrote, "Push comes to shove, you find exactly what you're made of." So let me start at the time when I began to learn exactly what I was made of.

Some might say that it was when I was in the Georgia Legislature, when it really started, but to paint the complete picture, I should go all the way back and start from the beginning. I believe this will explain why I never aspired to become a Washington insider if it meant selling out my constituents and killing my soul.

When I went away to the University of Southern California for college, I would get homesick. And, I had an album. Some young people don't even know what albums are, imagine that. But the album that I would play was of Dr. Martin Luther King, Jr.'s speeches. And I would imagine that there was nothing that I was feeling that could in any way rival what Dr. King had to be feeling as he confronted the powers of his day on his mission for all of us--and for me--in particular, so I could get an education at such an illustrious institution as the University of Southern California. So, after listening to the album all the way through, I would straighten myself up, collect my emotions, and hit the books again.

After undergraduate and graduate studies, I met and married a Jamaican and then left The United States of America for Jamaica where I had my child. A few years later, though, I was back at home with my child and a divorce on the way.

Unfortunately for Georgia's Good Ol' Boys, I ran for the Georgia Legislature for all the right reasons—mainly, to ensure that Georgia had a fair redistricting that would last ten years or more into the future. My reasoning was that I would serve for four years, but that people in Georgia would feel the impact of my service for a very long time after that. With that in my mind, I ran for office.

The seat I was running for had been created to maintain a White majority in the Fulton County House Delegation of the Georgia Legislature after Maynard Jackson had been elected (Atlanta's first black mayor). The seat was a countywide seat that was destined to be dismantled because it had been created out of White resistance to desegregation.

Certain Whites still wanted to be able to dictate City of Atlanta politics and if they could not do that from Atlanta's City Hall, then they intended to do it from under the Gold Dome of Georgia's Legislature. Their refuge was these abominations of at-large State House districts. The average State Representative represented 35,000 people at that time, but my at-large district was home to over 600,000 people—the size of a Congressional District! Needless to say, those at-large single member districts were the complete antithesis of the democratic systems of proportional representation and the legally enshrined "one person, one vote" requirement. I would later advocate as a Member of Congress when I introduced the Voter's Choice Act.

Of course, the media were full of naysayers because no Black had ever won in these at-large districts and certainly no Black woman. Funny how Ralph David Abernathy's son ran alongside me in the other at-large district that was created for the same reason, covering the same territory, but the press never said it was impossible for him to win. But they sure had a lot to say about the impossibility of me winning.

Despite what the pundits said and the Atlanta media wrote, I won. And so did he!

I went to the Georgia Legislature with a clear mission and purpose. I intended to stay for four years, take care of political justice for Georgians through redistricting, and then to resume my academic career, because I love school and learning.

That was 1988.

I won because my father, Billy McKinney, who was also a State Representative, had built up a career of service to the community—service without expectation of reward. People in the community knew that when they needed him, they could count on him to be there for them. They trusted me to be a fighter, too.

In 1989, I was sworn in. It had been agreed by "The Powers That Be" (TPTB) that the two at-large State House seats, one of which I had just won, violated the Voting Rights Act and had to be dismantled.

That's why I knew that I would only serve four years–until after the 1990 Census and the 1991 redistricting. And I was content with that because politics was never my thing: books and learning were.

Well, my father and the Speaker of the House, Tom Murphy—fitting every stereotype of a southern politician—got together, and I was appointed to the Reapportionment Committee, just as I had asked. What I didn't know was that Billy had assured the Speaker that I would be a good girl and go along with the program! Of course, even Billy couldn't imagine how unfair their program was going to be; I think he might have had an inkling about how "unmanageable" I could be.

(Did I mention that Billy and I were the first and only father-daughter legislative team in the entire country? That's worth a book all by itself because I almost never voted the way he expected! Our public disagreements were numerous and noticeable.)

Of course I went along with the program—just, not their program. I had been elected for the JUSTICE Program! That is, I would do what justice required—nothing short of that. Reapportionment, remember, was the only reason, I had run, anyway. And so, I became the champion for a fair reapportionment for Georgia.

I'll never forget one gentleman who came before the Reapportionment Committee from "Liberty" County, Georgia. I peered deep into his face as he made his presentation. I studied every line on his face. That he was there, standing before the Georgia House Reapportionment Committee, testifying for justice in Georgia's reapportionment also told me that each one of those lines created in whole a man whose impressive dignity was honed by years of struggle. I was filled with a tremendous amount of love as I watched this man. And then he spoke and I paraphrase:

> Mr. Chairman, Members of the Reapportionment Committee, I come from a county named Liberty, but the Black man is still not free.

Blacks from all over the state called on me and I responded to their plea for representation. They had always voted for representatives ever since they had the right to vote, but they yearned for representation, a still-unattained goal. I was going to do everything I could to make sure that Georgia's rural black belt communities not only got a chance to vote for representatives, but that they got representation, too.

Across the world, nearly every nation daring to call itself a democracy uses systems which guarantee voters representation in deliberative bodies in proportion to the support those representatives and their parties enjoy among the electorate. But in Georgia, in fact even across much of our country—as a result of the redistricting process--we let elected incumbents choose their voters before the voters get to choose their elected representatives.

Man! Georgia's Powers That Be were so angry with me. Good Ol' Boys were angry with me. My colleagues were angry with me. But Black people across the state found that they could count on me. I championed what became known as the "Black Max Plan," which used as its guidelines the exact current legal interpretation of the Voting Rights Act. Blacks from all over the State of Georgia came to me and we worked with the Justice Department to get Black-opportunity legislative and Congressional districts all over the state. Likewise, I created the City of Atlanta's first gay-opportunity City Council district.

Here, I must add that the American Civil Liberties Union (ACLU) Voting Rights Section was instrumental in helping us find fair map-drawing skills. This is pretty technical work and nothing I did as a Democrat using the facilities of the Legislature was either secure or secret, although it was supposed to be. Therefore, I spent hours that melted into days with Kathy Wilde and Laughlin MacDonald and Derek Alphran getting the numbers right for a state-wide Congressional and Legislative redistricting that lived up to the Voting Rights Act.

Now, this angered TPTB in Georgia because they had decided that Blacks would only get one new Congressional District! And they were really angry at me because I not only voiced my belief that Georgia needed to do better, but I sought out allies that were in a position to force the Georgia Democrats to do better. And sometimes that meant talking to and allying with my Republican colleagues in the Legislature who were motivated by other reasons.

The law mandated two new Black-opportunity Congressional districts and I wasn't going to budge on that. I was on the Reapportionment Committee; I had a voice, I had a vote and I used them. Black opportunity districts are called that because given the racially-polarized bloc voting that has been demonstrated to occur in certain jurisdictions, remedies have been fashioned to level the playing field so that Black (and other voters protected in the Voting Rights Act) can have a reasonable expectation to elect their candidate of choice.

Man, I must admit that it was lonely sitting up there on the rostrum at the Reapportionment Committee meetings with all my colleagues furious at me!

It was lonely at the Georgia Legislative Black Caucus meetings where my Black colleagues were furious at me, especially the senior ones. (The most vocal ones, of course, had found it more expedient to just sell out. By sell out, I mean accept what the Good Ol' Boys were willing to give them rather than to fight for what their constituents deserved.)

Everyone was "going along to get along" except "The Four

Horsemen." That's what we who stood fast became known as: the Four Horsemen were Tyrone Brooks, John White, Mary Young Cummings, and me. The Four Horsemen were responsible for Georgia having elected Sanford Bishop and me to Congress--of course, at the time I didn't know I was going to run—and dozens of new state legislative districts were created that elected Blacks and integrated Georgia's Legislature for the first time. Georgia now has the largest Legislative Black Caucus of any state in the United States. That, in and of itself, is not the goal; the goal is a shift in public policy that accounts for the priorities and values of all of our state's and country's residents.

My experience on the House Legislative Reapportionment Committee gave me my first contact with rural Georgians. I grew to love them for their rock solid innocence and honesty. I later was able to serve them in the U.S. Congress from the House Agriculture Committee. And more importantly, I was able to get to know rural Georgia, Black and White--very Southern--in the most intimate way because there's something special about that moment during which old Confederate customs are confronted with modern, post-Voting Rights Act realities.

My notoriety for having advanced and won the "Black Max Plan" for Georgia set the tone for everything else that was to follow. As a result of my fight for a just reapportionment for Georgia, I learned what it was like to infuriate the leadership; I learned what a prostrate Black leadership looked like; I learned that it was possible to stand one's ground on principle and win; and I learned how to understand and accept the vitriol that comes with taking a stand.

I also learned (because other people told me this) that when I take a stand that is popular with constituents but threatening to TPTB, those Black elected officials who are afraid or who disagree with that stand are then asked inconvenient questions by their constituents. This is very uncomfortable for the elected officials because it shows their constituents what their elected officials could or should be doing for them. I understood how this dynamic came into play after it was pointed out to me.

And if I ever had any fear because there were moments when all eyes were on me, and those eyes felt like daggers, I remembered my pedigree. I remembered my ancestors who braved the slave rebellions and the Civil Rights Movement. Africa's stolen children, who had nothing but their unity, used that as a hammer to club the United States out of its slavery first and then out of its apartheid.

I remembered what it must have been like for my own great-grandmother who could have passed for White, but instead chose to live in the segregated South and suffer the daily indignities of what it meant to be Black in the United States during her day.

I remembered my father, who picketed his place of employment by himself because the other Blacks were too afraid to walk with him and stand up for their own dignity. I remembered Malcolm X and Dr. Martin Luther King, Jr. who knew that their own government wanted them dead, but they never stopped and they never gave in.

I remembered the women: from the enslaved Sojourner Truth who plaintively asked "Ain't I a Woman" at a Woman's Convention where the issue was women's right to vote. And I remembered Fannie Lou Hamer, who stood up to the President of the United States of America when the Mississippi Democratic Party refused to seat Black delegates to the Democratic Party's national convention, when she said, "I'm sick and tired of being sick and tired."

And with political ancestry like that, people who've gone before me having struggled like that, there was no way I could give in to my fears. So, day after day, meeting after meeting, I went through the motions necessary to take the right stand for my community, my state, my country.

That's why I went to Congress with no illusions. I knew that if I held fast to my beliefs and the reason I ran for office in the first place, that it would make me popular only with the people. And, that's why I would never be an insider. Unless things dramatically changed in the U.S. My experience in the Georgia Legislature was a primer for leadership and the loneliness that comes with standing up for one's convictions. Dr. Martin Luther King, Jr. reminded us that our lives begin to end the moment we remain silent about the things that really matter. I took the lessons of Dr. King to heart and tried to live by them.

So, back to where we began, with my empty Washington, D.C. apartment. Not that I take my cues from pundits, but I remember that one female political pundit (if my memory serves me correctly, it was Ellen Goodwin, but I'm not sure on that) had written a column in which she describes the best representatives as the ones who have one foot inside the body to which they are elected and the other foot outside with the people who elected them. Her thesis was that the best representatives for the people are the ones who are willing to stand with the people at all costs. I cut that column out and it was one of the few items that I had hung on my wall.

# CHAPTER 3

# HOW TO STEAL
# AN ELECTION

When I returned to Congress in January of 2005, my first order of business was to make the definitive Congressional statement on the important issues that had started my troubles with the Bush Administration in the first place: election fraud; the war in Iraq; the expanding yet already-bloated Pentagon budget; corporate sweetheart contracting deals with Administration insiders; and the September 11th tragedy. The Administration's pitiful performance during and in the aftermath of Hurricane Katrina was another point in Congress that begged for my voice, rather than the usual political posturing (as now-retired Congressman David Obey used to say, "posing for holy pictures," that can be ensured during a tragedy.

Well, many people didn't know it until the movie American Blackout came out, but in 2001 I did the only Congressional investigation into the Republican theft of the 2000 election with sworn and transcribed testimony. An investigative journalist in London, Greg Palast, had written about his findings of election fraud in Florida and there was a Georgia connection--a company, Database Technologies (DBT), that had been acquired by the giant corporation, Choicepoint, a software company. I contacted Palast and got the scoop on how the "win" in Florida had been manufactured. Then, I put together a town hall meeting to explore the unexposed facts surrounding the 2000 vote.

**I did the only Congressional investigation into the Republican theft of the 2000 election with sworn and transcribed testimony.**

I invited Choicepoint to send a representative to my town hall meeting. (That's when I learned about the trick often used in Congressional investigations of sending in someone who knows absolutely nothing about the details of what is being investigated. Watch out for it, because that's one of the sure signs that a coverup might be underway.) The Choicepoint Vice President came and was sworn in, and I was loaded for bear with my questions. And even though he was relatively new on the job, I got the goods! His testimony revealed the worst about the Republican Party: that they tried mightily to suppress the Black vote—in violation of the Voting Rights Act—using highly unethical means that were later found to be illegal, too. But with a democracy and justice system like ours, hey, who's going to be held accountable? Certainly the Democratic Party was not going to hold the Republicans accountable because then it would seem like the Democrats were taking the side of their Black constituency. And, of course, the Democrats never actually have to do that because the Black vote is in the bag for them, anyway! So, nothing but cosmetics were applied to the situation and the fraudulent election was allowed to stand.

This is also an indictment on the media in this country who have never told the story of the orchestrated Black voter suppression and outright election theft that resulted in George W. Bush being sworn in as the 43rd President of the United States of America. The only people who have a clue as to what really happened are the ones directly involved in one way or another, or the people who have read Greg Palast's writings, or the people who have seen American Blackout. The myth floated by Democrats is that Ralph Nader's running as the Green Party nominee caused George Bush to be elected. This myth serves both the Democrats who can cover up their failure to protect Black voters and Republicans who can cover up their illegal election scheme to defraud the people of their right to vote and have their vote counted.

Here's how the Republicans stole the election, the Democrats did nothing, and gave the world George W. Bush and Dick Cheney. The rest, as they say, is history.

Basically, a few Republican Governors, (including George W. Bush who at the time was Governor of Texas) provided Jeb Bush's Florida with their lists of convicted felons. Those lists were then used to illegally construct a list of people in Florida who were not going to be allowed to vote. The problem was that the lists that were imported into Florida were not accurate: the people on them were not necessarily convicted felons, and not all of them were ineligible to vote. Never mind the intellectual leap of someone, convicted in Texas being put on an ineligible voter list in Florida. Except . . . and here is where it gets tricky . . . Florida requested an inaccurate list from Choicepoint just so it could move to step two of its fraudulent election operation scheme!

Aside from the fact that it was illegal for Florida to get a list of convicted felons from other states whose names it then banned from voting in Florida, the worst part of all of this is that the list that Choicepoint provided to Florida was not even of convicted felons!

For example, the state of Texas gave Choicepoint a list of people convicted of misdemeanors, and then Choicepoint provided the state of Florida a list of misdemeanor offenders which was used by Florida as a convicted felon list. Texas also did not tell Choicepoint that its list was composed of misdemeanor offenders. That was the testimony of the Choicepoint Vice President who testified at my Georgia town hall meeting after the election debacle. Video of this testimony from the town hall meeting can be seen in the documentary American Blackout.

The Democrats could have had the White House had they fought for it, but they settled instead for Republican hubris. And still, the American people largely don't even know what happened. They believe the lie that Ralph Nader who ran for President under the banner of the Green Party "spoiled" the election for Al Gore and the Democrats. Only the complicity of the special interest media allows this profound ignorance and baseless myth to persist.

Blacks in Florida had voted at nearly 100%. They were angry and they wanted their voices heard and their votes counted. Instead, they got deceived at the highest levels by the government of Florida. Jeb Bush won another term as Governor; and Kathryn Harris, the Secretary of State at the time who oversaw the election fraud, was rewarded with a Congressional seat. No one was punished except the mostly Black people who had gone to the polls and tried to vote but could not because they were on a list of convicted felons, and thus were ineligible to vote. It didn't matter that the list was inaccurate either because of duplicate names or because the people had not even committed felonies and therefore were actually eligible to vote.

And of course, America lost because America ended up with George W. Bush as President. And the world lost because the U.S. ended up with George W. Bush as President.

So, who cared enough about the sanctity of the Black vote (which ought to be treated like every other vote) to really do anything about it? Not even Al Gore, who prematurely announced that he was giving up the fight. I believe a recount of the entire state of Florida would have erased that 537 vote advantage for Bush and given Florida's electoral votes correctly to the winner: Al Gore. Al Gore would have become our President. I like to think that Gore would have made a better President than Bush. But, would we not have gone to war anyway? Depends on how well Gore could keep his war mongering Vice President in check—Joseph Lieberman. And that is an open question. The one thing we do know is that the Bush Administration proved toxic, not just for us, but for the world.

44

In fact, I see a few parallels between Gore and me. He was robbed of an election victory by the Republicans. He has a thought-provoking film, An Inconvenient Truth (like the American Blackout documentary about my elections). People know he was wronged. He did, in contrast, remain connected to Democratic Party insiders and has been rewarded handsomely as a result. I guess it pays to "take one on the chin" for the Party—or whoever he actually took it on the chin for.

I am reminded by those closest to me that I should not remain in my blissful reverie too long because Vice President Gore's family owned stock in the companies committing genocide against the indigenous U'Wa people of Colombia in order to access the oil under their sacred lands; that as Vice President, Gore helped the Clinton administration usher in NAFTA and GATT, Welfare "Deform," the effective Death Penalty Act (limiting access to Habeas appeals); that he failed to act to address obvious sentencing disparities resulting in massive Black and Brown incarceration rate disparities; and the list goes on.

Yes, I have to admit that Vice President Gore did not fight, even as the Presidency was being stolen from him. In the film, American Blackout, Barbara Boxer states that Gore even asked her not to challenge the Florida electors after that gross debacle! She admits in the film that she regrets having listened to him.

Thank goodness the Congressional Black Caucus did fight to the limited extent that it could—for naught, because not one Senator, including those elected because of Black votes, like Max Cleland, my Senator, would back the Black Caucus attempt to force a floor debate on what had happened in Florida in the 2000 Presidential election.

**In the film American Blackout, Barbara Boxer states that Gore even asked her not to challenge the Florida electors after that gross debacle! She admits in the film that she regrets having listened to him.**

All that is to say, yes, it was easy for me to get involved in the Ohio 2004 stolen election story when I had already been "primed" by what happened in Florida.

I'm proud of the film American Blackout. And it turns out that the title comes from me in the Floor Statement I gave during the Ohio Electoral College debate, when I said "This is not about bitterness or a recount, it's about a blackout. It's time to shine the light on our precious right to vote."

As Greg Palast says in the documentary American Blackout, I've got political tourette syndrome. I just can't keep myself from telling the truth!

# CHAPTER 4

# OVERSEEING
# THE PENTAGON

During a portion of my first tenure in Congress (my entire first tenure was from 1993 to 2003), I served on the House Armed Services Committee. I relished that seat on that Committee because I won it only after "America's Congresswoman" Patricia Schroeder and "America's Congressman" Ron Dellums (that's what I called them) both went to the House Leadership and asked that I be allowed to have the open seat on that Committee due to Pat Schroeder's decision to retire from the Congress.

That was important to me because Congresswoman Schroeder told me that she and Congressman Dellums, together, had been forced to share one seat in the Committee room. Congresswoman Schroeder told me that when they were first named to the Committee in the 1970s, its southern "Dixiecrat" Chairman felt that a body determining U.S. military policy was no place for women and Blacks. So, he literally made them share a chair! This made it difficult for the two of them to be present during deliberations at the same time.

Well, I was named to the House Armed Service Committee and Congresswoman Schroeder even came to Georgia and "passed the torch" to me as she retired from Congress. Shockingly, I was the lone "No" vote on the Pentagon budget each year but that allowed me to write the Congressional Dissent to the Committee Report which became a part of the Congressional Record accompanying the Report. My vote was "No" when it was the Clinton Administration as well as when it was the Bush Administration. How can one justify spending more than all the world's leading militaries combined on a war machine meant to kill people while the American people's needs continually go unaddressed? The American people should not have to beg for health care, quality education, modern infrastructure, and efficient energy.

How long can immigration, war, and debt serve as the labor, energy, and economic policies for this country?

I'm proudest of the dissent I wrote to the FY2007 Pentagon budget—it tells the American people everything the Bush Administration did not want anyone to know about what our military does around the world, and what the Pentagon does to our service men and women.

During my first year on the House Armed Service Committee, I called the Committee staff in to ask them to go over the budget authorization bill with me. Perplexed, one of them asked me if I really wanted to do that. I surmised at the time that such requests must have been rare. But how could one know what was in the bill if one had not read it and how could one vote for and pass a bill that one had not read? Boy, I was in for Congressional culture shock!

> **During my first year on the House Armed Service Committee, I called the Committee staff in to ask them to go over the budget authorization bill with me. Perplexed, one of them asked me if I really wanted to do that.**

I quickly found myself in the crosshairs of some of the largest Pentagon contractors, including Lockheed where certain Black employees had been targeted for nooses placed in various locations within the corporate complex. I challenged the sweetheart deals that were rife at the Pentagon. In particular, one of the earlier challenges occurred when the White House had requested money, I recall half a billion dollars or so, for a Carlyle Group weapon system (the Crusader) that the Pentagon did not even want. I mentioned it in my dissent, bringing unwanted attention to the issue, and that was the first time I had big trouble with the Bush Administration. The issue for me was the seeming conflict of interest inherent in the President requesting money for a company with which his father had financial ties while none of this had been officially disclosed. All of a sudden, the Congressional Office started getting phone calls from the Pentagon and we even had an incident caught by one of my Congressional staffers of "late night rifling through our files!" Needless to say, we let that "intern" go! But, the President's apparent conflict of interest was only the tip of the proverbial iceberg.

Dick Cheney's continued remuneration by Halliburton while he served as our country's Vice President did not escape my attention. Nor did Halliburton's no-bid contracts. And, if one did more than scratch the surface, conflicts of interest were rife. Secretary of Defense

CYNTHIA A. McKINNEY
4TH DISTRICT, GEORGIA

COMMITTEE ON
INTERNATIONAL RELATIONS
INTERNATIONAL OPERATIONS AND HUMAN RIGHTS
RANKING MEMBER

COMMITTEE ON ARMED SERVICES
MILITARY PROCUREMENT
MILITARY PERSONNEL

# Congress of the United States
## House of Representatives
### Washington, DC 20515-1011

WASHINGTON OFFICE:
☐  124 CANNON HOUSE OFFICE BUILDING
WASHINGTON, DC 20515
(202) 225-1605
FAX: (202) 226-0691

DISTRICT OFFICE
☐  ONE SOUTH DEKALB CENTER
2853 CANDLER ROAD, SUITE 9
DECATUR, GA 30034
(404) 377-6900
FAX: (404) 377-6909

WEB ADDRESS:
www.house.gov/mckinney

## Defense Spending Statement
### Congresswoman Cynthia McKinney

Ms. MCKINNEY. Mr. Speaker, on Wednesday, February 6th, Secretary of Defense Donald Rumsfeld testified before the House Armed Services Committee and asked for a record increase in defense spending. He pointed to the brave new world post-September 11th as justification for the largest hike in defense spending in 20 years. Sadly, Secretary Rumsfeld thinks that the brave new world of post-September gives us amnesia about 9/11 and the events before 9/11. He also mistakenly believes that all of his destabilizing proposals can be justified as a reasoned response to 9/11. And incredibly, both the Vice President and the President placed calls to TOM DASCHLE asking that the fog of ignorance around the events prior to and the day of 9/11 not be lifted.

The fact, however, is that September 11 was not a failure of our nation's defenses. Rather, September 11 was a colossal intelligence failure--a failure to act on timely and accurate warnings predicting massive terrorist attacks against our nation. The LA Times and other leading press agencies have identified some of these missed warnings. And this was not the first time that our intelligence agencies have let us down. The same failure to act on critical warnings happened with respect to the terror attacks against our embassies in Africa.

Even the CIA, the FBI and other senior Capitol Hill figures all now agree that there were serious lapses in the handling of perishable and highly significant warnings preceding the September 11th attacks. But instead of examining what went wrong with respect to these warnings and then trying to prevent it from ever happening again, President Bush and Vice President CHENEY now seek to actually prevent the Congress from investigating these and other events surrounding September 11th. Indeed, Senator RICHARD SHELBY, a member of the Senate Intelligence Committee told CNN: ``It was a real massive failure ..... In my judgment too many bureaucratic failures, not enough coordination between the Agencies.''

The active efforts to prevent a Congressional investigation into the events surrounding September 11 not only violate the principles of good government but are an affront to the memories of all those who perished in the September 11 attacks. But sadly, the Administration now chooses to direct us on a path of war while refusing to allow us to know how we got there.

I have been asked by my constituents to explain to them why and how September 11 happened. Indeed, the whole world community continues to search for answers to those exact questions. That cannot be done if the Executive Branch will not cooperative with the Legislative Branch in answering important questions about what was known before, during, and after the tragedies in New York and Pennsylvania and Washington, DC.

Why doesn't the Executive Branch want us to know answers to these questions? Is there something that they don't want the American public to know?

Instead of working with the Congress to search for answers to these questions the Administration has now become obsessed with finding ways to expand the U.S. military budget. The White House is now using our new War Against Terror as a means of siphoning public attention away from the events surrounding September 11th in order to generate widespread support for the largest increase in defense spending in a generation. The Administration has even identified a dubious ``axis of evil" to further justify this increased spending.

The President has requested an increase of $48.1 billion in defense spending. Sadly, many commenters have already pointed out that his father stands to personally gain immense profits from the President's proposals because of the former President's relationship with The Carlyle Group, a leading defense conglomerate. One particular defense contract, for the development and purchase of a mobile howitzer, the Crusader, exists with the Carlyle Group. Though the company has received millions for this, the Crusader is too hefty to transport, has not yet reached its production phase despite years of engineering and re-engineering, and is far from fulfilling its purpose or need.

In his testimony before the Congress Wednesday, Secretary of Defense Donald Rumsfeld said that America can afford this increase just fine. This comes after defense spending snared a whopping 62 percent of all new spending for the year 2002. This accounting is specious, as Rumsfeld himself noted on the eve of September 11th, that ``according to some estimates we cannot track $2.3 trillion in transactions." Increased spending should occur under no circumstances without increased financial accountability. Does Arthur Anderson keep the Pentagon's books?

Rumsfeld's trick of throwing bones to would-be critics in the form of pay raises for the troops should not obscure the fact that the bulk of this budget hike goes not for pay raises, but for expensive gadgets such as missile defense, three new, separate fighter planes and space-based lasers.

2

Of the $48.1 billion requested in more funding, less than 5 percent of that increase is for soldier pay raises. And let us not forget that the President's first act in this war on terrorism was to waive the high-deployment overtime pay for our troops who are on the front line of this war.

I might remind Mr. President that we still have veterans from the Vietnam war suffering from the ill effects of Agent Orange, we still have Vietnam veterans impoverished and sleeping on the streets of our Nation's Capital, we still have veterans from the Gulf War suffering the ill effects of Gulf War syndrome and we still have service men and women in our armed forces living on food stamps and residing in poor housing. How in good conscience can the Secretary of Defense come before this Committee and ask for yet more money for aircraft, ships and missiles and not adequately address these critical issues concerning the personal welfare of our veterans and serving men and women?

Sadly, however, at the same time that the President proposes the largest defense spending hike in 20 years, hisbudget also proposes to cut funds for programs that bridge the digital divide, reducing funds for highway construction and urban development and cutting funding for the EPA by $300 million. And despite the down-turned economic situation, the President has also proposed to cut back on job training, assistance for low income home heating, and rural housing and utility improvements. Moreover, funds to cleanup the Savannah River Site nuclear weapons complex are sliced, and abroad, international food aid and peacekeeping funds are also shrunk.

At $379.3 billion, the President's proposal will not tell us how just a few months ago during the trial of suspects charged with initially bombing the World Trade Center in 1993, a suspect told U.S. officials that bin Laden's group was trying to make war on the United States and in particular would bomb an embassy, yet we did nothing and lost hundreds of lives in Nairobi and Dar Es Salaam. Nor will this budget explain the Mossad warning of a major terrorist force of 200 individuals entering the U.S., which apparently again fell on deaf ears. What of the supposed warning to German police by an Iranian in Hamburg of an impending attack on the U.S. using hijacked planes? And nor will this budget illuminate for us who performed the unusual stock trades on the Friday and Monday before September 11th, but has since decided not to pick up the tidy profit that was made. The U.S. Government is now being sued by survivors of the African embassy blasts because it has become clear that the United States had ample warning but chose to do nothing rather than prevent the loss of life. Given the prior warnings, insider stock trades, and convoluted financial interrelationships, September 11th represents yet another wasted chance to save innocent lives.

The most shocking aspect of the President's request involves the New Defense Strategy to be implemented now. Secretary Rumsfeld testified that a major role now for the U.S. military will be to occupy an opponent's capital and replace his regime. In as much as the Secretary has identified some 60 countries,

including our own, that host terror cells, and publicly stated his intention to ``drain the swamp," we can only surmise that the U.S. military is now in the business of taking over capitals around the world and replacing regimes ..... starting with Washington, DC.

Donald Rumsfeld certainly had his own conflicts: This led me to object to Secretary Rumsfeld's purchase of Tamiflu by the Pentagon because he had a financial stake in its parent company. As was ultimately exposed, Deputy Secretary of Defense Paul Wolfowitz forced a Pentagon contractor to hire "a World Bank employee with whom he had a 'close personal relationship'" (yuk); Defense Policy Board Chairman Richard Perle, solicited a $100 million bribe from Saudi Arabia for his investment company, Trireme Partners LP, to stop possible U.S. attacks on Saudi Arabia during George Bush's Global War on Terror—the very targeting he was influencing for the President from his position on the Board!

I became interested in the Pentagon's program of forced vaccinations for our service men and women and the source of those vaccines from DynPort, a joint venture between DynCorp and Porton Down located in England. Wellness screenings before deployment to Iraq for our service members had been promised to them due to illnesses occurring as a result of toxic exposures during the First Gulf War, Operation Desert Storm; U.S. use of depleted uranium munitions (I introduced a resolution to completely stop the use of such munitions until the health effects were fully known), and the Pentagon's penchant for sweetheart deals with odious corporations like Halliburton and DynCorp. Underlying all of my activities was my firm belief in and commitment to the public's right to know.

I also held the first Afro-Latino Symposium on Capitol Hill, bringing Afro-Latinos from all over Latin America to Washington, D.C. I put the conditions experienced by Afro-Latinos into the annual U.S. Human Rights Report and worked to increase the visibility of all Blacks at the World Bank by increasing their numbers inside the institution, as well as paying particular attention to their policy needs. This led me to increase activities within the scope of my Committee assignments regarding U.S. activities in Latin America. I stepped into a lot of hypocrisy.

I sent a Congressional staffer to Colombia to see the effects of DynCorp spraying in the so-called "War on Drugs" and everything I had heard about the toxic effects on the people and their resultant displacement was corroborated. At this point, I became more vocal in my objection to Plan Colombia and the U.S. government's militarization of our bilateral relationship. My staffer confirmed that the majority of people affected by the loss of land were Afro-Latinos. Because of the work I did with the Afro-Latino communities in Latin America, I have relationships there that last to this day.

I forged a very special bond with undoubtedly the most popular elected official in Colombia: Piedad Cordoba. I can say this without reservation because I have tested her name in my travels throughout the United States and throughout the world. Colombians like her. But, she is a woman who will not back down. That makes her unacceptable to the Americans. I met her after she had been kidnapped and after her escape to Canada where she lived in exile. Had she been in the country, she could have contested the Presidency against America's choice, Alvaro Uribe. Instead, she was away from home and trying to find her way back to her beloved Colombia. She just happened to come to my Congressional Office and there we struck the bonds of sisterhood. What a strong and impressive woman. How wronged she had been. Incredibly, she had managed to escape her kidnappers, and now she was with me, seeking help.

I did what I could to help. I worked with then-Secretary of State Colin Powell to get Piedad back to Colombia where she was ultimately elected to serve in Colombia's Senate. That was certainly a triumph! And when I went to Colombia to sit on a panel for Afro-Colombians, Senadora Cordoba was in rare form. It was so refreshing to hear someone speak the truth so openly—even though I didn't understand all of the Spanish, but I understood enough.

Sadly, I met her for a second time in Washington, D.C. after her Chief of Staff had been murdered and his bones mailed to her. Clearly, this was a sign from the paramilitaries funded by U.S. interests for her to stop her activities on behalf of the people of Colombia. I took her to meet the Chairman of the Committee and I introduced the photos of the bones into the Committee Record. I routinely voted against Plan Colombia, but what more could I do? I introduced an amendment to the Pentagon budget bill to cut all funding for Plan Colombia and to make an equal amount of money available to the Black elected officials there to relieve the disproportionate impact that Plan Colombia has had on Afro-Colombians. It was quite interesting to hear all of the bogus reasons my Democratic Party colleagues (of whom I had higher hopes) gave for voting to support Plan Colombia.

Recently, Senator Cordoba was attacked—probably so that she would not get any ideas about running for President—something her supporters were pushing. She has been barred from serving in public office for 18 years because of accusations that she worked with FARC, the Revolutionary Armed Forces of Colombia, in ways that exceeded her authority to negotiate humanitarian hostage releases. Senator Cordoba's only activity was to work for peace in her fractured country.

Also after learning about U.S. efforts to desecrate the sacred lands of the Indigenous U'Wa people while in Colombia, I did everything I could to protect those lands and amplify the voice of the U'Wa leader inside our Congress and to the American people. Helping the Australia Aboriginal community to obtain a World Heritage designation for Kakadu National Forest in the Northern Territories sparked a relationship with that community that lasts to this day. I also reached out to Native American communities in this country fighting uranium and other mining on their lands to try and stop that activity, promote cleanup, and lend support in whatever way I could. This work directly led me to Tennessee to speak out on behalf of families living around Oak Ridge National Laboratory who had been exposed to the chemicals used by the U.S. Department of Energy in the production of nuclear weapons and who had been ignored by their own Congressional representatives in the U.S. House and Senate.

There was no more outspoken Congressional critic of Pentagon spending, especially for the wars, than I was. In fact, I remember one edict that had come down from on high that Members of Congress should stay away from the anti-war protests, particularly those sponsored by ANSWER (Act Now to Stop War and End Racism). A group of us anti-war Members met on the House Floor and decided that we wanted to participate, anyway. We set an hour to arrive and appear onstage together. At the appointed hour, no one was at the venue but me. It was then that I realized that what many of my colleagues said to me was one thing, what they were actually willing to do was quite another. For some, giving speeches on the Floor was enough, for others maybe a vote, but to give speeches, vote, and participate in street actions was just too much for many of them—even when reelection campaigns had been hypocritically based on their opposition to war.

Luke Thomas, FogCityJournal

**McKinney holding a graph that shows U.S. military spending in comparison with other countries in the world.**

A Zionist colleague from New York later commented to me that I should not be surprised that I'm the one paying the price: "Every vote," she said to me, "has its consequence."

Serving on the House Armed Service Committee was not just about being against the war on Iraq. It was also about the Congressional responsibility of oversight of the Pentagon. That's everything from policy to funding. And that means the largest chunk of discretionary spending in the entire U.S. budget. There's a lot of room for waste, fraud, abuse, and bad policy in that.

American Blackout captures an exchange between Secretary of Defense Donald Rumsfeld and me on the Pentagon's "loss" of $2.3 trillion from its accounting books. The scene is one of the most popular political offerings of mine on youtube. I can't say anything except: see it in the film. But the genesis of that exchange goes back to something my father told me a long time ago when I first entered the political arena: "Cynthia, they put on their pants just like you do: one pantleg at a time. Don't be afraid of them."

Those are probably the best of my father's lines that definitely got me into the most trouble, because guess what? When I looked at them, from the Georgia Legislature to the White House, I could see one thing: my father was right. There really was nothing special about these men—and they mostly were men—except that they had been given, and lived all or a portion of their lives in, great privilege.

Privilege was the great divider and, for me, education was the great equalizer. I'd put my brains up to theirs any time. And I won many times because I learned an ancillary lesson: "Those whom privilege blesses, forget excellence." I learned that I could beat them with my brain; and that after a defeat, they would retaliate every time with brute force. I won many battles; I won in the Georgia Legislature and in the U.S. Congress. But I also learned that with the support of like-minded people, I could survive the retaliations, too.

However, there was an important addendum to my lesson learned: while education is a great equalizer, money is the greatest political equalizer. And while we don't necessarily have to match our political opposition dollar for dollar, we do have to have enough money to organize and mobilize our supporters in order to accomplish our political goals.

Was I in store for retaliations when I theorized that because the people of the U.S. have spent trillions of dollars on a military and intelligence infrastructure, it could not possibly have failed four times on the same day: September 11th.

And, boy, was I in store for retaliations when I theorized that because the people of the U.S. have spent trillions of dollars on a military and intelligence infrastructure, it could not possibly have failed four times on the same day: September 11th. I was familiar with at least the contours of that infrastructure and what the Bush Administration was asking me to believe was just flat out, unbelievable to me. All we Members of Congress were told in the beginning was that the United States was hit because we are free. Talking points were distributed around the Congress containing, among other things, the message: We were hit because we are free; terrorists don't like us because they don't like our freedoms!

Now, as a Black American, the one thing I know more than anything else is that this isn't a "free" country—not for everybody, that is. Or maybe, it was that my freedom didn't count. At any rate, the Administration's talking points were not sufficient for me and I refused to go back to my District and tell my constituents that we were hit because we are free. So, I began to ask more questions and soon realized that it was the Administration that had come up with a hyperbolic conspiracy theory that just didn't fit the facts. So what did fit?

> **As a Black American, the one thing I know more than anything else is that this isn't a "free" country . . . The administration's talking points were not sufficient for me and I refused to go back to my District and tell my constituents that we were hit because we are free.**

Well, the first thing we needed to do was investigate. So, I went on a California radio station and broke the silence on the tragedy. I was the first Member of Congress to speak out on what the world witnessed on September 11, 2001. Then from out of left field on April 12, 2002 came the "plot/conspiracy theory" story from Juliet Eilperin at the Washington Post that started the tumult. And from there all of the national, what I call "special interest," media started piling on. All I had done was call for an investigation. What I did not know was that at the very moment that I was calling for an investigation, both President Bush and Vice President Cheney were working the Senate leadership to stall one.

On April 13, the day after the "plot/conspiracy theory" Washington Post story, I outlined my views in an oped calling for an investigation. Here is that op ed:

CYNTHIA A. McKINNEY
4th District, Georgia

COMMITTEE ON
INTERNATIONAL RELATIONS
International Operations and Human Rights
Ranking Member

COMMITTEE ON ARMED SERVICES
Military Procurement
Military Personnel

WASHINGTON OFFICE:
☐   124 Cannon House Office Building
Washington, DC 20515
(202) 225-1605
Fax: (202) 226-0691

DISTRICT OFFICE:
☐   One South DeKalb Center
2853 Candler Road, Suite 9
Decatur, GA 30034
(404) 377-6900
Fax: (404) 377-6909

WEB ADDRESS:
www.house.gov/mckinney

# Congress of the United States
## House of Representatives
### Washington, DC 20515-1011

# Statement of Congresswoman Cynthia McKinney,
# April 12, 2002

The need for an investigation of the events surrounding September 11 is as obvious as is the need for an investigation of the Enron debacle. Certainly, if the American people deserve answers about what went wrong with Enron and why (and we do), then we deserve to know what went wrong on September 11 and why.

Are we squandering our goodwill around the world with what many believe to be incoherent, warmongering policies that alienate our friends and antagonize our allies? How much of a role does our reliance on imported oil play in the military policies being put forward by the Bush Administration? And what role does the close relationship between the Bush Administration and the oil and defense industries play, if any, in the policies that are currently being pursued by this Administration?

We deserve to know what went wrong on September 11 and why. After all, we hold thorough public inquiries into rail disasters, plane crashes, and even natural disasters in order to understand what happened and to prevent them from happening again or minimizing the tragic effects when they do. Why then does the Administration remain steadfast in its opposition to an investigation into the biggest terrorism attack upon our nation?

News reports from Der Spiegel to the London Observer, from the Los Angeles Times to MSNBC to CNN, indicate that many different warnings were received by the Administration. In addition, it has even been reported that the United States government broke bin Laden's secure communications before September 11. Sadly, the United States government is being sued today by survivors of the Embassy bombings because, from court reports, it appears clear that the US had received prior warnings, but did little to secure and protect the staff at our embassies.

Did the same thing happen to us again?

I am not aware of any evidence showing that President Bush or members of his administration have personally profited from the attacks of 9-11. A complete investigation might reveal that to be the case. For example, it is known that President Bush's father, through the Carlyle Group had - at the time of the attacks - joint business interests with the bin Laden construction company and many defense industry holdings, the stocks of which, have soared since September 11.

On the other hand, what is undeniable is that corporations close to the Administration, have directly benefited from the increased defense spending arising from the aftermath of September 11. The Carlyle Group, DynCorp, and Halliburton certainly stand out as companies close to this Administration. Secretary Rumsfeld maintained in a hearing before Congress that we can afford the new spending, even though the request for more defense spending is the highest increase in twenty years and the Pentagon has lost $2.3 trillion.

All the American people are being asked to make sacrifices. Our young men and women in the military are being asked to risk their lives in our War Against Terrorism while our President's first act was to sign an executive order denying them high deployment overtime pay. The American people are being asked to make sacrifices by bearing massive budget cuts in the social welfare of our country, in the areas of health care, social security, and civil liberties for our enhanced military and security needs arising from the events of September 11; it is imperative that they know fully why we make the sacrifices. If the Secretary of Defense tells us that his new military objectives must be to occupy foreign capital cities and overthrow regimes, then the American people must know why. It should be easy for this Administration to explain fully to the American people in a thorough and methodical way why we are being asked to make these sacrifices and if, indeed, these sacrifices will make us more secure. If the Administration cannot articulate these answers to the American people, then the Congress must.

This is not a time for closed-door meetings and this is not a time for secrecy. America's credibility, both with the world and with her own people, rests upon securing credible answers to these questions. The world is teetering on the brink of conflicts while the Administration's policies are vague, wavering and unclear. Major financial conflicts of interest involving the President, the Attorney General, the Vice President and others in the Administration have been and continue to be exposed.

This is a time for leadership and judgment that is not compromised in any fashion. This is a time for transparency and a thorough investigation.

I became a voracious reader on all stories related to the September 11th attacks. I understood from my Congressional work that I wouldn't get but a part of the truth from the U.S. media, but the internet allowed me to read papers from around the world and so I did. Just as I had found Greg Palast in England on the 2000 Presidential Election fraud, I found breaking stories from Scotland, Ireland, Australia, and Israel that never appeared in the U.S. press. Finally, when I went on the radio and told all that I had learned, including that warnings about a disaster to come had come to the Administration from several countries, all heck broke loose.

From my perches on the House Armed Services and International Relations Committees, I understood that private and classified briefings about which one was forbidden to speak were really useless. I got more information from the international press than I got from the Pentagon "dog and pony shows," with all their slides and Powerpoint presentations and from the State Department briefings. (Of course, if I wanted gossip about a Head of State, what medication he or she was on and the like, such briefings were replete with that kind of information! I guess that's why Secretary of State Hillary Clinton was requesting her Ambassadors at their posts to collect DNA samples from targeted individuals, Ambassadors, even Heads of State!) So, I basically developed a coterie of trusted advisors who were active on the ground and I sought to verify my information directly from my original sources. I didn't rely on staff to do this: this was my activity because I considered it that important. This was not just on the topic of the 9/11/01 attacks, but on every aspect of my work in Congress.

The special 2005 eight-hour briefing that I did on September 11th and the 9/11 Commission's Report was the first time that government whistleblowers, family members, former CIA agents, academicians, researchers, and lawyers had all been brought together to discuss what we knew, didn't know, and should now know about September 11th. Congresswoman Carolyn Kilpatrick attended briefly and Congressman Raul Grijalva was supportive. In other words, despite all that we now know was a lie about the September 11th official story coming from the Bush Administration, neither Democrats nor Republicans wanted to open

---

### 9/11 Security Precautions and Exercise Impacts

Hon McKinney: Given the previously scheduled events at the United Nations in New York City that day, were any special security precautions being taken or heightened security alerts declared? Was it appropriate to conduct these training exercises given the responsibilities of the Department to ensure the security of the UN events on that day?

General Myers: No DOD special security precautions or heightened security alerts were in effect due to UN activities in New York City. The Army Director of Military Support, J-3 DDAT/HD, Joint Director of Military Support and Assistant Secretary for Homeland Defense, conducted records reviews. We did not find any requests to DOD for support of the UN events. Since no DOD support was requested, the DOD had no responsibilities associated with UN events.

A review of records determined that participation in air defense Exercise VIGILANT GUARDIAN and Operation NORTHERN VIGILANCE actually improved the military's ability to respond to the events of that day and clearly did not impair NORAD's ability to respond to the terrorist attacks.

that chapter and look critically at the events of and official response to that tragic day. To this very day, the representatives of the people in the United States Congress have remained silent. When I left the Congress, so too did any Congressional quest for 9/11 Truth. Given the global ramifications and the continued Presidential justifications for war after war after war, how on earth can that be?

The 9/11 Commission tried to close that book shut, even though it was clear that it didn't tell us the unvarnished truth. Even though the Bush Administration used the September 11th attacks to pass the Patriot Act, carry us to war, engulf our allies in war, attack our civil liberties, change the entire structure of government, change the focus of government agencies, spend even more for the war machine instead of for investments in the people, virtually no one else in Congress wanted to do anything more to get to the root of the issue. The briefing organized by my Congressional office remains the singular moment when Congress was seized of the issue in a thoughtful, insightful, inquiring way.

I used my voluminous reading and seat on the House International Relations Committee to confirm that the United States Government relationship with the Bin Laden family went back decades.

I confirmed on the Congressional record that that relationship was also a financial one involving the U.S. government's expenditures in the millions of dollars.

And then, after I came up short of votes in the 2006 primary election, I read in *Rolling Out*, a hip hop industry newspaper that Chuck D (of Public Enemy) wrote that I had set another record: being turned out of Congress two times in three years!

As I prepared to pack my things and head out of Washington, D.C. once again, the only thing I wondered was why the American people were so quiet in the face of so much criminal activity operating within the U.S. government.

**As I prepared to pack my things and head out of Washington, D.C. once again, the only thing I wondered was why the American people were so quiet in the face of so much criminal activity operating within the U.S. government.**

**Cynthia with Dennis Kucinich. They got him, too.**

MARCHING ACROSS THE GRETNA CITY BRIDGE AFTER KATRINA AND BEFORE EVERYONE ELSE DID IT. THEY THREATENED TO ARREST US; WE MARCHED ANYWAY.

*Hey, we didn't teach our young people Freedom Songs!* Pictured behind me are my Congressional Chief of Staff Adrienne Cole (on the right) and Black Panther Party Member Robert King (on the left), formerly of the Angola 3.

# CHAPTER 5

# WHAT HURRICANE KATRINA EXPOSED

The Democratic leadership had told Democrats not to participate in the House Select Committee on Katrina. I'm not sorry that I did
not obey. What the world witnessed of New Orleans in the aftermath
of Hurricane Katrina was a tragedy beyond belief. There was no way
Minority Leader (Republicans constituted the majority in Congress at
the time) Nancy Pelosi could even begin to explain to me why I should
not participate in a Committee formed to investigate what happened.
Certainly, my contention was that Congress must get to the truth and
expose that truth to the American people. How were we going to ensure
the people of the U.S. that a failure like that would never happen again
if there was never any true investigation into what happened and why?
Even more to the point, the faces and plight of the Black Katrina survivors
revealed the great racial and class divide in the United States. There was
no way I would allow Nancy Pelosi to effectively dictate to me what my
responsibility to the survivors and victims of Hurricane Katrina was in the
context of some kind of larger monopoly game of partisan politics. My
disappointment was magnified when I began to realize that this, too, was
yet another stand that I was going to have to make alone. Despite the
hoopla in the Black community about this being a "never again" moment
for us, the fact is that Democrats, including Black Democrats, refused to
participate in the proceedings of the Select Committee: in short, they
did as they were told.

So, I participated in the Select Committee alone and wrote an
important addendum to its Final Report. The Republicans offered other
Democrats the opportunity to add their words, but I was the consistent

Democratic attendee at the Hearings. The Republicans begged me to get the Democrats to participate and I, in turn, went to the Members of the Congressional Black Caucus and asked them to participate. From time to time, Bill Jefferson, the Representative of all of those desperate faces that were broadcast across the globe, came intermittently. On November 13, 2009, Jefferson was sentenced to thirteen years in federal prison for bribery after a corruption investigation, the longest sentence ever handed down to a congressman for bribery or any other crime. Two other White Democrats, Louisiana's Charlie Melançon and Mississippi's Gene Taylor came more often and were given a "pass" by the Democratic Leadership (as was Jefferson) to attend because they were directly affected by Katrina and Rita and their aftermath. Neither the Democratic Leadership nor the Democratic Party--not even the Congressional Black Caucus--paid any political price whatsoever for this perfidy against their own constituents and voting base.

It was at the proceedings of this Select Committee that I had the opportunity to ask Secretary of Homeland Security Michael Chertoff why he should not be prosecuted for homicide due to his failure to perform his job (or even report to his office!) as the tragedy that was to become known to the world began to unfold. (It was Michael Chertoff who had so skillfully orchestrated the roundup of approximately 700 Arab, Muslim, and South Asian men inside the United States after September 11, 2001 and who provided counsel to the Bush Administration in favor of torture.) But for Katrina, he was missing in action—except to ensure that Blackwater mercenaries were there to protect wealthy neighborhoods from desperate hordes and to make sure that Carnival Cruises could get a big chunk of the money action.

I requested that the Republicans allow me to put together my own hearing with my own witnesses and permission was granted. My hearing, "Race and Class in the Government's Response to Hurricane Katrina," was played and replayed several times on C-Span. Mama D became a national celebrity as she and the other Katrina survivors told their story of survival. They directly challenged the assumptions of White Republican Members of Congress, for whom life is a crystal stair. They told their experiences as only people too familiar with America's grimy, hard, and crusty underbelly of poverty and racism can. They testified about selective evacuation, police taunting of children with lasers and guns, and murder on the Danziger Bridge. The President of the Black Chamber of Commerce stunned the room when he revealed that the Lower 9th Ward (the established Black New Orleans neighborhood) had been deliberately flooded back in the 1920s in order to save the French Quarter. The response of the Republicans present at that Committee hearing was disbelief bordering on contempt, especially when the survivors told of police activity to deny them the opportunity to flee the floodwaters.

I offered important Katrina-related legislation and held a town hall meeting in Georgia with the U.S. Department of Housing and Urban Development (HUD) and the Federal Emergency Management Agency (FEMA) for Katrina survivors and individuals interested in their plight.

Upon hearing of the disgraceful turning away of Katrina survivors by racist authorities in Gretna, Louisiana, a New Orleans suburb, I was outraged. I expressed that outrage in two ways: One, I drove to New Orleans and participated in a reenactment of the attempted Gretna City Bridge crossing. Jefferson Parish Sheriff Harry Lee, who orchestrated a turn-around of fleeing Katrina survivors threatened to arrest any of us who marched across that bridge during the protest reenactment if we set foot on the other side. Undaunted, I marched anyway. All of us did, willing to be arrested if Sheriff Lee insisted on denying us just as he had denied the fleeing Katrina survivors. Suddenly, when faced with the reality of having to make arrests, because we were undeterred, the Sheriff relented and we successfully marched across the bridge to the other side. However, that was not the end of the incident because taxpayers' dollars were used to turn the Katrina survivors away and deny them their Civil Rights. This fact led to my second action.

I introduced legislation to take all federal funding away for the period of one year from any law enforcement agency that was involved in the turnaround of Katrina survivors seeking to escape the floodwaters. How dare weapons be discharged and insults hurtled in order to prevent the mostly black Katrina survivors from getting to the other side of the bridge to what just happens to be a mostly white suburb! Of course, I was vilified once again in the press for daring to introduce such a bill, but since then, five New Orleans police officers have been found guilty of deprivation of rights under color of law, conspiracy, civil rights conspiracy, and other crimes in the Danziger Bridge incident.

The second piece of legislation that I wrote in response to Hurricane Katrina revolved around my mother's initial reaction to seeing the 9/11 rescue efforts unfold before her very eyes. My mother's first remarks to me as we watched the rescue efforts on our televisions was that the rescuers were not being taken care of properly by authorities and that later there would be health after-effects suffered by the rescue personnel. She was concerned about toxic exposures and the inhalation of the dust that pervaded the Ground Zero site. (My mother is a retired nurse and her specialty was Emergency Nursing. She managed the Emergency Room of Atlanta's trauma hospital, Grady Memorial Hospital, now known as Grady Health System.)

I know she was right because now those 9/11 rescue workers are experiencing health effects, including premature death, due to those

Ground Zero exposures. Already 1,000 Ground Zero First Responders have died prematurely. Certainly, our government wouldn't let that happen again, would they? Oh, but I believed that the Bush Administration absolutely would and did. So I introduced a bill that would require testing and full public notification of the results of those tests on the residue from the "toxic brew" that bathed every structure in New Orleans in particular and the Gulf States in general. The bill didn't pass in the 109th Congress, but I hope its introduction sets a standard for what the future treatment of rescue and reconstruction workers ought to look like in what might prove to be unhealthy work environments in the aftermath of large-scale calamities.

In addition to the Georgia town hall meeting, I held my own town hall meeting in New Orleans when I traveled to the Gulf States as a part of the Select Katrina Panel delegation to the region. At that New Orleans town hall meeting I learned of the treatment of inmates who were in prison at the time of the cataclysm.

During the latter days of my second Congressional tenure, I received a phone call from a conscientious mother, disappointed that her son refused to go public about Katrina because he had signed a Pentagon confidentiality agreement. She called me because of my reputation for truth telling and because I had been quite involved, as I have outlined above, in the Hurricane Katrina events, including criticizing FEMA and the Red Cross for their poor organization and refusal to assist Black survivors or to reimburse Black Churches that had stepped in to lend assistance in the absence of government help. The mother who called me worked inside the Red Cross. Her testimony was corroborated by other Blacks with whom I spoke who also worked at the Red Cross. She told me and my Congressional staff of a large number of bullet-riddled bodies that had been catalogued by her son and then dumped in the bayous of Louisiana. To this day there are still missing individuals and the exact number of dead remains unknown. So, my Congressional office began its own investigation of the information. However, the results of my next election precluded us from going any further. When I left office, the investigation ended.

Is that why my voice has to be silenced? Because it is known that if given credible information on any aspect of government responsibility, I will demand an investigation of the report? I can guarantee one thing: that someone was poised to make some big money in the land grab that came after Hurricanes Katrina and Rita, and it wasn't the people of the Lower 9th Ward or the survivors who are now scattered in most of the 50 states. How inconvenient to have some pesky Member of Congress asking too many questions!

Upon reflection, it is clear that the way to remain in office is to do and say absolutely nothing. Those who constructed the U.S. political system as it is today are the ones who benefit from its current construction. Doing nothing is the way to ensure that those currently with positional and political power maintain that power over the rest of us. Too bad that most constituents—the voters—go to the polls and vote for candidates that they think are actually going to do something for them and change that power balance. Somehow, we've got to be able to discern the ones who are there for us and keep them there and get rid of the do-nothings. There are good people in Congress and then there are the rest.

What else are we to think when the Democratic Party's most loyal voters are shafted by the Congressional leadership of the Democratic Party? Clearly something untoward is afoot. Seems to me that someone in a responsible position ought to at least ask, for the record, what it is. Why does it usually boil down to me?

My father used to say to me all of the time that the U.S. political system will expand, but only so far; and that it will definitely not tolerate any structural attack on White Skin Privilege or white supremacy. He takes a rubber band and stretches it for emphasis. Nowhere has this been more evident than in the case of the survivors of Hurricane Katrina. One U.S. Representative, Richard Baker, was overheard stating the facts as he saw them:

"We finally cleaned up public housing in New Orleans. We couldn't do it, but God did."

"Chocolate City," the name given to New Orleans by former Mayor Ray Nagin, is now Whiter, wealthier, and emptier. According to the 2010 Census figures, New Orleans lost 30% of its population and is now down to 60% Black and is no longer in the top 50 largest U.S. cities. Chocolate City's mayor is now Mitch Landrieu, the brother of the state's senior U.S. Senator, Mary Landrieu. He is the first White mayor New Orleans has had in 30 years.

Efforts to force the government of Louisiana and the United States to recognize the rights of the Katrina survivors have largely come to naught. And no wonder why. The United States Supreme Court in the Dred Scott Decision informed us of the position of Blacks before the law. The Court wrote that Blacks had no rights that the White man was bound to respect. And when direct White opposition was inconvenient or didn't look right, Blacks were recruited to do the distasteful work of White resistance to their own brothers and sisters. Therefore, the Black community, the country, and the world have had to endure Black-skinned individuals

**The Black community, the country, and the world have had to endure Black-skinned individuals basically shilling for the status quo interests that preserve White skin and class privilege.**

My supporters from all over the state of Georgia loaded and then drove this truck to a shelter in Baton Rouge that I found full of Hurricane Katrina Survivors who needed help.

basically shilling for the status quo interests that preserve White skin and class privilege: e.g., a Ward Connerly, to counteract the good that Martin Luther King, Jr. accomplished; a Clarence Thomas to counteract the accomplishments of Thurgood Marshall before his ascent to and during his tenure on the United States Supreme Court; a Michael Steel (first Black head of the Republican Party who ran for the U.S. Senate from Maryland) to counteract a Kweisi Mfume (former Chair of the Congressional Black Caucus who pressed for a united Black community and a national Black agenda to govern Black participation in the political system) and who was thwarted in his attempt to gain the Democratic Party nomination by a Democratic Party pro-Israel Member of the U.S. House of Representatives who jumped into the race after Mfume announced (and after this Party perfidy, the Democrat, Ben Cardin, won the unquestioning Black vote). This explains why we get shills (men or women of any race, ethnicity, religion, or language) to protect entrenched interests and even publicly counter the effectiveness or block the popularity of an authentic voice promoted in the corporate-stream press. Glen Ford of BlackAgendaReport calls them the "misleadership" class. Dr. June Terpstra warns us that these misleaders can be of any gender. The challenge for us today is to be able to identify who these misleaders are. This is the quality of discernment. U.S. communities of conscience must be able to detect this new tactic and counter it accordingly. It is here that we can learn lessons from official U.S. government papers—the Reports of the Senator Frank Church Committee and the papers of the Counter Intelligence (COINTELPRO) Program.

11 May 1965

MEMORANDUM FOR THE RECORD

SUBJECT: ███████████, Conversation with

     1. The writer had a short discussion this morning with ██
██y concerning the involvement of A. Philip RANDOLPH, the distinguished
Negro leader, in the so-called "Declaration of Conscience" against participation in the war in Vietnam. In fact, this Declaration of Conscience goes
so far as to attempt to get Negroes to refuse to register for the draft
which is, in fact, illegal activity and against Federal law.

     2. In summarizing ███████ point of view, the problem appears
to be something like this. The Communist left is making an all out drive
to get into the Negro movement. If through any mechanism they can link
prominent Negro leaders to illegal activities and activity which is against
President Johnson's policy, this may cause a serious break between Johnson
and the Negro leadership which, in turn, may create a violent disruption
in the Negro Civil Rights Movement which would give the Communists an
opportunity to cause chaos and disruption.

     3. Furthermore, if the above is coupled with an exposure of
Martin Luther KING, Jr. by other then members of his own race, the damage
to the Negro movement would be impossible to estimate. ██████ is gravely
concerned that KING may be exposed by white sources, official or otherwise,
which would have no good effect and would probably only make KING a martyr.
██████ was also concerned that KING might possibly be assassinated before
his exposure which would have the effect of making him a martyr and would not
be at all helpful to the Negro movement. It is ██████ belief that somehow or other Martin Luther KING must be removed from the leadership of the
Negro movement, and his removal must come from within not from without.
██████ feels that somewhere in the Negro movement, at the top, there must
be a Negro leader who is "clean" who could step into the vacuum and chaos
if Martin Luther KING were either exposed or assassinated.

     4. In summary, ██████ feels that unless the Negro leaders,
other than KING, are informed and are capable of intelligent maneuvering,
the Communists or Negro elements who will be directed by the Communists
may be in a position to, if not take over the Negro movement, completely
disrupt it and hence cause extremely critical problems for the Government
of the United States.

SECRET

Morse Allen

70

# CHAPTER 6

# AMERICA THE BEAUTIFUL

My commitment to the environment and to human rights was the solid foundation upon which my "Green" philosophy was constructed. I have come to believe that most important of all is truth, because with truth, justice will not be far behind. With justice, peace will surely follow. And when we are in peace with each other and Mother Earth, our human dignity is reaffirmed. Therefore, truth, justice, peace, and dignity are my core values. I don't think it is possible to be anything but Green with these beliefs. The challenge is then to match our actions with our beliefs and that involves traveling the road of personal transformation that is necessary for all of us. Therefore, I am also proud of my environmental and human rights records while in Congress because they exposed my development as I became more aware of human and earth needs. During my years in Congress, I consistently scored very high on all of the environmental and human and civil rights legislative score cards. I was a reliable vote for putting the rights of human beings over the rights of corporations to profit from environmental degradation or human rights violations, especially where war and matters of health were concerned.

After my historic 1992 election in a contentious and often racially polarized environment, I immediately sought to bring the races together as best I could while putting an end to intolerable behavior that was rife in the Congressional District, given that many old Confederate practices continued into the present. For example, I had to appeal to the Justice Department and have one election overturned and re-voted due to obvious vote-rigging to prevent an outspoken Black candidate from winning the election. I had to report one school system to the Civil Rights

Division of the Department of Education because this particular school system basically ran a segregated school system within the confines of one set of school buildings. Another time, I reported parent complaints about the standard practice in one school system of drugging Black male children and labeling them uneducable, thus allowing these children to be segregated from the general school population and put into special programs for which the school system was paid extra money. Needless to say, one of the main complaints coming from the parents was that children rarely achieved well enough to graduate from the program; the Black parents felt that the school system had found a way to deny their children an education and then to financially profit from it.

I held a series of what I called "Unity Receptions," to which I invited all of the town to come out and socialize. At my most successful Reception, held at the home of the local mayor, the mayor whispered to me, "You even brought out the Klan!" By the time the Congressional District had been dismantled by the U.S. Supreme Court as a "racial gerrymander," I had worked to integrate the list of elected officials in all of the counties, totaling the election of approximately fifty Blacks to office covering 22 Georgia counties over a four-year period.

We really did make an effort to let everyone know that my door was open to them, and if their cause was just, I would become their strongest advocate. Not everyone believed me, and the White farmers in my District discovered the hard way that their prejudice was misguided.

Shortly after I was sworn in and assigned to the House Agriculture Committee, I decided that I would organize the farmers in my District and take them up to Washington, D.C. to meet and greet the officials in the new Clinton Administration that would make decisions affecting their farms and hence, their lives. This was a very important event for me and so the Congressional staff worked diligently to ensure the success of this event. I personally went to the Georgia Farm Bureau to inform them and the farmers in my District about the opportunity that I was working to make available to them. The Congressional Office spared no effort to inform and reach out to the farmers and extend an invitation to them all to participate.

When the day of departure arrived, the bus was set to leave from the designated spot. All we needed was farmers! Yes, the Black farmers came out in force; but the only White farmers who showed up were two farmers from another Congressional District who had heard about the trip. When I asked them, they shrugged their shoulders and said they didn't know why the farmers in my District wouldn't want to participate.

When we arrived in Washington, D.C., we were received by the officials at the United States Department of Agriculture, including the new Secretary of Agriculture, Mike Espy. Everyone whom the farmers had told me they wanted to meet responded positively to our request and met the farmers. Those who came marveled at the openness of everyone they met. They felt empowered. Black farmers finally felt that they had an open door among the power corridors. Then came the long bus ride home. Everyone was smiling, but me.

I was deeply hurt by the obvious snub by Georgia's White farmers. I was hurt for my staff who had worked so hard on the project and I was hurt that despite our vigorous outreach, there was no reciprocity to our extended hand. So, we redoubled our outreach efforts. I didn't have much time to indulge my hurt feelings, because in that District, there was always more work to do. So, I set aside my feelings and went back to work.

Weeks later, the very same farmers who refused to participate in our bus ride were frantically calling me to meet with them urgently; they said it was an emergency. They even wanted me to skip going to D.C. in order to arrange an emergency meeting with them. As it turned out during this time, Georgia was experiencing a pretty severe drought. The very farmers who refused to participate in my "farmers' trip" to Washington, D.C. were especially hard hit. They were the big farmers. They needed a "Disaster Declaration" from the United States Department of Agriculture and they told me: don't go to Washington, come to see us. I did. Then, I went to D.C. and asked the Administration to send someone to take care of my farmers. The Deputy Secretary of Agriculture did come to my District and we walked the parched fields of my farmers together. But I could not remain quiet. I had to ask them why had they not gone to D.C. on the trip that I had organized for them? I asked; they answered. Their answer was shocking, honest, and true: they had organized themselves to boycott me because they didn't think I would represent them, "too." The "too" at the end of their sentence was extremely important. They saw my Black skin as an impediment to me being able to or even wanting to represent them. Their disaster declaration in hand proved them wrong.

Unlike most Black elected officials who have White constituents, I refused to run away from my Black constituents in order to serve my White ones. I hope it becomes clear from these few anecdotes, of which there are many more that I could tell, that I served all of our constituents and I did it with zeal. It was this example that was a dangerous precedent for some; and as soon as we had become successful in establishing a "new normal" of respectful post-Civil Rights Act, post-Voting Rights Act coexistence, our efforts were stopped--dead in their tracks by bigger forces not looking on these developments (consistent with a New South) with approval.

The farmers' trip wasn't the only time racist fears were proved wrong.

I went throughout the District with my District Days—days during which I would set up a satellite office and remain there until every constituent who came had been seen. Soon, a familiar pattern began to emerge. For my White constituents, I was the call of last resort. Whether it was attendance at a District Day or a visit to the Congressional Office, my White constituents would have already called everyone possible before calling me. But, in too many cases, they were forced to approach the office because they just couldn't always get served elsewhere to satisfaction. So, they would call. We took our "don't-take-no-for-an-answer" attitude into the bureaucracy of the Federal Government and got results for our constituents. We had a reputation for getting what our constituents wanted. In one particularly impactful case, the Congressional Office literally worked a miracle for a constituent. This particular constituent contacted the Office in desperate need of an organ transplant. He got the transplant and actually came back to say thank you.

This gentleman then proceeded to shout from the rafters the good work that had been done by us for him! After that, the outreach to our White constituents became significantly easier.

I traveled to one small Georgia county and it was the first time that a Member of Congress had been there—ever. Although not many people came to District Day there, the County leadership was impressed and began to contemplate ways in which we could cooperate. We really had begun to break down the barrier walls.

During my first campaign for Congress in 1992, I had been warned by friendly Whites in a few counties to get out of town before the sun went down. What a long way we had come!

I learned a lot, too, about Georgia history. Because I started out having these District Days at the various County Courthouses. But month after month, I noticed that Black constituents would not attend. So, naturally, I asked why. Anyone who knew Georgia history well would not have even had to ask; the County Courthouse was where lynchings were either consented to or actually carried out. Long established behavior patterns had been molded by nooses and vigilante justice. Indeed, one of my rural Black supporters had her house shot at and had she sat up in her bed, to see what was happening, she would not be with us now. Another of my supporters put signs out one weekend only to find them all collected and placed back in his mailbox with gunshots over his house to alert him to look outside and see the commotion. Despite all of this, and more, after I was sworn into the Congress in 1993, I approached the people of my new Congressional District with compassion and a "can do" attitude. Still, my election threatened to completely upset the apple cart of White supremacy. Well, in my opinion, that apple cart deserved to be upset, but how to touch hearts and obliterate the practice of U.S.

apartheid when it was no longer legal was an ongoing challenge that I chose to openly confront rather than wish away.

This brings to mind a story of one of my typical challenges.

Jane Fonda was very active in Georgia politics; she had a successful program to combat teenaged pregnancy. Once, while Zell Miller was Georgia's Governor, Fonda commented on Georgia's poverty. Zell demanded an apology from Jane for the remark and he got it. Well, I jumped into the public conversation and seconded Fonda's observation and told of the excruciating poverty in my own Congressional District that I was working hard to correct. Of course, my intervention was certainly not welcome, but a national wire service journalist was sent to Georgia to see my District for herself. She ended her day-long tour in tears, I'm told by the staffer who escorted her, because she just did not know that we had that kind of poverty inside the United States. That's why self-empowerment and adequate financial support for community institutions was always one of my Congressional priorities.

One issue that was brought to me proved to be a very big one that brought me in direct confrontation with wealthy multinational mining corporations doing business in the red clay of Georgia: the chalk mines.

At one of my District Days, a talkative Black man came to me weaving an incredible yarn about mining leases being taken out by mining companies on private land that was never actually mined; payments as low as a nickel a ton for tons of kaolin mined; and non-existent reclamation of the land after mining. The kaolin deposits just happened to be situated in Georgia's Black Belt. Therefore, most of the non-union labor force was Black. I was told that a flyer was placed in one of the chalk mine break rooms instructing workers not to vote for me! One White landowner told me that I was the first elected official in twenty years to even return his phone call!

Kaolin was one of the first issues I tackled after being elected to the U.S. Congress. Kaolin? Yes, kaolin. Not the French rock band: kaolin is a mineral. One of my home state of Georgia's largest natural resources. And it's big business, too. Kaolin gives Kaopectate its name. Kaolin is used in cosmetics, paper, china, and toothpaste. About $1 billion per year! Georgia is the largest kaolin producer in the United States and one flyover of our state puts a lie to the reclamation claims that the industry boasted at the time that they repaired the land after mining it. As the Atlanta Constitution wrote, "Kaolin should not [have been] McKinney's fight. But because the state was filled with 'weak-kneed men,'" it became my fight. Kaolin, for me, was the perfect combination of Black and White issues where there was no fuzzy, gray line: environment, worker's rights, civil rights, and human rights.

I worked with the landowners in the region, both Black and

White, and got the kaolin companies to renegotiate their mining agreements with them. It would be a costly victory because when the matter of my victory in the Eleventh Congressional District of Georgia made its way to the United States Supreme Court, and the District was struck down, every revision of the District presented as a possible redraw took me out of Georgia's kaolin country. In fact, as if to erase even the memory of the Eleventh District, the entire Congressional map of Georgia was renumbered and in 2002, a White conservative U.S. Representative was elected in the area and I was out. Fast forward to 2008, when a Black woman State Senator decided to leave her Georgia Senate seat and run in the successor District against the conservative White incumbent U.S. Representative. Democratic Presidential nominee Barack Obama endorsed the conservative White Member of Congress over the conscious Black woman State Senator, consigning to the history books our pioneering work to bring the races together in Georgia's Black Belt and justice for those workers and landowners victimized by the Georgia chalk mines.

**Democratic Presidential nominee Barack Obama endorsed the conservative White Member of Congress over the conscious Black woman State Senator, consigning to the history books our pioneering work to bring the races together.**

With determination and presence, we made a difference. People dared to hope and act on behalf of change and change came. It was possibly the dawn of a new day and a different political script in Georgia that was then snuffed out by the Supreme Court which, with Clarence Thomas's vote, struck down the Eleventh District of Georgia, believing five White racists who argued that a Black Representative could not represent them, and who were joined in Court by the Anti-Defamation League, who wanted no part of minority-opportunity districts that gave the minority population an opportunity to have real representation and make real change for themselves and the country. Sadly, the Anti-Defamation League, a "civil rights organization" known primarily for its protection of Jews intervened in a situation related to Blacks to see to it that Blacks just have a representative rather than having true representation.

Before I left the Agriculture Committee and the Eleventh Congressional District, I added innocuous but momentous language to the Farm Bill that authorized a disparity study of the United States Department of Agriculture (U.S.D.A.) and its practices with respect to Black farmers. Secretary Espy took the language seriously and contracted with an experienced outside firm to conduct the study. It came back confirming what the Black farmers knew: U.S.D.A. practice was full of discriminatory effect and U.S.D.A. actions had led to Black land loss and to

Black farmers losing their farms and their lands. Sadly, President Obama's Department of Agriculture has done nothing yet to make the Black farmers, victimized by discrimination, whole. In fact, President Obama's latest effort, along with Congress, has been described by Black farmers as more of a severance than a settlement. Sadly, to date, the plaintiffs in the initial Black farmer lawsuit, known as the Pigford I farmers, have not received compensation for the admitted discrimination that they have suffered (this is worth another book just by itself), although millions of dollars have been spent. Who got the money? Maybe I need to go into this a bit more in-depth since the myth is that the Black Farmers have been made whole.

There are two classes of farmers involved in the Pigford Lawsuit: the original claimants who are active farmers and in whom the institutional knowledge of farming techniques is stored. Due to the admitted racial discrimination, these farmers by and large were never given the opportunity to convert their farms to "modern" farms. As a result, Black farmers have always done organic farming because they could not get the loans to build up the business side of their farming enterprises. Therefore, at a time of peak soil, when organic farming is in demand, it is the Black farmers who sit on the county's most fertile soil. The Pigford I farmers are the farmers who know what to do with a piece of land to keep it producing the nourishing foods that we all need. Then come along the lawyers who seek to enlarge the class to make the settlement even bigger. These are the Pigford II class: the people who might have thought about farming, maybe tried to start a farm and were turned down by one of the U.S.D.A. agencies and who, as a result, never put plow to the soil and within whom very little institutional knowledge is stored. The Pigford II class is the class to which the media announcements about settlements refer. Not the Pigford I class of actual farmers who own the remaining Black-owned farm land in production. This is like a cruel bait and switch on those farmers who have sustained the cruelest blow of admitted discrimination, and who are on the verge of losing their farms anyway because the discrimination never stopped! As a result of this continued discrimination, one and one half million Black-owned farm acres are at risk of being foreclosed on at any moment by the Obama U.S.D.A.—the very U.S.D.A. that is guilty of the acts of discrimination that led to the current crisis.

During my first years in the Congress, I also introduced what was to become one of the centerpieces of U.S. environmental legislation regarding our national forests—to provide for their protection from logging, road building, and clearcutting and to mandate their restoration. I helped write that bill and put my heart and soul into it. The National Forest Protection and Restoration Act (NFPRA) was the result. I worked on it with Chad Hanson (I could never forget you, Chad!)—who at the time was somehow indirectly affiliated with the Sierra Club. After that bill became my labor of love, and was introduced by me and Republican Jim Leach of Iowa, the folks in the national Sierra Club office decided that it would be better to have the bill introduced by the White male Republican, even though I had helped to write it!

I told the Sierra Club brass that, as far as I was concerned, their suggestion was racist. Needless to say, after I was defeated in 2002, the Sierra Club got its way. Upon my return to Congress in 2005, as I was attempting to reintroduce the bill, I found that it had already been reintroduced by Jim Leach. Of course, the bill still hasn't passed, despite successive Democratic and Republican majorities in Congress.

The Sierra Club wrote articles all the time about that bill and my environmental record in general. You could say I was their poster child for as long as they could use me. After they tried to take NFPRA away from me, the relationship certainly began to sour. So much so that, in 2004, when I was running to recapture my seat in Congress, the same Sierra Club that had featured me in their magazine too many times to count, didn't even endorse me for reelection.

I had always touted the environmental community for its apparent affinity for America's diversity. What I mean by that is that I felt welcomed into the environmental community, I felt a harmony of interests, I felt that I didn't have to leave my Blackness at the door when I entered a room with them. But my experience with the Sierra Club reminded me that Dr. Martin Luther King, Jr. also had choice words to say about this country's White "progressives" in his Letter from a Birmingham Jail —which goes directly back to what my father said about U.S. power centers not tolerating any dismantling whatsoever of White Skin Privilege or the ideological foundation of this country—White supremacy.

When I voiced my feelings about the Sierra Club and my experiences with them to others who consider themselves the "real" environmentalists, I was told that they considered the Sierra Club to be the "corporate wing" of the environmental movement and that there were many other organizations composed of true believers who did truly value America's diversity. These groups weren't afraid to acknowledge and struggle with the issue of White Skin Privilege as they also dealt with the degradation of our planet, starting inside our own country. Many of these people constituted the core of the "Green Movement."

One of my supporters, Mark Donham, called the Sierra Club out on their failure to even endorse me and Counterpunch.com carried his missive. I affectionately call environmentalists like Mark the "tree huggers" and "my people" because we truly seem to understand each other. After a few invitations to hike with these environmentalists, I now consider myself a bona fide tree hugger, too!

I was already a student of the FBI's Counter-Intelligence Program (COINTELPRO) and understood its devastating effect on the movement for complete liberation from oppression for all people in this country. I understood that the United States government had violated its own legal precepts and hortatory pronouncements in a secret war ordered to preserve White supremacy against attacks coming from Blacks, Whites, Native Americans, Puerto Ricans, and others daring to dissent. I quickly learned that environmentalists had to endure COINTELPRO of their own that resulted in FBI excesses and that targeting continues till today as environmentalists are labeled as terrorists. Anyone targeted by the government was subjected to character demonization at a minimum, prison or death at the other extreme.

The case of Judi Bari and Darryl Cherney were an example of what could happen to inconvenient environmentalists. The FBI was found guilty by a jury of violating Judi and Darryl's Constitutional rights when the FBI and the Oakland Police Department targeted the Earth First! Organizers, illegally arrested them, and illegally searched their home. After a motion-triggered pipe bomb exploded in Bari's car while she and Cherney were in it, the Oakland Police immediately looked to Bari and Cherney as their only suspects. The bombing was seized upon by the authorities as an opportunity to demonize the character of Bari and Cherney and politically neutralize them and their organization—in line with the mission statement of the FBI's COINTELPRO.

I had the great honor to meet Julia Butterfly, the tree-sitter who saved an area of forest on the West Coast because she was able to sit for 738 days in a 1,500 year-old California Redwood named Luna! I also met Woody Harrelson at Heartwood in Kentucky. I always liked Woody Harrelson, and was stunned to learn that his father was at Dealey Plaza on that fateful November day in 1963 when President John Kennedy was shot. While at Heartwood, I learned about the mining practice called "mountaintop removal" which, incredibly, does just that! Kentucky is rolling green hills and just full of beautiful greenery and beautiful people, but it is also at the epicenter of blowing the tops off mountains in order to facilitate mining!

As I was driving in from the airport to my lodge for the Heartwood Annual Conference, I noticed so many hospitals and I thought to myself, "This state is really taking care of its people." Then my guide informed me that we were in the heart of black lung territory. Yes, there are lots of hospitals because the people have given their lives in many instances and certainly their health in other instances, to provide coal to an energy-hungry country.

Energy is the foundation of the American "quality of life." And so the human toll that coal once took is now being felt globally in the race for oil. Is a "quality of life" something worth killing over? I don't think so.

Some time later, I read that the atmosphere over the United Kingdom is testing positive for depleted uranium. And U.S. soldiers are returning to the States and testing positive for uranium exposure. The articles seemed to justify language I had introduced to ban the use of depleted uranium weapons by the United States. I caught a lot of "inside-the-beltway" flak for that, too, but those articles proved to me that once again, I had been right.

When I returned to Congress in 2005, there was already pending legislation on depleted uranium, but I reintroduced mine because my bill was tougher. I have read the information on exposure levels and birth defects from Dr. Rokke, and I have had the opportunity to get to know Leuren Moret, a beautiful woman whose passion on the issue of depleted uranium is unsurpassed.

Unfortunately, the Pentagon's own policies fail to protect the lives of our soldiers. When Halliburton served our service men and women tainted food and water, it was not disqualified from obtaining further Pentagon contracts. On the contrary, it was rewarded with even more contracts. If the Pentagon were truly interested in promoting the health and welfare of our soldiers, it would not have reneged on the promise the Bush Administration made to provide pre-deployment health screenings for our young men and women deployed in Iraq and Afghanistan. It wouldn't have forced our soldiers to take those vaccines that made them sick and weren't even approved by the FDA. And, the use of depleted uranium would have long ago been halted. The birth defects being seen in Iraq and experienced in the offspring of our exposed soldiers should be enough to stop the use of these weapons. But it is not. Depleted uranium's armor-piercing capability is deemed more important, so the Pentagon continues to use these weapons in its war machine, despite the cost to our environment and the human toll that is taken.

**If the Pentagon were truly interested in promoting the health and welfare of our soldiers, the use of depleted uranium would have long ago been halted.**

My interest in human rights preceded my tenure in Congress. My concern for Africa had always pushed me to be concerned about the primacy of morality and human rights in the formulation of U.S. foreign policy. Of course, in academic circles, such a reality-based idea was anathema to the higher status of "realpolitik." It all seemed very "masculine" to me, this Cold Warrior talk about nuclear weapon throw weights, electro-magnetic pulses, and total body displacement from nuclear blasts. After I arrived in Congress, I was convinced that war and use of the U.S. military arsenal is metaphor for the impotent men who order their use. Due to my seniority on the House International Relations Committee, I became the highest-ranking Democrat on its Human Rights and International

Operations Subcommittee. Honestly, I didn't have much competition for this position because it wasn't perceived as a "money committee." But I loved it. From this perch, I could focus the work of the International Relations Committee toward a centrality of human rights as the name of the Subcommittee suggested. I took every human rights claim seriously.

However, I gained a valuable glimpse at the real way business was conducted in Congressional hearings after one of my International Relations Committee hearings. One of my colleagues ranted and raved at one of the hearings convened by the International Relations Committee. I was really into the subject matter, it was about the Western Hemisphere, and I couldn't wait until my command of the facts was so great that I could run a hearing like that, too. But then after the hearing was over, I heard the same Member of Congress who had railed on this and railed on that, laughing, joking, and backslapping with the very people he had lambasted during the hearing. Was all that just theatrics? Was it just a big show? Were all the Hearings like that? In the end, I concluded that it seemed to be a good acting job tailor-made for the C-Span cameras. I had a really bad feeling after that because my balloon was punctured. Sadly, I began to wonder if all hearings on Capitol Hill were like that.

That experience caused me to open my eyes a little wider. And to view things, not through the prism of a wide-eyed visitor, but through the eyes of someone who had struggled to be in that "seat at the table" of public policy making. That unpleasant moment shook me back into the grimy reality of what was really happening there. I served on the House International Relations Committee from 1993 to 2003. I accrued ten years seniority on that Committee and on the Human Rights Subcommittee. I soon became a respected authority on matters pertaining to human rights. People from all over the world knew that if they could just get to me, I'd give them a fair hearing and that I'd do my best to alleviate their suffering—if it was within the power of a Congressional Office to do so. And I vowed that, when my turn came to direct the content of or manage as Chair or Ranking Member my Subcommittee, my input would be serious at all times, not like the duplicity I had witnessed. When my turn came, I was exposed to the way things really work on Capitol Hill, stunned at the opportunities for corruption.

**Stunned at the opportunities for corruption, I grasped the reason why conditions of the people deteriorate despite the fact that we have representatives who are supposed to represent our best interests.**

I grasped the reason why conditions of the people deteriorate despite the fact that we have representatives who are supposed to represent our best interests. I became aware, like Shakespeare's Marcellus, that: "Something is rotten in the state of Denmark."

# CHAPTER 7

# A GLOBAL VIEW

John Stockwell. *In Search of Enemies: A CIA Story*. The author and the book that changed my life. John Stockwell is the highest-ranking Central Intelligence Agency (CIA) agent to leave the Agency and go public. In 1978, his book In Search of Enemies was published and I devoured it. As a student of International Relations at the University of Southern California, I began my exploration of the world. From the date of my birth and my coming of age and the recognition of my African-ness, my exploration of the world was through African eyes. So, when John Stockwell wrote about his experiences in Africa, I paid attention.

John Stockwell confirmed for me my father's basic lesson. Earlier in his careeer, Stockwell had been told that the guys on top had the big picture and until he reached the top he needed to do as he was told. Well, when he finally reached a high-enough position to see those people at the top, here's what he found:

> I wanted to know if wise men were making difficult decisions based on truly important, threatening information, threatening to our national security interests. If that had been the case, I still planned to get out of the CIA, but I would know that the system, the invisible government, our national security complex, was in fact justified and worthwhile. And so I took the job . . . Suffice it to say I wouldn't be standing in front of you tonight if I had found these wise men making these tough decisions. What I found, quite frankly, was fat old men sleeping through sub-committee meetings of the NSC in which we were making decisions that

Cynthia hosts Mozambican woman who had given birth in a tree due to severe flooding there.

were killing people in Africa. I mean literally. Senior
Ambassador Ed Mulcahy . . . would go to sleep in nearly
every one of these meetings . . .

Stockwell confirmed something that deep in my bones I "knew:"
that CIA case officer Larry Devlin had Patrice Lumumba killed. And
importantly, he warned the attentive public of the American people that
they were being lied to—along with Congress. In one of his many lectures
now available on the internet, Stockwell said:

Our Ambassador to the United Nations, Patrick
Moynihan, he read continuous statements of our
position to the Security Council, the general assembly,
and the press conferences, saying the Russians and
Cubans were responsible for the conflict, and that
we were staying out, and that we deplored the
militarization of the conflict.

And every statement he made was false. And
every statement he made was originated in the subcommittee of the NSC that I sat on as we managed this
thing. The State Department press person read these
position papers daily to the press. We would write
papers for him. Four paragraphs. We would call him
on the phone and say, call us 10 minutes before you
go on, the situation could change overnight, we'll tell
you which paragraph to read. And all four paragraphs
would be false. Nothing to do with the truth. Designed
to play on events, to create this impression of Soviet
and Cuba aggression in Angola. When they were in
fact responding to our initiatives.

And the CIA Director was required by law to brief
the Congress. This CIA Director, Bill Colby--the same
one that dumped our people in Vietnam----gave 36
briefings of the Congress, the oversight committees,
about what we were doing in Angola. And he lied. At
36 formal briefings. And such lies are perjury, and it's
a felony to lie to the Congress.

He lied about our relationship with South Africa.
We were working closely with the South African Army,
giving them our arms, coordinating battles with them,
giving them fuel for their tanks and armored cars.
He said we were staying well away from them. They
were concerned about these White mercenaries that

were appearing in Angola, a very sensitive issue, hiring Whites to go into a Black African country, to help you impose your will on that Black African country by killing the Blacks, a very sensitive issue. The Congress was concerned we might be involved in that, and he assured them we had nothing to do with it.

We had in fact formed four little mercenary armies and delivered them into Angola to do this dirty business for the CIA. And he lied to them about that. They asked if we were putting arms into the conflict, and he said no, and we were. They asked if we had advisors inside the country, training in the use of weapons, installing communications systems, planning battles, and he said, we didn't have anybody inside the country.

In summary about Angola, without U.S. intervention, 10,000 people would be alive that were killed in the thing. The outcome might have been peaceful, or at least much less bloody. The MPLA was winning when we went in, and they went ahead and won, which was, according to our consul, the best thing for the country.

And of the press, Stockwell had this to say: "The First Amendment does not require anyone to publish the truth."

After reading Stockwell, it became clear to me that powerful U.S. leaders cynically used Black power advocates in the United States, who were unaware of U.S. policy actions against liberation groups in Africa, to fight as volunteers (mercenaries) on the side of the U.S. and against the very movements that these people, with more information, would have supported. In other words, as a result of our lack of preparation and accurate understanding of our political environment, Black people, especially, but in a more general sense, many people, get twisted into supporting U.S. policies that are exactly counter to their values and their interests. At this moment, I vowed that I would never be unprepared or make a policy position without personally obtaining enough reliable information from trusted sources. This meant that I needed to weave my own information network that did not solely rely on "official" sources, and so, that is exactly what I did.

Thus, appropriately armed by one of the Central Intelligence Agency's own, I entered the United States Congress. I never met John Stockwell, and little did he know, but by his courageous act of conscience, he prepared me to function as an effective voice for the people as a United States Congresswoman sculpted by his mold, serving on the House International Relations, House Agriculture, House Armed Services, and

Budget Committees and the Select Committee on Hurricanes Katrina and Rita.

There are many others, inside my Congressional Districts, who served as role models and nourished my heart. John Stockwell's truths fed my brain.

I had seen firsthand how Congressional hearings could be all theatre, but as I became more comfortable in my role, I began to ask more questions and became more assertive—I was using the people's seat the way it was intended at the policy-making table.

I remember one post-9/11 House International Relations Committee meeting at which the State Department was making a presentation about how dangerous Osama bin Laden was. I had recently read that, for all the hoopla about bin Laden, the fact of the matter was that the United States covertly maintained a relationship with the family and had even given the family hundreds of millions of dollars for a covert construction project in Afghanistan during the U.S. bid to oust the Soviet Union from there. In fact, the United States had begun funneling money and support to Afghanistan in 1979 after a pro-Soviet government took control in Kabul. U.S. policymakers were giddy with the prospect of handing to the Soviet Union what the Vietnamese people had handed to the U.S.: military defeat.

The trap was sprung in December 1979 when the Soviets crossed their military into Afghanistan. The United States became even more involved in its Afghanistan project. Aid to the mujahideen, whom President Reagan called "freedom fighters" was targeted to the most extreme elements within the Islamic community with a view to fomenting unrest inside the Soviet Union, itself, with its own large Muslim population. The Afghanistan project quickly became the largest covert operation of the U.S. government at that time. Eventually, it is believed that Osama bin Laden controlled as many as one dozen training camps in Afghanistan. I had read all about the U.S. effort, had watched the testosterone flow as the male Members of Congress either bragged of their exploits in the Afghani bunkers or reported on the billions of dollars spent to embarrass the Soviets. What the world didn't know, was that the creation of what has become known as "radical Islam" was a policy option theorized and acted on by individuals in and out of universities, the U.S. government, and think tanks. Thus "radical Islam" had been made strong with U.S. tax dollars as a part of U.S. policy. Professors Peter Dale Scott and Michel Chossudovsky have written extensively on U.S. involvement with terrorist groups created by U.S. policy that the U.S. now purports to fight in its Global War on Terror. The unwillingness of the U.S. government representatives that came before Congressional Committees to tell the whole truth to the American people was what sent me searching for a more robust reflection of reality by cultivating my own sources of information on the ground and in affected communities. The Ronald Reagan dictum, "Trust, but verify," became my watchword. And that's what got me into so much trouble in Washington, D.C.! I trusted that I needed to verify everything I was being sold in a "dog and pony" show. Not only did I question those in authority, as can be seen on the many C-Span and youtube clips, I also attempted to verify for myself everything that they told me!

> **The Ronald Reagan dictum, "Trust, but verify," became my watchword. And that's what got me into so much trouble in Washington, D.C.! I trusted that I needed to verify everything I was being sold in a "dog and pony" show.**

This is reminiscent of the project that I appointed for myself while I was in the Georgia Legislature. I wanted to write an "op ed" about the Georgia State Flag. In the early 1990s, the State of Georgia was still fighting its "Flag Wars." The Saint Andrew's Cross, the battle flag of the Confederacy, was emblazoned on our State Flag. This had been done back in the 1950s after the Brown versus Board of Education Supreme Court decision mandated desegregation of Georgia's public schools. I decided to interview the members of the Georgia Legislature who were still around, venerated as the "Noble Old Guard" to whom I must look up. In reality, they were just a bunch of old cigar-chewing White men who had become comfortable with state power and who used that power to benefit themselves and entrench their values. So, for one day, I fancied myself a journalist and marched right up to them one by one and I asked them their feelings about the role they had played in putting the Saint Andrew's Cross on Georgia's state flag. My last question, "Are you a racist?" took them by surprise. One thought about it and told me seriously that he was "a man of the time." That, to me, was a very honest answer. And in my opinion, it was the truth. Denmark Groover was the one who owned up. I liked and respected him after that, even when I disagreed with him; I respected him because when it mattered, he told me the truth.

So, I expected to be told the truth when I went to Congress and I grew impatient with the representatives from the Executive Branch who told half-truths or none of the truth when questions were put to them. And just as I had intervened with my sister Congresswoman to clarify that the United States had, indeed, contracted with the bin Laden family while the State Department representative was accounting to us the dangers of Osama, he had to admit the U.S. government relationship with the family. When I asked him the right question, he had no wiggle room and responded honestly. This was the lesson I learned; the onus was on me to ask the right question, knowing enough background to be able to go three or four rounds deep into the issue so as to leave no wiggle room when the time came to get an important answer.

The Caribbean, Africa, and Asia all became areas of interest for me, all under the important rubric of human rights and correcting the wrongs done to innocent people by U.S. policy. I got my first taste of the power of a commitment combined with fresh ideas when selected Members of the Congressional Black Caucus demanded of the new Clinton Administration that Haiti's priest-become-President Jean Bertrand Aristide be reinstated and allowed to serve out his term.

It was clear that the George Herbert Walker Bush Administration, acting on the loathing of the idea of self-determination for Black people in general and for Haitians in particular had green-lighted the coup that overthrew Aristide in 1991. Honestly, at the time, I didn't realize the precious history in the Western Hemisphere that Haiti represented; but I did know that my responsibility as a conscious Member of Congress was to restore the will of the Haitian people as expressed in their election—and that meant that President Aristide should be restored to power. Therefore, in 1993 when we were sworn in as freshman Members of Congress, Carrie Meek, Corrine Brown and I formed a special bond with Haiti as our project.

[*The following section on Haiti was done after a series of interviews of Haitians and U.S. citizens of Haitian descent, including Attorney Marguerite Laurent and David Josué.*]

Christopher Columbus landed in Haiti in December 1492 on his first voyage to the New World. He claimed it for Spain, and named the island La Isla Espanola, The Spanish Island. The island became known as Hispaniola in English. The native population of Taino of the Arawak people, were wiped out by enslavement, imported germs that Columbus and subsequent European settlers brought with them, to say nothing of the sheer brutality that accompanies settler colonialism. Africans were brought to the island in 1503, when the slave trade started in earnest. It was Bartholomew de las Casas, a Catholic priest, who blessed the operation. After the defeat of the Emperor of France, Napoleon Bonaparte, and the declaration of the Haitian Republic in 1804, successive punitive invasions, occupations, and dictatorships propped up by the United States, it would be another Catholic priest, a modern-day liberation theology Catholic priest who would arouse the dreams of the Haitian people to be free from domination once again. That Catholic priest was Jean Bertrand Aristide. Rooted in the Haitian experience, Father Aristide was deeply affected by the plight of the Haitian people under the weight of U.S. domination; and he found the solution in liberation theology, along the lines of the practices of Archbishop Romero who was gunned down in El Salvador while saying Mass. Father Aristide could have become a part of the bourgeoisie. Instead, he preached a brand of sermon that told the people that everyone was worthy. He set up a children's charity, La Famille, C'est la Vie (Family is Life), and encouraged the children of the street to become family to each other. He went among the poor and helped them to become family to each other. He identified for them the dignity already inside of them. He was known as a selfless priest who used his resources to help the poor. It was because of his actions that the people implored him to become their President.

Aristide spoke out against the U.S.-supported autocratic dictator, Jean Claude Duvalier, known as "Baby Doc," who followed in his father's footsteps as a brutal but reliable U.S. ally in its struggle against Communism. For over 30 years of anti-Communism, Haiti paid a high price in blood for the U.S. Cold War against the Soviet Union. However, when U.S. propaganda began to champion democracy and self-determination for the peoples of the Soviet Union, then the Haitian people understood that if it was good for the people of Russia, then it was time for self-determination to be good for them. Aristide played a pivotal role in bringing down "Baby Doc" and his violent death squad known as the ton ton macoute. Aristide used the Church to organize people. And by 1987, they had organized so well that they brought down the Duvalier regime. The Vatican forced Father Aristide and all of its priests to choose between The Church and their activism as elected officials. Father Aristide chose the Haitian people.

It was The Lavalas Movement (the Flood) that washed out the Haitian dictatorship and marked the beginning of the formal politicization of Aristide culminating in his run for President. Fanmi Lavalas was the political party formed by Jean-Bertrand Aristide. And when Aristide was sworn in, the children of his charity led the procession into the national palace. President Aristide gave the children a broadcasting radio station, something that empowered them. Krayol became the national language, not French, the language of Haiti's powerful and oppressive elite. President Aristide purposely did not speak French to the people; he was the first Haitian President not to do so. Consequently, he was heard and understood by the masses of Haitian people who also spoke Krayol and not French. President Aristide respected vodun even though he was a Catholic. He brought literacy to the adults. For all of these reasons and more, Jean-Bertrand Aristide was and is loved by all of the Haitian people, except those allied with the United States and who constitute the Haitian elite.

The Haitian elite don't have the votes to ever win a free or fair election. So they resort to all measure of propaganda, lies, spin, and outright attempted theft in order to prevent the people from having their choice elected. The U.S. has walked in lockstep with these efforts to deny self-determination to the Haitian people. In reality, it is clear that the real problem with Haitians as far as the U.S. is concerned, is that special Haitian spirit that compelled Toussaint l'Ouverture to defeat on the battlefield a European power led by an Emperor known for his military acumen. Jean-Bertrand Aristide was the first democratically-elected President of Haiti. The United States, meanwhile, attempted to turn the Parliament against Aristide and the country experienced legislative gridlock. It was at the end of the Bush Administration that Raoul Cedras, trained at the U.S. School of the Americas, toppled President Aristide who went into exile in 1991. And so, with that backdrop, the size of the Congressional Black Caucus (CBC) nearly doubled in 1993 with the addition of freshman Members from the South, and we actively bolstered the CBC call for the return of President Aristide to Haiti. It was clear to the Clinton Administration that on this issue it had little wiggle room—it was boxed in: it had to overtly support the call for Aristide's return to power.

Soft-spoken Aristide made the case directly to Members of Congress. I was in all of those meetings. By his side was his lovely lawyer Marguerite Laurent, who spoke my language—she spoke forcefully of the injustice that had been done to the Haitian people and that it was the United States that needed to correct this wrong. President Aristide had served only 7 months of a five-year term. The demand was that Aristide be allowed to return and serve out the remainder of his term. Haiti was the rallying cry for millions of Blacks across the United States, the very people who had just overwhelmingly voted Bill Clinton into the U.S. Presidency.

Randall Robinson of TransAfrica was one of the major players in the U.S. wing of the anti-apartheid movement and Katherine Dunham, famed Black ballerina, went on a hunger strike. The informed Black electorate was galvanized around this issue. The Congressional Black Caucus worked very hard for the restoration of Aristide. From 1991 to 1994 Aristide was in the U.S. lobbying for his return, and I had entered the Congress in 1993, along with my other colleagues from the South. It was during this time that I met Randall Robinson, his wife Hazel, Marguerite, and Aristide. On Capitol Hill, we were all working together. But that was not all. The Haitian Diaspora was extremely active; some women camped in front of the United Nations Headquarters in New York City for years, even in the rain, asking for the return of Aristide.

"Operation Uphold Democracy" was what Clinton called the return of Aristide. Between his swearing in, in 1991, and his exile seven months later, Aristide had survived nine assassination attempts and lost many of his close mentors. The U.S. returned him with 20,000 troops. This was in 1994. He returned behind plexiglass—which for him must have been a kind of prison. The Clinton Administration made him agree that he wouldn't recoup the time not served; he only had one year left onto his term, and that was to be spent transitioning to the next President. Aristide didn't even return with the lawyer, Marguerite Laurent, who had worked so diligently for him with me and other Caucus Members. Instead,

Aristide was accompanied by Ira Kurzban who was to lead efforts on behalf of Aristide and Haiti. Aristide didn't even return with Haitian security guards, but rather a U.S. security team from a San Francisco, California firm that failed to protect him when the boys led by Guy Philippe were on their way from the Dominican Republic to topple his Administration and the U.S. Marines forced Aristide onto a plane to take him away from Haiti. A friend of mine often remarks that President Aristide returned to Haiti as President Harry Steed, because the form of Aristide was there, but something of the substance was missing.

President Aristide, fundamentally, was a priest. He was not a realpolitik theoretician or practitioner. In the one year left in his term, Aristide was expected to prepare for the transition to different leadership, privatize state entities, form a coalition government comprised of people chosen by the U.S., and allow the U.S. to reestablish the Haitian military that, as President, Aristide had demobilized because of its history of oppression of the people. Interestingly, the U.S. Ambassador at the time was Larry Swing, whom I would later meet in South Africa at the twilight of apartheid, and again speaking perfect Lingala in Laurent Kabila's Democratic Republic of Congo.

At the same time that we were fighting this monumental battle for Haiti, I had become the target of a redistricting lawsuit filed by my White male opponent who had lost to me joined by four other Whites who said that the District as drawn was a racial gerrymander. As you now know, that lawsuit went all the way to the Supreme Court and the people of that District lost. Our work on behalf of Haiti was even used in a similar redistricting lawsuit targeting Corrine Brown in Florida with the plaintiff, also her former White male opponent, arguing that a redistricting favoring the election of Blacks to Congress would change U.S. foreign policy—Haiti being a case in point.

**A similar redistricting lawsuit argued that a redistricting favoring the election of Blacks to Congress would change U.S. foreign policy—Haiti being a case in point.**

Haiti was and is indeed a case in point. Just as I had vowed when I read the Stockwell book that I would never allow U.S. policy to hurt innocent people and deny them their basic human rights without some effort on my part to correct the wrong, we went all out for Haiti— meaning persons both inside and outside of the Congress. As far as Haiti is concerned, at the time of this writing, there is still much wrong to be corrected: the gold stolen from Haiti and stored at Fort Knox for "safekeeping" has never been returned to the Haitian people, Guy Philippe walks free in Haiti today while President Aristide was never allowed to complete his term, and a Clinton-appointed protégé serves

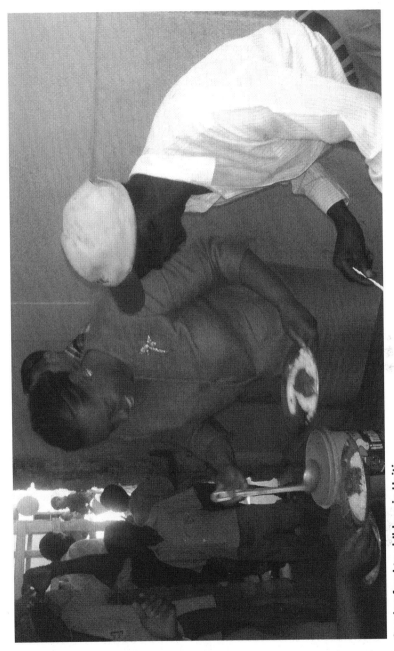

**Serving food to children in Haiti.**

as its Head of State. Moreover, a mockery was made of the elections by Clinton's selection of Michel Martelly, a performer who once mooned his audience, to be President of Haiti.

The story of Haiti is important because it shows what a determined people can do to change U.S. policy. That ingredient of vigilance and determination on the part of the Congressional Black Caucus was missing in the most recent Haiti elections whose outcome was dictated by Secretary of State Hillary Clinton. The elections were held under the worst possible conditions, including United Nations occupation, and smacked of U.S. dictatorship rather than Haitian self-determination while Congressional voices of dissent remained muted.

My next project involved trying to repair the damage done to Africa by successive U.S. policies of terror against African peoples. Of course, John Stockwell had chronicled U.S. policy against the authentic liberation groups of Angola and Mozambique, MPLA (Popular Movement for the Liberation of Angola) and FRELIMO (Front for the Liberation of Mozambique). In graduate school, I had met a young FRELIMO freedom fighter who actually had carried arms in The Bush to liberate his country from colonialism: that same colonialism that I read about in Franz Fanon's Black Skin, White Masks and in Wretched of the Earth. But here was someone who had lived it. And I was studying with him and amazed that I could touch him and in so doing, touch a part of the African Revolution. In Congress, I was able to work as a partner in the results of that struggle and extend a hand of friendship. I met the leaders of Angola who alerted me to the possibility that what I was hearing about Rwanda might not be the whole truth and thus began my travel back in time through the wormhole of truth through which I would view events transpiring in Rwanda and Zaire.

**Thus began my travel back in time through the wormhole of truth through which I would view events transpiring in Rwanda and Zaire.**

I eventually nominated Joaquim Chissano, President of Mozambique, for the Nobel Peace Prize and my next big project after Haiti involved Rwanda and Zaire's transformation into Democratic Republic of Congo.

My involvement in Zaire/Democratic Republic of Congo began as I read the headlines of impending regime change. Can you imagine how excited I felt? Silly me, I thought it was real. Little did I know that behind those headlines was really the hidden hand of the U.S., again interfering in African affairs. At any rate, the thought of Mobutu Sese Seko, longtime autocratic dictator installed by the U.S. getting kicked out of power in Congo by a rebel army sweeping westward toward Kinshasa was music to my mind. I determined that I needed to be there with the people of Congo to usher in a new era of real self-determination and to finally correct a tremendous wrong visited upon the Congolese people by the United States with the earlier murder of their democratically-elected leader, Patrice Lumumba.

The United States Department of State had issued a travel advisory and was telling U.S. citizens to stay away from the region. Well, by this time I had had enough experience with State Department advisories to know that that just meant that they didn't want anyone to interfere in what they had going on. So, despite the admonishment from the State Department not to go, I continued my search to figure out a way to get there. Destination: Lubumbashi!

Lubumbashi served as the headquarters of the resistance before it marched triumphantly into Kinshasa and was where Laurent Kabila had camped out. Now, how in the world was I going to get there?

Well, my staff went scouring the newspapers to find any mention at all of how I could get to Lubumbashi. Well. Just my luck, it turned out that one of my staffers found a newspaper article stating some businessmen with roots in Arkansas were making their way exactly to Lubumbashi. So, we called them and asked if I could hitch a ride. They loved the idea! And that's how I came to know that the real reason the State Department didn't want anyone meandering into the Lubumbashi backwoods or The Bush: the U.S. was running a covert operation.

Well, when the State Department figured that I was not going to be deterred, they helped me obtain the meeting I was looking for. I wanted to meet Laurent Kabila. And so, the U.S. government representative in Lubumbashi went to inform Kabila that "Congresswoman Cynthia McKinney" wanted to meet him. According to the story I got back from the State Department and the Democratic Republic of Congo—and in Rwanda, too—Kabila asked the White male representative of the U.S. government stationed there in Lubumbashi, upon mention of my name: "Did she win?"

It seems that my pleas for a fair redistricting for Black people in the Southern part of the United States, and even my own pleas for myself and my own redistricting case, had reverberated from C-Span, CBS, ABC, 60Minutes, and all the U.S. news channels across the Atlantic Ocean, across the Congo River, to the outback in the middle of political upheaval. Everywhere I went, Africans knew my name. They knew of the heroic struggle that I was waging just to stay in Congress. And they cared about my winning! The year was 1996 and yes I did win. My victory presaged their own ability to win in a system terribly tilted against them. They were one with me. I was so proud to be able to tell them that I was one with them.

Kabila and I hit it off immediately. He seemed to me to be the very definition of a Congolese Patriot and I sensed that he longed for someone in whom he could confide and trust. He gave me all of his telephone numbers and those of his family, too. This would later become important symbolically when I received a phone call from Madeleine Albright asking for his phone number because he wasn't returning her calls.

It turned out that Laurent Kabila had Revolutionary pedigree. He was a Lumumbist who had even spent time with Che Guevara, working toward an African Revolution. He shared everything with me. Even how insulted he was when Susan Rice put the word to him that he was going to have to betray Congo. I was on the steps of the U.S. Capitol when the phone call came in from him. He was livid. He wanted to give me a blow-by-blow of what had happened in the meeting; he told her that he would never betray Congo. I knew that he was in danger. I went back to my Congressional office and tried to call him: the Office phone would not ring the Congo number. We tested the Congressional Office next door and its phone worked. It was just my Congressional Office phone that had stopped working. I tried my cell phone. My cell phone did not work to call to Congo. I could call other numbers fine, but not the Congo numbers. Both the Office phone and my personal phone had been shut down. Undeterred, I sat down and wrote a memo to him advising him of my appreciation of how grim the situation had become. I had to go through a very circuitous route to get that fax to him. But he did receive it. Sadly, one month later, he was dead. Assassinated.

There's so much more to this very sad story that I won't tell here. But suffice it to say that I personally know that the United States was in partnership with the massive military mobilization of Rwanda and its occupation of and attempted overthrow of Laurent Kabila. In the middle of the night someone from the Pentagon phoned me—awakening me—to tell me to phone Kabila and tell him to release the Tutsis because they'd better not be detained when the Rwandan Army made it to Kinshasa. Well, they never made it to Kinshasa because the Zimbabweans, Namibians, and Angolans thwarted the U.S. move to topple their man because he chose to love Africa more. To this day, Zimbabwe is hated partially because it thwarted this attempted coup.

The perfidy of the Rwandans and the Ugandans in the Congo affair, at the behest of the United States, certain European countries, and Israel was outrageous. In my opinion, Paul Kagame of Rwanda has become the Jonas Savimbi of Africa. And that's whose police were dispatched to Haiti after the earthquake. Rwanda's. As I looked deeper down the rabbit hole of truth, I saw another operation just like the John Stockwell type of operation, staring me in the face. The entire onion of layered

**I was to learn what only a few people in the entire world would come to know about the full story of the Rwandan Genocide.**

lies came sharply in full view. And because of my work, I was to learn what only a few people in the entire world would come to know about the full story of the Rwandan Genocide and I shook my head in disgust as I saw history being rewritten right before my very eyes. The "rest of the story" was one of the strategy and political intrigue that comes with an operation of regime change. And if one million African souls had to die to achieve the goal, then as far as U.S. policy makers were concerned, that was perfectly all right. After all, 500,000 dead Iraqi children was a price that those same policy makers found worth paying for U.S. objectives. Only thing, they weren't the ones paying any price. Then I witnessed the cover story "Hutus don't like Tutsis," "Africans can't help killing each other," being written and promoted on television, in newspaper, and even in film. And sadly, Black actors on and off the screen, were the main characters assisting in the misdirection of the truth and the development of the plot.

A generation before, it was the murders of Patrice Lumumba, Salvadore Allende, and Dag Hammarskjold that shocked the conscience. What I was a witness to was nothing new; I had read about it, was a student of it; even sought out whistleblower and family accounts of what had happened. It was just that this time, it wasn't in a book, it was up close and personal to me. I was living it. It was my introduction to what the U.S. will do in pursuit of what it perceives to be the most expedient way to achieve its interests, despite human rights abuses. That's the story that everyone knows about, but no one will talk about: U.S. pursuit of its strategic and resource interests in that region of the world with utter disrespect and disregard for the needs, hopes, dreams, even humanity, of the people whose land and resources the U.S. is interested in stealing. My shame was the willingness of Black Americans to go along with the program despite it being blatantly wrong, unethical, and illegal. I didn't go looking for this story, it, instead, was fumbled into my hands because the international community as well as the U.S. "progressives" and activists and "liberals" lacked the will to catch it and stop it. So, I did several things: one, I wrote a letter to President Clinton and the international community blowing the cover off the entire dismal affair and, two, I traveled to Spain and testified before the Spanish Court on behalf of victims of the U.S. policy to support corporations and political leaders that abused human rights. Three, I went to France to testify before its Terrorism Judge about what I had learned about the Rwandan Genocide. Four, I held a hearing on Capitol Hill and asked Wayne Madsen to testify at it; and Five, I held a Congressional Briefing where I asked Janine Roberts, Wayne Madsen, Keith Snow, and Jim Lyons to testify about the plane crash, an act of terror that sparked the Rwandan Genocide, killing two democratically-elected African Presidents and one million innocent African souls. What none of the popular press dared to expose was that it all started as U.S.-concocted regime change and certain Administration Blacks and certain

Administration women were responsible for overseeing this African nightmare and orchestrating the cover up. You can imagine my horror when the same people resurfaced in the Obama Administration!

President Eisenhower had talked about the military industrial complex and I chanced upon its dealings in full throttle. Perhaps, that phrase should have remained as I'm told it was originally put: military-industrial-Congressional complex. And it was also so much more than that. Because with the situation in Rwanda, my eyes were

**What none of the popular press dared to expose was that it all started as U.S.-concoted regime change and certain Administration Blacks and certain Administration women were responsible for overseeing this African nightmare.**

opened to the delicate interplay between human rights groups, Non-Governmental Organizations (NGOs), journalists, and the U.S. and its interests. I learned that in order to truly understand a situation, it is insufficient to merely look at the readily visible. With Rwanda, every time I peeled back a layer, I got yet another layer. And, for me, it all started when I met the Angolan Minister, a young man who visited me and commended me on my actions thus far on Africa. When I made a comment about the Rwandan Genocide along the lines as popularly cast, his simple response to me was, "Which one?" Which genocide! It was no accident that the Angolans would rally to assist Kabila against U.S./European/Israeli and Rwandan designs. Popularly explained as "Blacks killing Blacks" or "Hutus killing Tutsis," far more important questions were never popularly explored, like: Who gave Kagame the equipment, the training, the funding to rampage and kill across Africa? Who fed his army, and then, most importantly, gave him the nod to kill two sitting Presidents? (Discredited war criminal and former United Kingdom Prime Minister Tony Blair reportedly made the following comment, according to the opposition Rwandan People's Party: "Paul Kagame is a visionary leader who has ushered in development in Rwanda and should be given allowance for genocide.") Who crippled the United Nations Security Council and stopped it from doing its job? That's what happened. And then, I watched as everyone associated with the repeated crimes and cover up got promotions. From Kofi Annan, who as head of the Department of Peace Keeping Operations failed to protect the Rwandan elected leadership in his promotion to Secretary General, to Madeleine Albright who was the United States Ambassador to the United Nations and then became Secretary of State. Louise Arbour stopped the U.N. investigation of the plane crash and was rewarded with a seat on the Canadian Supreme Court. Susan Rice left the National Security Council and headed over to the State Department with Albright and Jendaye Frazier followed her.

CYNTHIA A. McKINNEY
4TH DISTRICT, GEORGIA

COMMITTEE ON INTERNATIONAL
RELATIONS
INTERNATIONAL OPERATIONS AND HUMAN RIGHTS

COMMITTEE ON
ARMED SERVICES

MILITARY PROCUREMENT
MILITARY PERSONNEL

# Congress of the United States
## House of Representatives
### Washington, DC 20515-1011

WASHINGTON OFFICE:
☐  124 CANNON BUILDING
WASHINGTON, DC 20515
(202) 225-1605
FAX (202) 225-0691

DISTRICT OFFICE:
☐  246 SYCAMORE STREET
SUITE 110
DECATUR, GA 30030
(404) 377-6900
FAX (404) 377-6909

INTERNET ADDRESS:
cymck@hr.house.gov

November 10, 1999

His Excellency Pasteur Bizimungu
President, The Republic of Rwanda
Embassy of Rwanda
1714 New Hampshire Avenue, NW
Washington, DC 20009

Dear President Bizimungu:

I join your outrage at the release of Jean-Bosco Barayagwiza by the International Criminal Tribunal for Rwanda. People around the world who cherish peace and justice must speak out against this grave injustice. Certainly, for the innocent people of Rwanda, this is yet another slap in the face by the international community. I believe that Rwanda should sue the United Nations and seek reparations for the damages it has suffered.

I am pained by the instability, war, disease, and poverty that mark the Great Lakes today. And unfortunately, the resort to violence most often leads only to more violence. The "international community" has let Rwanda down. But in my opinion, only because individuals who made critical decisions in 1994 and its aftermath have been allowed to hide behind their governments and the United Nations. Kofi Annan just earlier this year said that no individual who commits crimes against humanity should be shielded by any government or organization. Surely, Kofi Annan's own United Nations should not attempt to hide itself behind the shield of immunity. I believe it is now time for Rwanda to rip away the edifices of immunity that the "international community" has built around itself, denying accountability to all of us who care about peace and justice and development in Rwanda and in Africa and who support the United Nations.

As you well know, in 1994, Rwanda suffered one of this centuries greatest human calamities and, as the world looked on silent, an estimated 1,000,000 of your fellow citizens died. The failure of the world to assist Rwanda in her hour of need must surely rank as one of the darkest hours in the long history of mankind.

The United Nations' Secretary-General, Mr. Kofi Annan, has maintained the position that the United Nations is not to blame for this catastrophe, but rather, the entire world is at fault, a form of collective guilt which we must all share. However, I do not accept his explanation and believe that the United Nations has much of Rwanda's blood on its hands.

It is now becoming clear that the United Nations and certain world powers were receiving special intelligence warning of the Rwandan genocide well in advance of the outbreak of fighting on April 6, 1994. For some inexplicable reason, the warnings that were forwarded to the Department of Peace Keeping Operations, headed by Kofi Annan, were kept secret from the Security Council. Indeed, even after the genocide had erupted, General Dallaire continued to forward daily reports to Kofi Annan's department warning of "ethnic cleansing" and "crimes against humanity" but this information too was kept from the Security Council. My own country, together with Britain, France and Belgian, also

His Excellency Pasteur Bizimungu
President, Republic of Rwanda
page 2

participated in this active suppression of the truth and all refused to call the crisis in Rwanda by its rightful name, genocide. The Security Council was deliberately kept blind from learning the truth in order to ensure that the western world would not be required to respond to Rwanda's urgent calls for help.

Significantly, the experience of two Rwandan families well illustrate the cowardly abandonment of Rwandan civilians by the United Nations. I have now received a copy of a UNAMIR intelligence report dated February 17, 1994, which was forwarded to General Dallaire. The report details a secret murder plot by the dangerous "Death Escadron" against his honor Mr. Joseph Kavaruganda, Chief of the Supreme Court, and Mr. Landoald Ndasingwa, the Minister of Labor and Social Affairs. It also provides the names of the leaders of the group and the names of the assassins selected to commit the murders. Incredibly, nothing was done with this information and, as was predicted, both men were among the very first persons murdered early on the morning of April 7, 1994. In the case of Mr. Ndasingwa, his mother, wife and two teenage children were also murdered with him. To make matters worse, United Nations troops positioned as guards at each of the Kavaruganda and Ndasingwa homes, failed to protect the families and instead surrendered them to their killers. To my understanding, this is the first time United Nations' troops have become complicit in genocide.

I have fought hard to have Kofi Annan tell the truth about the tragic events of 1994. Just last month, I confronted him in United Nations' Headquarters in New York at the opening of the General Assembly, and personally gave him a letter demanding that he inquire into the circumstances surrounding the murders of his honor Judge Kavaruganda and Mr. Ndasingwa. I have enclosed a copy of this letter for your information.

I have been told that there is a possibility that Rwanda may be able to make a claim against the United Nations for reparations for the loss of life, injuries and damages that flowed from the United Nations' decision to keep critical information secret from the Security Council and its subsequent decision to withdraw from Rwanda. I am also told that a similar claim for reparations may also be made by the surviving family members of the Kavaruganda and Ndasingwa families.

A decision by the International Court of Justice in April of this year confirmed that the United Nations is responsible to pay reparations for all damages which flow from the conduct of its staff.

I have been an untiring champion of peace and justice for Rwanda and the Great Lakes region. Today, there is neither. And as we have seen, war only begets more war. Peace and justice can be won in many ways. Holding accountable those who made the decisions that left these two families and an entire nation vulnerable to one of the most heinous crimes of the century is a better path toward lasting peace and justice, I believe.

Rwanda should seek reparations from the United Nations for the damages suffered by these two families and the millions of Rwandan families affected by the genocide. No one would ever have imagined a few years ago, that Chilean President General Augusto Pinochet would have had his sacred sovereign immunity stripped from him in order that he could be arrested in London and face trial in Spain. Similarly, with respect to Rwanda, no one would ever have imagined until 1994 that the United Nations and certain world powers would have shown such wanton disregard for the laws of nations by deliberately turning

His Excellency Pasteur Bizimungu
President, Republic of Rwanda
page 3

their backs on the mass extermination of an entire people. In my mind, I could only imagine that, as with Pinochet, international law will change and hold world leaders responsible for the damage caused by their decisions to turn their backs on such a monstrous crime.

I remain always a friend of Rwanda

Yours sincerely,


Cynthia McKinney
Member of Congress

So, as my outrage grew, so did my determination to have a proper investigation of both genocides in Rwanda and the role of the United Nations. Amazingly, President Clinton invited me to accompany him to the United Nations and that was my opportunity to present my letter of demand for an independent investigation to Secretary General Annan. My letter stated that there was credible evidence of U.N. negligence and complicity in the deaths of targeted Rwandan families that it had been charged to protect. The U.N. was asked to form an independent investigation, and it did. This is how the Carlsson Commission was formed. The Commission was very limited in its scope, but it was an important public win because the U.N., for the first time, admitted its wrongdoing in the Rwandan Genocide. The Carlsson Commission came to D.C. and I brought the Rwandan survivor who witnessed the death of the brother of Rwanda's current Minister of Foreign Affairs and Cooperation (Louse Mushikiwabo), the hotel gardener. He was at the house when the Presidential Guard officers came to him, put a pistol to his head, and the pistol failed. So, the Presidential Guard officer tried to kill him again and the pistol failed again and the gardener recounted this absolutely terrifying, but true story.

The Rwandan chief Justice was murdered while the U.N. peacekeepers sat by drinking beer; the Chief Justice family members were being tortured, according to eyewitness testimony. No intervention from the U.N. peacekeepers. The Carlsson Commission reviewed all the evidence we could find: U.N. Peackeepers had fled and left a family to be murdered. On the one hand were the facts that we had gathered

Cynthia forces creation of Carlsson Commission and brings witness to testify, right: Louise Mushikiwabo, current Rwandan Minister.

and put forward to the U.N. On the other was the political reality that Senator Jesse Helms really could hold up United Nations money if he wanted to. And then there was the legal matter arising from its own negligence from which the United Nations could not escape. It's my "no wiggle room" theory in operation all over again. The United Nations was morally, legally, and politically liable for what happened in Rwanda after a missile blew a plane out of the sky, killing two sitting Presidents. So what could be done about that act of terror?

Journalist Steven Edwards wrote a compelling story in Canada's newspaper, *The National Post*, about the plane crash and the fact that the United Nations was suppressing the investigation into the murder of two sitting Presidents. This led to more stories about the plane crash and how the U.N. refused to investigate or prosecute Paul Kagame. But, eventually, the truth came out. The Spanish Court indicted 40 of Paul Kagame's soldiers for genocide; Judge Bruguiere released the findings of his investigation showing that the missile that shot the plane down came from the United States and was transferred to Kagame who had taken it from the Ugandan military and used it in an act of terror against two countries and ultimately against the entire democratic process of a Continent. As a result of my work on Rwanda, I began to realize that there is always a story behind the official story. That is what probably, also, led me to ask of the Bush Administration what it knew about September 11th and when did it know it. We knew what we saw, but we didn't know what happened. And the American people were owed an explanation.

**As a result of my work on Rwanda, I began to realize that there is always a story behind the official story . . . I came to grips with the total loss of moral authority of my country and the wanton killing of Black life on this planet.**

Rwanda became my International Politics 101, my introduction to the realpolitik that I studied in Graduate School: I came to grips with the total loss of moral authority of my country and the wanton killing of Black life on this planet. For private gain, for money.

For those who understand the signs, it is clear that the same exigencies have unfolded and are still unfolding in Afghanistan, Iraq, Pakistan, Sudan, and Somalia. Yet, I wonder if the American people are any wiser. Certain individuals can even launch wars for their own pecuniary interests against the interests of the people of the U.S.; they can move the machinery of state for greed and Administrations become their accomplices, even in war crimes and crimes against humanity. In Sierra Leone, it was for diamonds and little girls were raped and little boys had their hands chopped off. And Jesse Jackson was trotted out to seal the

In Barcelona with Jordi Palou at Lawyers Committee for Justice for Democratic Republic of Congo.

deal. I blew the whistle on that, too, and had the Administration backing off their commitment to put Foday Sankoh in as Minister of Mines, directly answerable only to the President of Sierra Leone—and since Sankoh had guns and his own army—in essence, he would have been answerable to no one. He would have been answerable, however, to the person who was going to buy all of those diamonds and had provided all of those weapons. These individuals, who don't like to have their names called in public, have done it before and they'll do it again. As long as they are allowed to get away with it. That's why we need courageous, non-complicit Members of Congress willing to tackle the corruption, create a good name for the U.S., and stop the global death and destruction.

Now, contrast how stubbornly the wheels of justice roll in the case of Rwanda's and Congo's victims of Uganda's Museveni and Rwanda's Paul Kagame with the swift and dubious empowering of the Special Tribunal on Lebanon investigating the murder of Lebanese President Hariri. The plane crash that killed two sitting African Presidents has never been investigated by the United Nations. Why do we have a specially-created Lebanon Tribunal and nothing for the 1994 plane crash? By acts of omission or commission, injustice can be fixed.

And it just doesn't stop with the United Nations and other multilateral organizations. When I tried to interest various international human rights groups in the truth about Rwanda and Congo, I was rebuffed by all of them. From the Center for Constitutional Rights, to the Red Cross, to Human Rights Watch, and Amnesty International, the targeting of human rights interest groups seems to go hand in hand with certain strategic interests. One part of the world warrants a story and then another part of the world merits only silence. Why? In the end, the pattern became clear. This was a part of the overall message manipulation strategy that had not been revealed to me before, but with Sudan it happened and I was enlisted to become a part of it. Between my Rwanda and Democratic Republic of Congo experiences—and I've only scratched the surface of them here—I was ready when the offer came in, of press sufficient to keep me in Congress for as long as I might like, if all I would do is get arrested in front of the Sudan Embassy, turning my sights and lending my considerable "human rights champion" branding to the cause of attacking and dismantling the state of Sudan.

This is the account of my legal representative, Michael Hourigan, who was at the initial meeting where the Congressional attack on Sudan was planned:

> I am an Australian lawyer who worked for the United Nations Rwanda War Crimes Tribunal during 1996-1997. I got to experience first hand the way the UN and

other countries used war crimes prosecutions to target governments on the African continent. I resigned from the UN tribunal in 1997 because I was angry at the way the UN manipulated the work on the Tribunal. In 1998 I worked at the UN Inspector General's Office in NY. I resigned from the UN in 1998 because I felt our work was subject to too much political interference by senior UN officials. In 1999 I volunteered as an attorney for Congresswoman Cynthia McKinney in Washington DC. The congresswoman had a great love of Africa and I got to work with her closely on her inquiries into the US involvement in the Rwandan genocide, as well as work with her on US foreign policy issues in Africa and around the world. I have always maintained a great fondness for her and we have maintained our friendship to this day. As you well know she lost her office because of the efforts of Zionists in the US who did not accept that the Muslims should have a voice in America. After working with Congresswoman McKinney, in 2000, I joined a US trial law firm in Atlanta. Our law firm asked me to work on general litigation matters. Being a former war crimes lawyer who had worked in Africa I was soon approached by a group of Christian activists from South Carolina USA wanting me to become involved in a potential lawsuit against Talisman Energy, a Canadian oil company extracting oil in southern Sudan. They said the lawsuit was to disrupt the Sudanese oil industry. I conducted some preliminary investigations and expressed an interest at becoming involved – I was soon introduced to Zionist lawyers from Philadelphia and they aggressively pursued the legal action. I told them of my concerns at the lack of evidence to link Talisman in human rights violations but they were not interested in hearing my views. They insisted that a lawsuit should be filed against Talisman in US federal court under the Alien Tort Claims Act as soon as possible. I didn't like their aggressive nature and wasn't comfortable with their conduct of the case. I refused to work them. Some months later in 2000-2001 I was called by a prominent African radio announcer who was working with the southern Christian activists. I was invited to attend a meeting in Washington DC to discuss Sudan. I flew to Washington DC and attended the meeting. I found the meeting was being chaired by a very high profile Zionist lawyer. At the meeting were NGOs, a number of African American media personalities and me the only lawyer. The chairman of the meeting said the purpose of the meeting was to begin a media and legal strategy to focus world attention on the human rights violations in Sudan. He said that he could fund the NGOs, set up web sites, help meet expenses associated with law suits and generally assist us in any way that was necessary to bring the public spot light on Sudan. I noticed that he wasn't going to do anything publicly himself. Everything appeared to be being done through us non-Jewish people. It was clear that the chairman was working with other people at the same time. He explained how he was involved in coordinating with Hollywood celebrities and other high profile US political figures to picket the Sudanese Embassy in Washington DC. I left the meeting and never became involved in the group. I didn't agree with their conduct toward Sudan. It was clear they were not interested in human rights but instead political activities and interference with Sudan. In my view the recent indictment of President Bashir is just the end game of a long process which I saw being born in Washington DC in 2000. As I said I am a former war crimes lawyer familiar with the ICC and its prosecutorial functions. I have already spoken with other war crimes lawyers in Africa, Europe and the US and they agree with me that the prosecution of President Bashir is politically motivated. However that may be, President Bashir now needs to defend against the indictment. I am convinced that the Zionists will not stop until he is convicted or out of office or both. But in my view they will not stop there. They will want to break the independence of your government – they will prosecute other members of the Sudanese government, as well as, target other international companies doing business there. I am 100% sure that this entire present crisis confronting Sudan is being run by the same people that I met in 2000 in Washington DC. I would love the opportunity to be able to serve your President and your government.

I, too, refused to be used. However, acting in good faith, my alternative policy proposal was to apply a corporate code of conduct to companies doing business in Sudan. My legislation sought to alleviate human rights suffering by restricting the behavior of U.S. corporations in conflict zones. I focused on the role of U.S. corporations in the human rights abuses occurring in Sudan and sought to delist corporations from the stock exchange if they were complicit in human rights abuses. Opposition abounded from the very people who wanted me to champion the cause their way. I was told that this was not an appropriate strategy because it would hurt Coca Cola and other corporations that use gum arabic from Sudan.

So, when President Bashir of Sudan was indicted for war crimes, the familiar pattern reemerged; to this day, people continue to die in Congo, the Congolese people are still denied self-determination; Paul Kagame still sits in Kigali, ironically with $100 million in executive Bombardier jets outfitted with anti-missile technology to ferry friends like Tony Blair around the world while the act of terrorism that killed two sitting African Presidents remains uninvestigated. But then, so does 9/11—and that's a crime against America, itself.

Haiti, Congo, Rwanda, Sudan, and more. All happened during my tenure on the House International Relations Committee from 1993 to 2003. So, when I returned to Congress in 2005 after the 2004 election, I sought a return to my same Committees: HIRC (House International Relations Committee) and HASC (House Armed Services Committee). I stated my case to the Committee that makes recommendations to the House Leadership on Committee selections. Some Members even spoke in favor of the recommendation that I be returned to HIRC and HASC with seniority accrued from my previous Congressional tenure. And just as the recommendation was about to be voted upon, Robert Wexler, Member of Congress from Florida rose to speak. My mother, campaign manager, and District Director were all in the room with me as Congressman Wexler spoke. And here's what he said, "My district is 50% Jewish and my constituents would be upset if she goes back to the International Relations Committee." He went on to say that someone with my views should be able to express them on HASC, but not on HIRC. And with that, you could hear a pin drop. Everyone in the room understood what that meant. Nancy Pelosi called me to tell me that I would not be able to serve on HIRC and that I should tell her another Committee on which I would be willing to serve. And while one Republican came back to Congress after a fifteen-year hiatus and received all of his Committee seniority, I got none of mine. I was denied HIRC altogether and sat so close to the witnesses in HASC that I could see them sweating. That set up the scenario that is so popular on www.youtube.com today, when I heard Pentagon Secretary Donald Rumsfeld whisper that he had to go to lunch just before it was my time to question him. And since my questions were about September 11th, I needed to eliminate Rumsfeld's wiggle room. I had stayed there all day to get my question asked—near last since I didn't have any seniority. But the important thing is no matter where I sat, I was there to ask my question. And Rumsfeld had to respond. The man who wrote in the margins of a torture memo that prisoners should have no problem standing for eight hours at a time, couldn't sit still long enough for me to ask my question.

So, in typical Cynthia McKinney style, I objected to the Secretary's announced departure for lunch and asked my question anyway about the war games taking place on September 11th.

```
                    QUESTION FOR THE RECORD
               HOUSE ARMED SERVICES COMMITTEE
                      MARCH 10, 2005
                       QUESTION 1
                                           Page 1 of 1
------------------------------------------------------------
    Exercises and War Games the Department of Defense conducted on
                      September 11th, 2001

Hon McKinney:  Please name each such exercise and identify which
agencies and individuals were in charge of and aware of each of these
exercises?  What was the impact of these exercises on the ability of
the Department to respond appropriately to the attacks on that day?

General Myers:  On 9/11 Exercise VIGILANT GUARDIAN and Operation
NORTHERN VIGILANCE were in progress.  North American Air Defense
Command (NORAD) was the controlling headquarters for Exercise VIGILANT
GUARDIAN.  VIGILANT GUARDIAN was a command post exercise designed to
exercise NORAD missions from an increased intelligence watch to war.
VIGILANT GUARDIAN exercised region-specific issues in coordination with
the NORAD headquarters battle staff.  All NORAD regions and sectors
were to participate.  The key training objectives of VIGILANT GUARDIAN
were to improve system effectiveness while maintaining a high level of
operational readiness.

The key participants involved in Exercise VIGILANT GUARDIAN were:

        o  NORAD Cheyenne Mountain OPS Center
        o  Canadian NORAD Region
        o  Alaskan NORAD Region
        o  CONUS NORAD Region

On 9/11, Operation NORTHERN VIGILANCE was an ongoing, routine
operational response to a Russian Air Force exercise in the Russian
Arctic and North Pacific Ocean.  It involved eight fighter aircraft,
three tanker aircraft and an E-3 AWACs aircraft.  All aircraft that
supported NORTHERN VIGILANCE were based in Alaska.  These aircraft were
controlled by the Alaskan NORAD Region, with NORAD as the controlling
headquarters.  The NORTHERN VIGILANCE aircraft moved from their normal
operating bases to forward basing locations in Alaska to meet the
Russian aircraft.  In response to the 9/11 attacks, the Russians
concluded their air exercises, thus ending the requirement for
Operation NORTHERN VIGILANCE.

NORAD's Exercise VIGILANT GUARDIAN and Operation NORTHERN VIGILANCE
improved responsiveness to the 9/11 attacks.  When the 9/11 Commission
questioned General Eberhart, then Commander of NORAD and USSPACECOM,
whether the exercise posture helped or hurt NORAD's response, General
Eberhart responded, "Sir, my belief is that it helped because of the
manning, because of the focus, because the crews--they have to be
airborne in 15 minutes and that morning, because of the exercise, they
were airborne in 6 or 8 minutes.  And so I believe that focus helped."
```

# CHAPTER 8

# THE U.S./ WORLD CONFERENCE AGAINST RACISM FIASCO

It was a long time before I could organize my own hearings because Capitol Hill is run by seniority. During my first ten-year stint, it was only after I had been there for a while that my turn came to organize hearings. Of course, by this time, the Republicans were in the majority, and so the only "organizing" I did was as the lead Democrat on the House International Relations Committee, Human Rights Subcommittee, and that was subject to only what the Republicans would allow.

In 2001, Ileana Ros-Lehtinen was the Chair of the Subcommittee (she is now Chair of the entire Committee!), and that meant that, as a Republican, she ran the show. The issue was the United Nations World Conference Against Racism in Durban, South Africa—a hearing that I had requested the Committee to convene. Congressman Ben Gillman was the Chair of the Committee and was such a wonderful man. His wife's name was Georgia and we always kidded each other about traveling to Georgia! Chairman Gilman always chided me for not going to Israel. And I told him that I would not go on an AIPAC (American Israel Public Affairs Committee) trip, but that I would go to Israel one day another way. Which turned out to be the truth, in spades!

Chairman Gilman ended up being done in by his own Party— they sacrificed him after New York State fell short in the Census and had to lose one of its Congressional House of Representatives Districts. Of course Chairman Gilman would get squeezed out because he was so darn nice! However, nice or not nice, it probably doesn't matter because the way things work in politics is, the big boys get together and decide who has to go. Like for example, the State of Ohio lost two House of Rep-

CYNTHIA A. McKINNEY
4TH DISTRICT, GEORGIA

COMMITTEE ON INTERNATIONAL
RELATIONS

INTERNATIONAL OPERATIONS AND HUMAN RIGHTS

COMMITTEE ON
ARMED SERVICES

MILITARY PROCUREMENT
MILITARY PERSONNEL

# Congress of the United States
### House of Representatives
### Washington, DC 20515-1011

WASHINGTON OFFICE

☐ 124 CANNON BUILDING
WASHINGTON, DC 20515
(202) 225-1605
FAX (202) 226-0691

DISTRICT OFFICE:

☐ 246 SYCAMORE STREET
SUITE 110
DECATUR, GA 30030
(404) 377-6900
FAX (404) 377-6909

INTERNET ADDRESS:
cymck@hr.house.gov

June 25, 2001

The Honorable Ileana Ros-Lehtinen
Chairwoman,
The International Operation and Human Rights Subcommittee
2610 Rayburn House Office Building
Washington, DC 20515

Dear Representative Ros-Lehtinen:

Please accept this letter as my official request for the House International Relations Committee, Subcommittee on International Operations and Human Rights, to convene a hearing on the upcoming World Conference Against Racism, Racial Discrimination, Xenophobia and Related Intolerance (WCAR). This historic conference will be held in Durban, South Africa from August 31 to September 7, 2001.

Hosted by the United Nations, WCAR will offer the unique opportunity to take a global look at how racism has adversely and unjustly affected people of color throughout this world and how we can begin to realistically develop a plan of action to address this issue. As Chair of the Subcommittee on International Operations and Human Rights, I know you are committed to the struggle to combat racism and intolerance not just here at home, but on an international level as well. It is for this very reason that I am sure you will find the issue of racism, one of humanity's most destructive ills, a worthy topic for a Congressional hearing.

Madame Chair, I am a firm believer that the WCAR will provide the necessary international platform to develop and implement concrete steps to combating the phenomenon of racism. It is my sincere hope that you will convene this hearing no later than Monday, July 16, 2001. Together, we can take the proactive steps necessary to eliminate this longstanding social affliction.

Please contact Mr. Merwyn Scott, my Chief of Staff, at x51605 with questions and or concerns.

With warm personal regards, I remain

Sincerely,

Cynthia McKinney
Member of Congress

CM/dcm

resentatives Congressional seats as a result of the 2010 Census results. Rapidly growing states like my state of Georgia gain population and hence, gain Congressional House seats. Georgia picked up one additional seat while Ohio lost two. Because the number of Members of Congress is fixed at 535 (435 in the House and 100 in the Senate), the entire country then has to be reapportioned to reflect the demographic changes that have taken place after the Census is taken every ten years. After each state is given the number of House seats that it will have based on those Census figures, then redistricting takes place to accommodate that new number. And because of "one-person-one-vote," every Congressional District in the state must have the same number of people in it—plus or minus no more than 1%. It all sounds so fair until they actually get down and start doing it! And every level of government is redistricted to reflect population shifts and demographic changes. Supposedly. Representative Dennis Kucinich from Ohio early on sent messages to supporters saying that he was being targeted for elimination because of Ohio's Census figures. Redistricting, about as exciting as watching paint dry, is the bread and butter of our political system because the way the districts are drawn determines which set of voters has the most chance of electing their candidate of choice. Therefore, for me, redistricting is invigorating! Redistricting is where the gladiators meet in the arena. And the stakes are just as high.

So, this particular time around, in New York, Chairman Gillman got the boot. At any rate, I recommended the Hearing on the Durban World Conference Against Racism, just as in subsequent years I would recommend the Katrina Hearing that, in the end, proved to be so popular with the public.

Well, in 2001, the issue was racism—that's what the Durban Conference was supposed to tackle. It was an opportunity for the world's dispossessed and marginalized to come together under the auspices of the United Nations, a world body charged with protecting humankind from global conflagration. Somehow, all the dispossessed of the world, people of African descent on the Continent and in the Diaspora, Latinos, Indigenous peoples from all over the world, Dalits in India--we were all there hearing from each other, interacting with each other, gaining strength, encouragement, and inspiration from one another, all jointly pressing our claims before the United Nations. For me, it was a beautiful sight.

As for me, I wanted to follow in the footsteps of my leaders. I understood that leaders before me had taken the plight of injustice in America, and particularly the plight of African Americans in the United States, to international bodies. Malcolm X had been the most recent one. And so, it was important to me that the Congressional Black Caucus

(CBC) be represented at this momentous occasion. That's why I asked our Congressional Black Caucus Chairwoman at the time, Eddie Bernice Johnson from Texas, to appoint me as the Chair of the Congressional Black Caucus Task Force on the Durban World Conference Against Racism.

Now, ordinarily, this would have been an easy one. But U.S. politics, global politics, and a sense of fair play all collided. The real loser threatened to be all the peoples of the globe who legitimately have injustice thrown into their lives on a daily basis for no other reason than someone else's prejudice and acts of discrimination. The peoples who always come up short on the power index wanted to get together to talk about solutions.

I was determined that the United States would participate in this Conference and that the Congressional Black Caucus would not only be officially present, but that the CBC would make a submission to the United Nations High Commissioner for Human Rights describing little-known facts about racial discrimination in the United States.

I contacted Kathleen Cleaver and Paul Wolf and asked them to please help craft a paper suitable for submission to the United Nations, subject: The Counter-Intelligence Program known as COINTELPRO. This FBI program was set up to spy on, penetrate and disrupt the growing civil rights and anti-war movements of the 1960s and all efforts to secure social change and justice in America. I specifically asked Cleaver and Wolf to focus on assassination as a policy tool of the U.S. government to stop the advance, during the heyday of the CONTELPRO program, of what the U.S. Government called "black nationalism."

And what a paper they wrote: cataloguing the use of murder by the United States government through COINTELPRO targeting of individuals and other things!

I asked them to focus on the members of the Black Panther Party who were unnecessarily targeted and murdered. Because they were committed by or for the government, few people were ever punished. One well-known example would be the murders of Fred Hampton and Dr. Martin Luther King, Jr. The COINTELPRO papers contain euphoric messages actually bragging after the murder of Malcolm X. I loved every word of the document prepared by Cleaver and Wolf and was pleased at its thoroughness. This is the document that I handed to United Nations High Commissioner for Human Rights at the time, Mary Robinson. And because these are unsolved crimes of murder with no statute of limitations, perhaps every U.N. Rapporteur who investigates the United States should have a copy of this document, too. Perhaps, that is work that needs to be done in the future. But, back to 2001 and the Durban World Conference Against Racism.

Durban represented a momentous occasion for the world's dispossessed to come together and try to fashion strategies for uplifting

CYNTHIA A. McKINNEY
4th District, Georgia

COMMITTEE ON INTERNATIONAL
RELATIONS

INTERNATIONAL OPERATIONS AND HUMAN RIGHTS

COMMITTEE ON
ARMED SERVICES

MILITARY PROCUREMENT
MILITARY PERSONNEL

WASHINGTON OFFICE:
124 CANNON BUILDING
WASHINGTON, DC 20515
(202) 225-1605
FAX (202) 226-0691

DISTRICT OFFICE:
246 SYCAMORE STREET
Suite 110
DECATUR, GA 30030
(404) 377-6900
FAX (404) 377-6909

INTERNET ADDRESS:
cynthia@tr.house.gov

# Congress of the United States
## House of Representatives
### Washington, DC 20515–1011

Opening Remarks
CBC Task Force - Hearing on the UN World Conference Against Racism
Tuesday, June 19, 2001
Washington, DC

Welcome, and let the spirit of Juneteenth pervade our discussions here today.

I am please to introduce my colleagues who are with us this morning. More will come throughout the morning.

The World Conference Against Racism, to be held in late August this year in Durban, South Africa, is an important world event. It seeks to focus world attention on examining the causes of racism as well as providing an opportunity for nations to formulate practical measures to prevent, and where possible, to eradicate racism and other discriminatory practices.

What could be more important than for the family of nations to come together as one and to seek to end racism in the world today.

The United States should fulfill its leadership position as a major world power and attend the conference. We should send a delegation consisting of highly respected and extremely capable individuals who hold high aspirations and deep convictions on ending the scourge of racism in the world today.

The Congressional Black Caucus can play a critical role in ensuring that this current administration fully appreciates the importance of this World Conference to people of color in this country. The members of the CBC all represent districts affected by poverty and race hatred, stricken with incarceration, overcrowding, violence, and all the other familiar ills of modern black urban life.

To our nation's great shame it has had much experience with racism. That experience spans almost every generation of our nation's history: from the early years of slavery during the establishment of our nation, through the apartheid practices of the southern United States, and finally through the federal government's physical destruction of the black political movement here in this country during the 1960s and 1970s.

But our nation's journey with racism will not end until it faces the truth of its past.

By drawing upon our nation's history and forging with it a willingness to confront these horrible truths, our delegation should be able to make substantive contributions to the World Conference forum examining the causes of racism.

I wish to briefly address two important issues which I think should feature as center points in our discussion today. The American slave trade and the destruction of the black political movement here in the US in the 1960s and the 1970s under the federal government's COINTELPRO (counter intelligence) program.

From 1490 until about 1870 one of the most elaborate maritime and commercial ventures arose, a result of which 30 - 60 million black men, women and children were enslaved in Africa and carried packed in ships wearing leg irons, in foul overcrowded conditions, and transported to the Americas to work on plantations, in mines or as servants in fine houses. Tragically, many tens of millions of them did not survive the journey and died en route during the Middle Passage from disease, cruel treatment, and the rigors of sea travel.

Slavery stretched several hundred years, involved every maritime European nation, every Atlantic-facing African people (and some others), and every country of the Americas. On any view, this slave trade must rank as one of the greatest crimes of all time.

Upon arrival in the Americas black families were broken up, men separated from their wives, and mothers and fathers permanently separated from their children. These slaves then suffered the further indignity of losing their African names, as well as, their own histories, cultures and languages. Their combined labors generated fabulous wealth for their white masters and they provided much of the financial foundation for modern America. Despite centuries of back breaking labor, black Americans never shared in the wealth and instead, to this day, remain poorer than whites, enjoy lower standards of living, suffer lower standards of health care, and figure disproportionately in incarceration levels in our state and federal prisons.

Incredibly, this history of slavery is largely unknown to the vast majority of Americans. Our nation has refused to confront the enormity of this crime and has instead sought to create the myth that slaves were better off being manacled and brought to the Americas. Nothing is ever said of the millions of slaves who died, of the destruction of whole African communities by ill health, violence, and separation. And nothing is ever said of the sheer injustice that nations which committed this crime still, to this day, refuse to even apologize for their conduct let alone pay reparations for the damage caused by their actions.

I remember only too well when Congressman Tony Hall introduced legislation asking for the Congress to apologize for slavery. To my horror I overheard other Members on the House Floor laughing behind Mr. Hall's back because he was foolish enough to introduce the Slavery Bill.

Not surprisingly the bill never got out of committee and was never voted on.

One other matter I think important for discussion in Durban is the federal governments COINTELPRO program. Important research is revealing that during the 1960s and the 1970s the FBI and other sections of the US military and intelligence apparatus conducted a secret war against black political groups and the Native American movement. To our collective shame we are now learning that the federal government conducted a secret, systematic and at times, savage use of force and fraud against a small political minority exercising fundamental freedoms considered sacred by our Constitution.

Many of our black political leaders were wrongly accused of crimes and imprisoned, and some were even murdered. The black political movement in this country was totally destroyed by our own government. The Native American movement suffered the same fate.

What I am telling you about didn't happen in Nazi Germany under Hitler, China under Mao, Chile under Pinochet or Uganda under Idi Amin. No, it happened here in the United States, under Lyndon Johnson, Richard Nixon, and others.

That this happened to people in this country in the 1960s and 1970s is no longer conjecture. It is a shocking fact that the federal government wrongly imprisoned and even murdered innocent black Americans.

On this generation of Americans falls the burden of proving to the world that we really mean it when we say that all men are created free and equal before the law. The real history of slavery in this country must be publicly recorded and there must be a reckoning with black America for its sacrifice in building this nation to what it is today. In addition, our federal government should reveal the truth about the full extent of the COINTELPRO program and make its records open to public examination.

themselves. You could say that we were all singing Kumbayyah because there was such unity of purpose.

And then, out of nowhere, the entire Conference gets side-swiped by the global Zionist contingent, in an attempt to veer it off course. The question of "Zionism equals Racism" became the topic. And so if the diversion had been successful, people from all over the world would have their issues ignored because Zionists didn't want to allow a discussion of Zionism. They used their political power to encourage the United States to boycott the Conference.

Colin Powell, the first African American Secretary of State, really wanted to participate, but was powerless to go if [P]resident Bush said no. ([P]resident because he was really the illegitimate resident, not the rightful President—I got that from Lori Price at Citizens for Legitimate Government!) Congresswoman Johnson reached out to Powell and had several discussions with him. But in the end, he would have to do as his President commanded.

And as scripted by the Zionist Lobby, President Bush said no. But as Chair of the Congressional Black Caucus Task Force, independently elected by the people as their Representative, I was determined that the United States would have a delegation in attendance and that we would not have our issues dictated to by others who, quite frankly, didn't share our interest in addressing structural racism in this country.

After much consultation, Chairwoman Eddie Bernice Johnson reiterated her interest in seeing that the Congressional Black Caucus was represented at this historic world event. Therefore, I went about the task of making our voices heard and our presence felt as the debate over U.S. participation in and the validity of the Conference, itself, was joined.

Now, to be honest, the Congressional Black Caucus was split and some of our more senior Members favored the boycott, saying that there were other ways to deal with our (Black) issues rather than at the contentious UN Conference. (Of course, in my view, that was the Zionist-influenced position being played out inside the deliberations of the Congressional Black Caucus.) However, if one looked at the statistics of Black life in the United States, it was clear that our issues were not being dealt with successfully, and if I did a quick glance at certain votes, it would further be clear that when it came to the issues on which Congressional Black Caucus votes could make a difference or be leveraged for improving the lot of Black masses inside the United States, even that was not done by the very same Representatives who favored U.S.boycott of the Conference. Clearly, this was a matter of some people inside the Congressional Black Caucus being thankful to the Black community for their votes, but being loyal to others for the money they contributed to enable them to run their campaigns in the first place. With campaign coffers full of special interest money, it was easier to wax eloquent about the problems in the Black community rather than use the power of their positions to actually try to solve those problems. That would be contentious and, according to them, it was always better to stay away from contention for Black people—although contention to benefit the special interests always seemed to be alright.

To further prove their point, these anti-Durban Black Members of Congress, joined by selected Jewish Members of Congress, circulated a letter saying that they supported reparations. Well now, that was news to me, so I immediately went to John Conyers's reparations legislation, H.R. 40, and noticed that none—not one--of the Jewish Members who had signed the reparations letter had cosponsored the Conyers bill! In fact, as of January 16, 2013, John Conyers had zero (0) cosponsors on his reintroduced H.R. 40. As I am not convinced by arguments of support (that aren't even made today, by the way), in 2001, when the specious argument was advanced, I wasn't convinced. My father had taught me a thing or two about politics and poly-tricks. John Stockwell had revealed the rest. I couldn't engage this confrontation half-heartedly. And I had seen my father, as he fought for Black opportunity, betrayed by his own Black colleagues. I knew from the COINTELPRO papers that the people closest to our leaders had somehow managed to find an FBI or CIA payoff. From the time of Marcus Garvey up to today, this has been the case. The most recent revelation of this type was that the photographer closest to Dr. Martin Luther King, Jr. was on the FBI payroll all along.

I knew that the Black community in the United States couldn't continue to be so bad off with such a powerful Caucus unless there was deep division or fear to the point of paralysis on the inside of that Caucus. And then, I had seen the Georgia Legislative Black Caucus split on the issue of redistricting with some favoring a limit in the application of the Voting Rights Act which meant limiting the number of Blacks that could enter the Legislature and the Congress! I was just surprised at who the opponents to participation in the Conference and the signatories to the reparations letter were. And I shook my head in disgust.

> I knew that the Black community in the United States couldn't continue to be so bad off with such a powerful Caucus unless there was a deep division or fear to the point of paralysis on the inside of that Caucus.

Herein is the lesson for us all: legislators who favor legislation cosponsor that legislation; they don't just sign letters when the issue is hot, just because the issue is hot and the outcome is not going their way.

OK, this was their first diversion and it did not work. What would they pull next? In the meantime, I continued to fight for Congressional

Black Caucus and U.S. participation in the Durban World Conference Against Racism.

So, I pressed to have a Congressional hearing on the Durban Conference which was under the jurisdiction of my House International Relations Committee subcommittee: International Operations and Human Rights. I was the Ranking Member on that subcommittee, meaning that I was its highest-ranking Democrat. But I was only allowed to have one panelist at the hearing, because Democrats were in the minority. Human Rights Subcommittee Chairwoman Ileana Ros-Lehtinen had complete run of the entire hearing. That was all right with me, in the end, because I was certain I could get key points on the record—for history's sake. So, I agreed to the ground rules and Congresswoman Ros-Lehtinen approved the Hearing.

I was pleased to see that she had invited the Anti-Defamation League to participate in the Hearing. Finally, I would get to ask them the question that I had been asking them for years, to which deafening silence thus far had been my only answer. Here is why I was happy to see them on the witness list.

The old 11th District that first sent me to Congress was Georgia's second poorest district. People paid rent, but didn't have running water in their homes. Why was it, then, that when Blacks finally did get representation, the Anti-Defamation League, an organization that purports to be a "civil rights organization," filed an amicus curiae brief on the side of the five White plaintiffs, and against the 649,995 Blacks and Whites who were working together in that district, in a lawsuit designed to dismantle that district and allow insensitive representatives to continue to fail to serve Georgia's poor, rural, and much-neglected Black Belt? Surely, the Anti-Defamation League would support poor Blacks who had never had authentic Congressional representation, right? Wrong.

And as I think about it, it might have also had something to do with me not signing the pledge for Israel. At any rate, here was my chance to get them on the Congressional Record. This was clearly something that they had done in the shadows, because when I would bring the matter up with my Jewish constituents who visited the Congressional office, they knew nothing about it and were surprised that the ADL might be involved in something like that. They promised to go back home and check into it. I never heard back, but at least I gave them food for thought.

So, on the day of the Hearing, I was ready to ask my question, for the first time, able to pose it and get a response directly from the organization, itself--on the Congressional record!

I started out by describing the desperate poverty that marked my District. That people paid rent, but did not have running water in their homes. That these same hard-working people sent their children to

**ADL** Anti-Defamation League®

August 14, 2001

The Honorable Ileana Ros-Lehtinen
Chair, Subcommittee on International Operations and Human Rights
257 Ford House Office Building
Washington, DC 20515

Dear Representative Ros-Lehtinen:

We write in response to a question Representative Cynthia McKinney directed to our representative, ADL National Commissioner Michael Salberg, during the July 31 hearing on the UN World Conference Against Racism.

We believe that Representative McKinney's question to Mr. Salberg regarding the 1995 Supreme Court case *Miller v. Johnson* was unwarranted and inappropriate in the context of the Subcommittee's timely examination of the critical issues relating to the World Conference Against Racism. It was clearly outside the scope of the hearing, unrelated to the work of the Subcommittee on International Operations and Human Rights, and unfairly antagonistic to ADL.

Of course we recognize that reasonable people can have opposing views on the highly-charged issues present in *Miller v. Johnson*. ADL filed an *amicus* brief in that case because we firmly believe that race should not be the "substantial and motivating" factor in drawing congressional districts, in large measure because we categorically reject the presumption that only a member of a certain race can or will effectively represent his or her constituents of that same race. The Supreme Court agreed. We continue to hold this position today.

We also believe that our democratic system of government provides effective mechanisms for resolving disagreements over law and public policy. We do not expect to agree with every legislator on every issue, nor do we expect our view to prevail on every issue. However, we were deeply disappointed that ADL and Mr. Salberg were not accorded the same respect given to the other organizational representatives on the panel with him.

We request that this response be made a part of the permanent hearings record.

Sincerely,

Abraham H. Foxman
National Director

cc: The Honorable Cynthia McKinney
Jess N. Hordes, ADL Washington Director

school so that their lives could be better, they went to community meetings to make their own lives better, and that in many places it was not as if either the Civil Rights Act or the Voting Rights Act had been passed. But just at the moment when we were making progress, and giving people hope that their circumstances could indeed change with hard work and dedication, a lawsuit was filed to dismantle their representation and to dismantle their dreams. And that shockingly, the Anti-Defamation League had taken sides in this dispute, against the people whose lives were being changed, and in favor of the Whites who were resisting change. I asked that Representative for an explanation of ADL's behavior.

Gosh, you would have thought I had struck a match under him, the way the Anti-Defamation League representative fired up at me for asking what he characterized as a totally irrelevant question. If I had had thinner skin, I would have been embarrassed at the ferocity of the response. But, being my daddy's daughter, I knew I had found the vein. And, as if it were ore, this was a deep, rich one.

Of course, Congresswoman Ros-Lehtinen agreed with him that my question was out of order. But the Conference was about racism and the Hearing was about the Conference and if anything, my redistricting ordeal that went all the way up to the Supreme Court—reportedly financed with fish fries in South Georgia—was about racism; I was perfectly in order to raise that question.

But, you see, I think there is more to it. I am a Black woman, descendant of enslaved Africans. I am not supposed to question the acts of certain individuals. I was out of "my place." That goes to the core, I believe, of my treatment on this issue and on the September 11th questions that I raised. That mindset was established in writing by the highest Court in this land, the United States Supreme Court, when Justice Taney wrote in the Dred Scott Decision that Blacks had no rights which the White man was bound to respect.

But there, I had it. In 1996, the United States Supreme Court dismantled the District that sent me to Congress in 1993 and I had been asking that one question at least that long with no response. After all, given the history of this country, and the cold shoulder that I got, it appeared to me that whoever was behind all of this just felt that I wasn't owed a response. But, finally, I had a response on the Congressional Record and finally I had a response that came later in writing. Never again would anyone from that organization be able to feign ignorance of the issue and just blow me off. And, the reason this is important is because every time we have redistricting or application of the Voting Rights Act, we now know the position of the Anti-Defamation League. And in this case, it is not a civil rights group fighting with other civil rights groups to protect the voting rights of protected classes of individuals and communities against whom discrimination has been documented.

Basically, the Anti-Defamation League response was that they have a right to do what they feel is in the interest of the Jewish community in the United States and they admitted what I already knew was fact: that yes, they, the Anti-Defamation League—a member of the Leadership Conference on Civil Rights-- had filed an amicus curiae brief against the voting rights of Black people in Georgia. Years and years of ADL-supportive visitors came to the Congressional Office and I posed the question to them of why the ADL would do such a thing to poor Blacks in the Blackbelt of Georgia and not a single one knew anything of what I was asking. They all would promise to get back to me, and of course, I never heard anything back. But this one time I was able to use the Congressional Record to get an answer to my question. Of course, none of those ADL supporters had ever marched with me in South Georgia, or helped me get our kids off ritalin, or reverse stolen election results, or even for that matter helped me or my constituents address their issues--even as they went home to houses with no running water or indoor toilets: the very communities that were supposed to benefit from the passage of the Voting Rights Act--nullified with the help of the Anti-Defamation League.

In addition to that, I also knew that similar organizations and groups that one would have expected to support the new minority opportunity districts, actually sided with the White plaintiffs, who were protesting the creation of a new set of black opportunity districts in North Carolina. In particular, the Zionist organizations sided, not with the Blacks in North Carolina fighting to have Congressional representation for the first time since 1901 when George White left the Congress, but with the Whites of the Old Confederacy still resisting Black empowerment.

This brought to my mind an important question: to what extent was the larger Jewish community for whom the Anti-Defamation League and other organizations were purportedly acting even aware of what was being done in their name? It would take me eight years and the loss of familiar Jewish friends, but I finally got my answer.

As for redistricting, the practical impact of the 1993 North Carolina Shaw v. Reno Supreme Court decision, and the Georgia Johnson v. Miller Supreme Court decision, on the country was that in the South, what Southern Whites would call "radical" or "militant" Blacks would not be tolerated; reinforcing my father's idea that the system was like a rubber band, tolerating only so much "stretch" or "tension" on its fundamental structure built upon White supremacy. Imagine, a kind of institutional, structural statement like the one given to me earlier: "If you can't pick strong friends, pick weak enemies." The system was not ready to allow a Black voice to go unchecked. Actually, there are quite a few structural hurdles that limit opportunities for authentic Black voices to be heard, that instead pick COINTELPRO-type leaders who have already been vetted by responsible people in authority before the people they're supposed to lead even have a chance to select or elect them.

I had also introduced a bill affirming the principles of the Durban Conference; amazingly, I beat pro-Zionist Congressman Lantos to the Clerk and my bill was introduced before his bill. Congresswoman Johnson had secured from Dick Gephard, the Minority Leader at the time, a commitment for an up or down vote on my resolution. Unfortunately, the weight of the Congressional Black Caucus was not enough to get Gephardt to keep his promise. I felt that this also reflected the lack of respect that White Democrats have for the Black vote because they know they can count on getting it no matter what they do or do not do to or for the Black community. My bill never saw the House Floor, but Lantos's did and was supported, as all of his resolutions were, with few dissenting votes.

In the end, Colin Powell did not attend the Durban Conference; but the United States did send a low-level delegation headed by Congressman Tom Lantos. That was because the Congressional Black Caucus was there in force—five members strong. Our Chairwoman went and made an impassioned statement. And with her being from Texas and knowing George W. Bush well, her presence was all the more appreciated by the other Conference delegates. Congresswoman Johnson later told me that she was under a lot of pressure to buckle to Zionist wishes. She never showed it at the time and she never gave in. Her presence there, along with the written documentation that we gave to Mary Robinson, proved to me that despite all of the odds, and especially with fewer resources,

**Cynthia fighting for the World Conference Against Racism along with UN High Commissioner for Human Rights, Mary Robinson (left).**

when we are united, it is possible to go up against the Zionist Lobby in the Congress and win. At least on some issues.

Predictably, as soon as the Black Caucus Members left Durban to resume Congressional work in Washington, D.C., Representative Lantos left Durban, too. And when he left, the United States propaganda machine went into high gear and announced that the U.S. was pulling out of the Conference for its failure to adequately counter the "Zionism equals Racism" charge. It never mentioned what the Congressional Black Caucus had been able to achieve. That's why I looked with some sadness at the refusal of the 2010 Congressional Black Caucus to challenge President Obama when he walked down the trodden path of George W. Bush and refused U.S. participation in Durban III held in Geneva, Switzerland ten years later. We, the people of conscience, could have scored another victory if only the Congressional Black Caucus had dared.

The collision over the World Conference Against Racism taught me that, with the support of the Congressional Black Caucus, I could out-organize and out-think the most potent of our rivals. The only thing we didn't have was the political muscle to make our will happen. And that's only because Black people, and the progressive left in general, were losing the will to mobilize and fight, not because our positions weren't correct, but because we no longer finance what we want to see become political reality.

FOR IMMEDIATE RELEASE                     Contact: Jocco Baccus
July 31, 2001                                        (202) 225-1605
                                          Email: Jocco.Baccus@mail.house.gov

## McKinney Calls for Bush Administration to Issue a Formal Apology for Slavery

**(WASHINGTON, DC)** Today, Congresswoman Cynthia McKinney, Chair of the Congressional Black Caucus Task Force on the World Conference Against Racism (WCAR), met with Senior White House officials to discuss U.S. participation at the upcoming conference to be held in Durban, South Africa from August 31 to September 7, 2001.

The White House meeting was called during a pivotal time in the planning process for the WCAR as the final Preparatory Committee for the conference is currently being held in Geneva, Switzerland. This meeting will determine the language that will comprise the Draft Declaration and Program of Action that will be discussed at the WCAR in Durban.

McKinney, who has been a strong proponent of the US participating in the conference, delivered her own language to the White House which she urged the Bush Administration to adopt as its official position going into the WCAR. "The practice of slavery has long been recognized as a crime against humanity and a violation of the laws of civilized nations. As we approach the largest meeting ever specifically devoted to combating the scourge of racism, I implore the United States to apologize for its participation in the world slave trade of the 18th and 19th centuries." stated McKinney.

CHAPTER 9

# TREESHAKERS
# AND
# JELLYMAKERS

I write all of my speeches because I love to write and I love to research. I guess you could say it's the nerd in me. I have several favorite speeches that I'll discuss right now.

The first favorite speech I will discuss is entitled, "Which Way Will You Go When the Conductor Calls?" The story is about my father's grandmother who could pass for White. Looking at her on the outside, no one would know her identity. But she knew her identity. She knew who she was and so there was never any question as to which way she would go when the conductor called to her. What conductor?

During the days of U.S. "Jim Crow" apartheid, my great-grandmother could have escaped the indignities visited upon Blacks of that day because she could pass. But she chose to bear those indignities because to her, her identity was Black. So, when she entered the racially segregated trains of her native Georgia in the U.S. South, the White conductor would direct her to the White train car. When the conductor called to her, which way did she choose to go? She turned away from the conductor's call to the easy life of a White woman and went, instead, to the segregated Black train car with my father in tow. And her gift to me was that from my earliest days as a toddler, she would rock me on her crossed legs and say to me over and over and over again, "Gal, be proud of your color." So, from a very early age, I was steeped in pride for who I am and what I look like—something that in a colonized world of White Supremacy constitutes a challenge to the core of the current global structure.

I originally wrote this speech for an important national organization of Gay executives. It was an encouragement to members of the gay community to embrace the totality of their identity, no matter what difficulties would come with that. I told them to imagine what not "passing" meant in the times of my great-grandmother. And if she could do it then, certainly they could come out now. I eventually took that speech, by popular demand, across the United States. I had people coming to me in tears after giving it because it touched them in their core. I loved giving that speech because of the way it made people feel and because of the way they then made me feel.

Another of my favorite speeches is entitled, "Street Lights." In it, I tell the story of a time in Black America when life teemed underneath the street lights. Children played with "June bugs," young men played with dice, older men solved the world's problems and talked about their women. Underneath the street lights, life was vibrant. Then, all of a sudden, for one week, there was nothing underneath the street lights. All across America there was nothing at all happening. For one week across America, even the crime rate went down. What on earth could bring Black life underneath the street lights to a screeching halt? Alex Haley's "Roots" was playing on national television and for once, the descendants of Africa's stolen children could luxuriate in self-awareness and self-knowledge. Alex Haley's search for his own roots provided a vicarious experience for millions of Black people in the United States.

"Street Lights" was delivered to African Transportation Ministers who had been invited to a Conference in the U.S. by President Clinton's Secretary of Transportation Rodney Slater and the Secretary had asked me to give them an address. Again, that speech was received to thunderous applause. Every one of those Transportation Ministers was spoken to in his or her heart.

The final of the favorite speeches I will write about involves "treeshakers" and "jellymakers." My mother even had a keychain made for me and on it she had the word "treeshaker" inscribed.

The tree shakers of yesterday, Thurgood Marshall, Malcolm X, Martin Luther King, Jr., Hosea Williams, members of the National Association for the Advancement of Colored People (NAACP), Southern Christian Leadership Conference (SCLC), Student Nonviolent Coordinating Committee (SNCC), the Black Panther Party, the Nation of Islam, and other activist groups produced "fruit" for America: the Brown v. Board of Education Supreme Court Decision, the Civil Rights Act, the Voting Rights Act, and the Fair Housing Act.

I am a product of the treeshakers. I'm their "jelly," formed from the fruit of Brown, the Civil Rights Act, and the Voting Rights Act.

The central question my speech on this issue poses is what happens to a community--whose lifeblood is fruit and the jellies produced from treeshaking--when all the fruit is gone? What happens to a community when it fails to raise a new generation of tree shakers? In the wake of several crippling Supreme Court decisions rolling back political, economic, and educational affirmative action programs, how does a community sustain itself when there are no more treeshakers to shake the fruit down so the community can make jelly? In 2013, the U.S. Supreme Court is expected to issue yet another ruling on educational affirmative action. We must do more to support the community that believes in programs that afford racial or ethnic groups who have historically suffered discrimination and who still feel the effects of that collective discrimination today a way to collectively repair the damage that has been done. In fact, the entire U.S. jurisprudence relies on this notion of repair. However, when it comes to repairing the damage of slavery, Jim Crow, segregation, unequal access to opportunity, mouths get mute or even worse, veil their contempt in the acceptable phraseology of Dr. Martin Luther King, Jr. and talk about post-racial societies as if the United States has reached this promised land. It is these people who contemptibly put the "post" before the horse. The United States has not lived up to the Convention for the Elimination of All Forms of Racial Discrimination (CERD) to which it is a signatory and has ratified. CERD calls for Special Measures for so long as a group has comparatively negative standing and further, it stipulates that this is not to be viewed as reverse discrimination. Why is this not argued? It's the law! And it is the minimum that could be applied to the community of slave-descendant African-Americans in the U.S. today.

No more treeshakers?

In another of my other favorite speeches that went around the country several times, I liken myself to a paramedic for the Black body politic and, due to the objective reality that embroils the Black community as described by its statistics, I render a diagnosis and a prognosis: I pronounce the patient near comatose. Linking back to the other speech, I assert that this is what happens when a community stops producing treeshakers. Sadly, the numbers tell the story.

The Department of Labor announced that the wealth divide by race just got bigger. And so it goes with many indices. From the National Urban League to United for a Fair Economy to Harvard University Kaiser Family Foundation to Hull House and Loyola University, you name the study, and the record will reflect a Black community in deep distress. Even in the best of times, deep structural flaws exist to deny Blacks access to what the U.S. has to offer. University of Dayton Law Professor Vernellia Randall offers a 21st Century Anti-Discrimination Act as an effective antidote to the continued discrimination that makes disparities by race persistent. It is important to note here, that on some indexes, racial disparities comparing Blacks and Whites in the U.S. indicate that Blacks are worse-off today than they were at the time of the murder of

Dr. Martin Luther King, jr. The findings of United for a Fair Economy, in back-to-back studies, reveal islands of deep poverty characterized by race and ethnicity. Dr. Iris Marion Young writes that there is one way to respectfully deal with this very thorny issue that cuts to the very foundations of U.S society--a country that expanded by genocide of indigenous peoples and that developed economically as a result of the Trans-Atlantic Slave Trade and then after that, slavery by another name--convict labor,that continues to this very day:  by people of the United States accepting collective responsibility for what happened in the past and by working collectively to address the glaring disparities that continue to exist and that are well documented in government studies and reports. This can be done by way of public policy that addresses these issues forthrightly as a result of engaged and committed authentic leaders, instead of the many transactional misleaders who currently hold positions of authority.

In addition to failing to produce leaders willing to be treeshakers and experiencing a contraction of opportunity as a result, another phenomenon was explored in a speech that I wrote for Women's History Month when I explored an essay by Dr. June Terpstra entitled, "Beware the Women of the Hegemon." That speech is about avatars who are accepted by the people because they look like something they are not. Dr. Terpstra concludes that some women are not the peace promoters that we once assumed all women to be, and that some women can, and indeed do, zealously defend and advance policies of the hegemonic imperial powers. I concluded that voters cannot just vote for a woman in the hopes that she will not be a warmonger, but that we all must cast our votes for people with strong backgrounds representative of the values that we hold dear.

I have always maintained that White progressives and Blacks have in common too many values to let race get in the way of cooperation and opportunities for the kind of deep and fundamental change that we both know is needed in public policy.. And the key to unlocking unfettered cooperation means that White progressives will have to allow Blacks and other minorities to lead our own struggles, and give their energies and devotion to playing a supporting role, particularly in their own communities, in the struggles faced by peoples of color.. I say unfettered because the Black or person of color has to be able to call the shots rather than merely taking orders from some unseen donor manipulating strings on a Black or person-of-color marionette.

**The key to unlocking unfettered cooperation means that White progressives will have to allow Blacks and other minorities to lead our own struggles, and give their energies and devotion to playing a supporting role, particularly in their own communities.**

What do I want for my community and my country? I want my community to live in peace with access to all the opportunities for self-expression and self-fulfillment that exist in the United States. I want my country to respect human rights around the world and at home. I want the Bill of Rights and U.S. laws to be apply to every U.S. citizen and resident equally. I want Nature to be respected or else the ultimate victory for the planet might very well come at humanity's expense.

That's all. Simple, isn't it? Then why is it so darn hard to accomplish?

In the film American Blackout, I ask aloud: what was the progressive community thinking when I got kicked out of a Congressional seat for challenging the George W. Bush Administration while Kathryn Harris (the Florida Secretary of State who helped Bush steal the election) had a Congressional seat drawn specifically for her? Where were they? Until today, I thought that the Black community's quest for justice was an insurance policy for the progressive community, therefore linking the two communities in aspiration if not in practice. Securing Black voting rights would assure a progressive agenda for America and therefore, we both had politically consistent goals and objectives. That is what I thought. Then, I was stunned by an idea provoked by a friend and supporter whose words began to eat away at me and undermined my thinking.

In a discussion with one of my very dear White supporters who was lamenting the ease with which my progressive White base was lured away from me when AIPAC painted the target on my forehead, a frightening thought entered my mind: Suppose the more important insurance policy for progressives is that of White skin privilege. What then? The thought was frightening to me because everything I've based my outlook on has been that it is possible to form a true rainbow coalition (notice no caps, meaning not the organization, but the spirit) and move our country forward, with fairness for everyone. Now if that's not possible, we all have to regroup and reexamine what we're really fighting for. And what we really stand for.

This stunning realization that there might be some divergence between what White progressives said and did only deepened upon a reread of Dr. King's "Letter From A Birmingham Jail." Dr. King wrote of his disappointment in the progressive Whites of his day. Here's what Dr. King had to say in his Letter readily available on the internet. (N. B. All typographical errors are from the original source and therefore have not been corrected here):

> I must make two honest confessions to you, my Christian and Jewish brothers. First, I must confess that over the past few years I have been gravely disappointed with the white moderate. I have almost reached the regrettable conclusion that the Negro's great stumbling block in his stride toward freedom is not the White Citizen's Counciler or the Ku Klux Klanner, but the white moderate, who is more devoted to "order" than to justice; who prefers a negative peace which is the absence of tension to a positive peace which is the presence of justice; who constantly says: "I agree with you in the goal you seek, but I cannot agree with your methods of direct action"; who paternalistically believes he can set the timetable for another man's freedom; who lives by a mythical concept of time and who constantly advises the Negro to wait for a "more convenient season." Shallow understanding from people of good will is more frustrating than absolute misunderstanding from people of ill will. Lukewarm acceptance is much more bewildering than outright rejection.
>
> I had hoped that the white moderate would understand that law and order exist for the purpose of establishing justice and that when they fan in this purpose they become the dangerously structured dams that block the flow of social progress. I had hoped that the white moderate would understand that the present tension in the South is a necessary phase of the transition from an obnoxious negative peace, in which the Negro passively accepted his unjust plight, to a substantive and positive peace, in which all men will respect the dignity and worth of human personality. Actually, we who engage in nonviolent direct action are not the creators of tension. We merely bring to the surface the hidden tension that is already alive. We bring it out in the open, where it can be seen and dealt with. Like a boil that can never be cured so long as it is covered up but must be opened with an its ugliness to the natural medicines of air and light, injustice must be exposed,

with all the tension its exposure creates, to the light of human conscience and the air of national opinion before it can be cured. . . .

But though I was initially disappointed at being categorized as an extremist, as I continued to think about the matter I gradually gained a measure of satisfaction from the label. Was not Jesus an extremist for love: "Love your enemies, bless them that curse you, do good to them that hate you, and pray for them which despitefully use you, and persecute you." Was not Amos an extremist for justice: "Let justice roll down like waters and righteousness like an ever-flowing stream." Was not Paul an extremist for the Christian gospel: "I bear in my body the marks of the Lord Jesus." Was not Martin Luther an extremist: "Here I stand; I cannot do otherwise, so help me God." And John Bunyan: "I will stay in jail to the end of my days before I make a butchery of my conscience." And Abraham Lincoln: "This nation cannot survive half slave and half free." And Thomas Jefferson: "We hold these truths to be self-evident, that all men are created equal ..." So the question is not whether we will be extremists, but what kind of extremists we will be. Will we be extremists for hate or for love? Will we be extremist for the preservation of injustice or for the extension of justice? In that dramatic scene on Calvary's hill three men were crucified. We must never forget that all three were crucified for the same crime---the crime of extremism. Two were extremists for immorality, and thus fell below their environment. The other, Jesus Christ, was an extremist for love, truth and goodness, and thereby rose above his environment. Perhaps the South, the nation and the world are in dire need of creative extremists.

I had hoped that the white moderate would see this need. Perhaps I was too optimistic; perhaps I expected too much. I suppose I should have realized that few members of the oppressor race can understand the deep groans and passionate yearnings of the oppressed race, and still fewer have the vision to see that injustice must be rooted out by strong, persistent and determined action. I am thankful, however, that some of our white brothers in the South have grasped the meaning of this social revolution and committed themselves to it. They are still too few in quantity, but they are big in quality. Some-such as Ralph McGill, Lillian Smith, Harry Golden, James McBride Dabbs, Ann Braden and Sarah Patton Boyle---have written about our struggle in eloquent and prophetic terms. Others have marched with us down nameless streets of the South. They have languished in filthy, roach-infested jails, suffering the abuse and brutality of policemen who view them as "dirty nigger lovers." Unlike so many of their moderate brothers and sisters, they have recognized the urgency of the moment and sensed the need for powerful "action" antidotes to combat the disease of segregation.

Let me take note of my other major disappointment. I have been so greatly disappointed with the white church and its leadership. Of course, there are some notable exceptions. I am not unmindful of the fact that each of you has taken some significant stands on this issue. I commend you, Reverend Stallings, for your Christian stand on this past Sunday, in welcoming Negroes to your worship service on a non segregated basis. I commend the Catholic leaders of this state for integrating Spring Hill College several years ago.

But despite these notable exceptions, I must honestly reiterate that I have been disappointed with the church. I do not say this as one of those negative critics who can always find something wrong with the church. I say this as a minister of the gospel, who loves the church; who was nurtured in its bosom; who 'has been sustained by its spiritual blessings and who will remain true to it as long as the cord of Rio shall lengthen.

When I was suddenly catapulted into the leadership of the bus protest in Montgomery, Alabama, a few years ago, I felt we would be supported by the white church, felt that the white ministers, priests and rabbis of the South would be among our strongest allies. Instead, some have been outright opponents, refusing to understand the freedom movement and misrepresenting its leader era; an too many others have been more cautious than courageous and have remained silent behind the anesthetizing security of stained-glass windows.

I didn't mean to include all of that from Dr. King, but it was just so appropriate. And of course, if I wrote the very same thing, all heck would break loose, but somehow, it's more acceptable when Dr. King says it, because he's dead and the government accepted to recognize his heroism. Well, unfortunately, we still have work to do in this regard.

The only thing, though, is that if White supremacy and White-skin privilege are the unshakeable foundations of this country—and this is when I shuddered—then is my dream of being a part of a true rainbow coalition just a dream? I remember that activists that I spoke to who were with the Occupy Movement even admitted that Occupy still couldn't transcend race and so "People of color" caucuses had to form to deal with the racial contradictions they were experiencing even inside the Occupy Movement. Right now, there is a very strong "Liberty" movement. Will "Liberty" activists be able to work respectfully with Black activists and activists of color who want freedom, respect for the Bill of Rights, and the shared Kingian goals of an end to U.S. militarism, racism, and material-ism? I so much don't want it to be a dream.

So, for now, I'm going to put that thought in the back of my mind and organize like heck to make a true rainbow coalition based on America's most noble ideals.

In the end, it really is up to us to diagnose our situation and then prescribe the best corrective action. I'm making my way back to the treeshakers and the jelly makers and to my conclusion.

I remember my outrage at the New York Police Department's (NYPD) murder of Amadou Diallo. Amadou Diallo, an African immigrant from Guinea, came to the United States in search of his dream. Instead, he was gunned down by NYPD in the vestibule of his own apartment building holding a wallet. The White police officers who killed him said they thought he was pulling a gun. That is always the line that White police officers use when they kill unarmed Black and Latino men. And it happens all the time.

I was outraged then, as I am still outraged now. And there have been many more killings since Diallo. I went to a few of the Members of the New York City Congressional Delegation and told them that we should organize a march of Black men from all over America to come, and demonstrate solidarity with Blacks who are subjected to NYPD rogue police misconduct. It would be a way for all of us, Black and White, to come together to demand better. In addition, I just had to do something because Amadou was my child. What I mean by that is that my outrage centered on the fact that Amadou could have been any of us. Another innocent, unarmed Black man gunned down by White fears.

Well, it was not to be. I was told by one Member of Congress in particular from New York City that "marching" was what we Southerners did. New Yorkers didn't do things that way.

That exchange probably typifies my situation in Congress from Day One. I came from an activist orientation and carried my activism into Congress. But increasingly, Congress consisted of people who were only avatars of that mold. So, when the time came for the Hurricane Katrina Committee, I went to almost every Black Caucus Member, but was finally told by one Member who leveled with me and told me that I just had to accept that when the leadership says something, Members will do it, even if they shouldn't—including that usually outspoken Member. Of course, I was disappointed, but again, not surprised. I'd kinda' been there before. I was thankful that this particular Member of Congress at least told me the truth.

I guess, what I'm suggesting is that if there's this disconnect, even in the Congressional Black Caucus, also known as the "Conscience of the Congress," then why should I expect more from America's progressive establishment? Professor Ricky L. Jones puts it succinctly: if the Congressional Black Caucus is the conscience of the Congress, what do we do when the CBC loses its conscience? In my estimation, that's a clue as to what happens when a community loses its treeshakers and its jelly makers. It also loses its soul.

The Network **Journal**
*Black Professionals and Small Business Magazine*

**21st Century Leadership**
She took on the Bush Administration over 9/11 and Iraq when no one else dared. Will she be the next leader of the African American community?

**LEARNING BOOM**
*Professionals are going back to school*
*Tips for choosing an online course*

**POUNDING THE CYBERWALK**
*Web sites for job hunters*

**Cynthia A. McKinney**

SEPTEMBER 2005    $2.95

web site: www.tnj.com

# CHAPTER 10

# THE POLITICS OF HATE AND LOVE

It became clear that I was to be ousted by AIPAC. We found one letter written by a once-supportive constituent detailing that no matter how effective my Congressional office had been in serving the needs of my constituents, because of my perceived anti-Israel votes, I was no longer deserving of Jewish support. Another letter indicated that the writer was raising money nationally against two Black Congresspeople perceived to be anti-Israel: Earl Hilliard, the first Black Member of Congress from Alabama since Reconstruction and me, the first Black Congresswoman from Georgia. There is a kind of "Zionist sifter" that U.S. leadership must survive to stay intact. Anyone who doesn't conform to the litmus test of loyalty to Israel, a foreign country after all, ceases politically to exist. It has come to the point now where this state of affairs is openly discussed—in Israeli newspapers, and moreso here since the publication of *The Israel Lobby and U.S. Foreign Policy* in 2008 by noted White academics, John Mearsheimer and Stephen Walt. Here is an example of what *Ha'aretz* wrote in 2009.

Published 12:44 04.12.09
Latest update 15:01 04.12.09

**American Jews eye Obama's 'anti-Israel' appointees**
**Nominees have been accused of being anti-Israel and touted as evidence showing Obama's bias.**
By Natasha Mozgovaya

Every appointee to the American government must

endure a thorough background check by the American Jewish community.

In the case of Obama's government in particular, every criticism against Israel made by a potential government appointee has become a catalyst for debate about whether appointing "another leftist" offers proof that Obama does not truly support Israel.

A few months ago, boisterous protests by the American Jewish community helped foil the appointment of Chaz Freeman to chair the National Intelligence Council, citing his "anti-Israel leaning."

The next attempt to appoint an intelligence aide, in this case, former Republican senator Chuck Hagel, also resulted in vast criticism over his not having a pro-Israel record.

American Zionists are urging Obama to cancel Hagel's appointment because of what they call a long and problematic record of hostility toward Israel.

The president of the Zionist Organization of America, Morton A. Klein, described Hagel's nomination as such: "Any American who is concerned about Iran's drive to obtain nuclear weapons, maintaining the Israeli-U.S. relationship and supporting Israel in its legitimate fight to protect her citizens from terrorism should oppose this appointment."

Republican Jews have also protested Hagel's appointment, citing an incident in 2004 when Hagel refused to sign a letter calling on then-president George Bush to speak about Iran's nuclear program at the G8 summit that year.

In August of 2006, Hagel refused to sign a letter requesting the UN declare Hezbollah a terrorist organization.

In a speech at the conference of self-declared "pro-peace, pro-Israel" lobby J Street, Hagel spoke about his views on the issue of Israel and the Middle East.

"The United States' support for Israel need not be - nor should it be - an either-or proposition that dictates our relationships with our Arab allies and friends. The U.S. has a long and special relationship with Israel, but it must not come at the expense of our Arab relationships," Hagel said.

The latest round of heated debate has been over

the nomination of Hannah Rosenthal to head the Office to Monitor and Combat Anti-Semitism in the Obama administration.

Rosenthal, who is the daughter of a Holocaust survivor, served as a Health Department regional director under the Clinton administration, and held positions in different left-leaning Jewish organizations.

Between 2000 and 2005, Rosenthal was the head of the Jewish Council for Public Affairs; she was also the executive director of the Chicago Foundation for Women. In recent years, she has served on the advisory board of the J Street lobby.

The president of Americans for Peace Now lauded Obama's appointment of Rosenthal. Even Anti-Defamation League chairman Abraham Foxman came out in support of Rosenthal's appointment.

"This appointment signals the continued seriousness of America'?s resolve to fight anti-Semitism," Foxman said in a statement.

Shortly after the announcement of Rosenthal's nomination, conservative Jewish web sites began to attack her, some of them declaring that Obama appointed an anti-Israeli to fight anti-Semitism.

Rumors brewed that she had accused Israel of systemically strengthening anti-Semitism. Bloggers argued that her appointment would cause Jews and Israelis to cast doubt on Obama and his relationship with Israel.

In one of her articles, Rosenthal criticized conservative voices in the Jewish community whom she accused of taking over the discourse regarding the Israeli-Palestinian conflict.

"It's a scary time, with people losing the ability to differentiate between a Jew, any Jew, and what's going on in Israel," Rosenthal said.

In an interview with the new online Jewish magazine, Tablet, Rosenthal said that she loves Israel.

"I have lived in Israel. I go back and visit every chance I can. I consider it part of my heart. And because I love it so much, I want to see it safe and secure and free and democratic and living safely," Rosenthal said.*

---

* See <http://www.haaretz.com/news/american-jews-eye-obama-s-anti-israel-appointees-1.2773>

**From:**

**Sent:** Wednesday, April 24, 2002 10:04 AM

**To:**

**Subject:** Invitation to meet Harvard alumnus running against Congressman who is unfriendly to Israel

I hope all is well. I am writing to invite you to a MID-PAC lobbying meeting with Artur Davis who is running against Congressman Earl Hilliard for the Democratic nomination in the 7th Congressional District in Alabama. MID-PAC is the Upper East Side pro-Israel political action committee. Attached is some information on both of them. Congressman Hilliard is considered to be one of the members who is most antagonistic to Israel. For example, he has visited Libya to meet with Mummar Gadhafi. Davis is a graduate of the Harvard College Class of 1990 and the Harvard Law School Class of 1993. Davis has written a policy paper on the Middle East which is attached as part of his bio. Davis ran against Hilliard in the 2000 election and is trying again. MID-PAC's goals are to try to help unseat Congressman Hilliard and develop a relationship with a young African American leader who appears to be destined for influence in that community. I believe that lobbying members of Congress is probably the most worthwhile thing that we can do to help Israel in getting its message out and building support for its survival in the face its numerous enemies and significant disinformation and misunderstanding of the issues. Please join me to lend support to Artur Davis and to help us get our message across to him and his staff. The meeting will take place on Monday, April 29 at 12:00pm at the offices of the law firm, Wachtell Lipton (our host is Mitchell Presser). The address is 51 West 52nd Street (Conference Room 33c). Please RSVP so that I can get your name to security at the building. I look forward to your joining me in this crucial work on behalf of the Jewish people. There will he no solicitation at the event.

# McKinney, seen as a foe of Israel, to run for her old seat in Congress

By Matthew E. Berger

WASHINGTON, March 30 (JTA) — Jewish fund-raisers are looking for ways to prevent former Rep. Cynthia McKinney from returning to Congress.

Jewish leaders were caught off-guard Monday when Rep. Denise Majette (D-Ga.) announced she would seek the Democratic nomination for Georgia's open Senate seat, and would not run for re-election in the House.

Just two days earlier, McKinney, a lightning rod in the Jewish community who has been called stridently anti-Israel, announced her intentions to seek the seat she lost in 2002.

Majette received strong financial support from the Jewish community when she defeated the incumbent McKinney in the Democratic primary with more than 70 percent of the vote, and she was considered a favorite for re-election in the House this year.

Her absence is expected to greatly aide McKinney's chances, unless another Democratic primary challenger can be found.

Morris Amitay, a leading fund-raiser in the Jewish community, said it was too early to determine how much effort the Jewish community would put into defeating McKinney this year, though he suggested there would be enough time to rally around a candidate before the July primary.

"It depends if there is a viable candidate," said Amitay, founder of the pro-Israel Washington PAC. "There is some time, but I haven't heard anything."

Cathy Woolard, the openly gay president of Atlanta's city council, announced her entry into the Democratic race for Majette's seat Tuesday. Several other local candidates told the Atlanta Journal-Constitution on Monday that they were considering challenging McKinney in the primary as well.

During her 10 years in Congress, McKinney angered many in the Jewish community with her anti-Israel comments and votes against resolutions supporting Israel's right to self-defense.

Notably, she asked a Saudi prince for the $10 million donation he had pledged for disaster relief after the Sept. 11, 2001 attacks. New York City mayor Rudolph Giuliani had rejected the money because the prince suggested U.S. support for Israel provoked the attacks.

McKinney also suggested that President Bush knew of the terrorist plans to attack the World Trade Center, but did not prevent them because he wanted to launch a war.

McKinney has enjoyed strong support from the Arab and Muslim communities. which view her as a strong proponent of a Palestinian state.

Several Jewish officials said they were surprised with Majette's decision, and predicted she would have an uphill battle to win the Senate seat in a state that is trending Republican.

However, there is speculation that Majette was pressured into the run because no viable Democrat had emerged for the race, and several Republican congressmen were expected to fight for their party's nomination.

Majette's entry could force Republicans to shift resources to Georgia from other competitive races.

Amitay said he had been planning to support Majette's re-election bid in the House, particularly if McKinney decided to run.

"I would have been happier if she had run again," he said, "and I don't think she's going to be the next senator from Georgia."

Print This Story

Back to top ^

Sure enough, with those forces ranged against me, as far as Congress went, thanks to the crossover voting in the Georgia Democratic primary,* I was, at last, history. And I have to say that it was not without a measure of sadness that I left the U.S. Capitol for what was likely my very last time. It's not so much the place that I miss, but being able to work on behalf of the people at a level that can make big differences in people's lives when we push hard enough for it. I'm proud that in our Congressional Office work, we gained a reputation for not accepting "no" from government agencies for our constituents.

*See my lawsuit against crossover voting in Appendix VII and Gus Savage's take on AIPAC election interference to defeat candidates critical of Israel in Appendix VI.

Some people weren't so sorry to see me go.

I'm sorry for the contents of the following e-mail section. While the e-mail addresses and the names of the senders have been removed, this is but a sampling of what I receive in my inbox. I get hate messages every way they can be sent—through the postal service, into my e-mail inbox (as you will see below), on online news postings, and via the airwaves on the radio! But I thought I would share a sampling of these with you so that you, too, can get a taste of what my life is really like. And what it has been like ever since the day I was sworn in as a Member of Congress. And, I'll tell you one thing more: my faith in the goodness of people remains unshaken despite the fact that I get an unhealthy dose from the worst of them. In fact, it's messages like these that keep me motivated to find a better way.

1. From: 'Mike K_____' _____nvestments@earthlink.net
   Sent: Tue Aug 8 21:50
   Subject: Adios
   Watching Cynthia on TV tonight just confirms what I have believed for years.
   She's a classless thug, totally illiterate regarding world affairs and generally has no business in the U.S. Congress.
   Why doesn't she do us all a favor and pull a Michael Jackson? Pack it all up and go run for congress in one of those other countries she loves so much.
   Adios, Muchacha!

2. From: 'KARL K_____' <k_____@msn.com>
   Sent: Tue Jun 27 13:26
   Subject: HAIRDO
   MAYBE IF YOUR HAIRDO LOOKED LIKE THIS THE GUARD WOULD HAVE RECOGNIZED YOU BETTER .

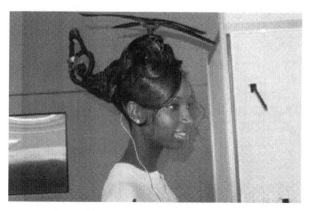

3. From: 'Kerry _____' <kerry@_____.com>
   Sent: Wed Aug 9 6:37
   Subject: Talkin about hard work??
   Have you ever stopped to consider that if you're working for minimum wage, you shouldn't be having a baby? Instead of hard work, lets talk about personal responsibility.

4. From: 'Richard _____' <_____@bellsouth.net>
   Sent: Wed Aug 9 5:30
   Subject: You got what you deserved
   Well I guess the people of the 4th district aren't so stupid after all. Finally, the people have gotten rid of the most racist, do nothing, unethical, thug that ever walked the halls of the United States Capitol building. Good Riddance.

5. From: 'Bud T_____ <b_____@cox.net>
   Sent: Wed Aug 9 4:31
   Subject: YOU LOST
   So long....How did you get an Irish name ???

6. From: 'Dan S_____' <dans_____@hotmail.com>
   Subject: Racist!
   Congressman McKinney,
   After your latest speech, I can only assume that you are the biggest RACIST I have ever known. Please move to Cuba or Venezuela, I no longer care to hear another thing about you. You have done more to tear down your race and constituency than any politician in the history of this great country!!!!!!!!!!!!!!!!!!!!!!!!!!!!!!
   Please Leave...............................the sooner the better

7. From: 'Steve B_____' < steve_____@bellsouth.net>
   Subject:  sha naaaa na na sha naaaa na na hey hey hey
   Fuck you and good bye

8. From: 'Randy S_____'
   Sent: Wed Aug 9 1:15
   Subject: Good Ridance! <rspeir@bellsouth.net>
   I am so glad to hear that the McKinney bunch (Cynthia and Daddy Billy) are soon to be out of Congress! You have been a total embarrssment not only to DeKalb County and the State of Georgia, but to the entire nation and the World!
   What job will you take on next? I hear that there is a position available at the local Way-Low Grocery store. You can continue to stay in touch with your former constituants as you bag their groceries while they pay for their merchandise with food stamps! Good ridance!

9. From: Robert J_____ <ro_____ <@yahoo.de>
   Sent: Tue Aug 8 22:38

Subject: I am so happy!!!!
8 August 2006
I am so glad that a racist, piece of shit, dumbass
like you has lost her re-election bid. You are a
disgrace to congress, and I'm so glad that there will
be one less nigger in Congress now. I don't say that
because you're black; Not all blacks are niggers.
If you were white, you'd be trailer trash, bitch.

10. From: Preston W_____ <pw_____ <@yahoo.com>
   Sent: Fri Aug 11 4:52
   Subject: Bye Bye, Nutball
   Outa here you nutball. Bye Bye. Please do us a favor and don't
   run again. You're an embarassment to the state and the country.

11. From: 'Jim S_____ <jim_s_____ <@hotmail.com>
   Sent: Wed Aug 9 7:25
   Subject: Yeah! The Nigger McKinney Loses!
   Now you can start a new website:
   www.niggercuntsdontprosper.com
   Use your asshole attitude as a warning to others.

I THINK THIS SIGN SPEAKS FOR ITSELF AND ITS OWNER
IN FRONT OF A STORE IN ATLANTA

I realize that some people reading this are too young to even know who Buckwheat is! And there will be readers from other cultures who will not know. So, I think I'd better explain Buckwheat.

Buckwheat is a character in 1950s U.S. television who really was a caricature of what White people thought of Black people. The depictions of Buckwheat were racist to the core. But, for the young Black person who played the role, it was employment. Here is Buckwheat in action—what this restaurant owner in Georgia likens me to:

THIS IS BUCKWHEAT.

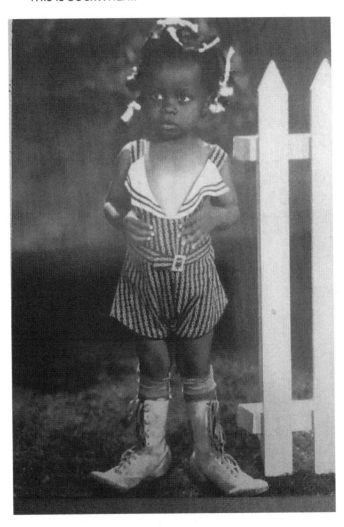

Paid for by
New Leadership for DeKalb
3577-A Chamblee Tucker Road
Atlanta, GA 30341

Then there was the postcard sent out to white voters during the campaign. I call it the "ABC" postcard: Anybody But Cynthia.

144

The above, as I said, is a "sprinkling."
On the other hand, there was also this:

August 12, 2006

Dear Cynthia

I watched the 'closing ceremony' at your election headquarters the night of August 8, and continue to be moved by your captivating speech.

The way your chose the quotations linked the past spiritually based challenges to racist injustice with the future struggle we must now construct. You gave a vision of that struggle to advance our claims, as a people, to justice and to peace, instead of obscuring them as the many public voices clamor to do these days.

Howard Zinn explained that in the Movement context, it is important to distinguish between a defeat that is a defeat, and a defeat that is a victory. We have all witnessed how viciously you are smeared and undermined by the power structure. Remember, they mount these attacks and cover-ups because they fear you. If you were not an effective advocate for your principled objectives, nor such a clear spokesman for an alternative social politics, it wouldn't be so important to remove you from office.

As you pointed out, however, a "change is sweeping the world," and you stand in the center of that effort to make sure it sweeps the United States. Congratulations – continue the fight. I support you.

Love

Kathleen Cleaver

And from my beloved son, Coy:

There are a lot of things in this world that I will never understand. For example, how the internet works, how in the world Ashlee Simpson got a record deal, how Brazil did not win the World Cup, or how the Golden State Warriors are still in the NBA. The most important concept that I will never understand is how American politics work. Although I have grown up

145

around politics all my life, it has never made any sense to me. I believe that each member of Congress has exactly the same job. They are to go up to Washington D.C., pass bills, bring back money that will help the people within their district, inform their constituents of what their government is doing, and to ask their government questions about their policies. Sounds simple enough, right? Well, you would be surprised at how many Congressional members fail to do any of those items. I know for a fact, that my mom does not fall into that category. To prove to you that this is not just a show of son-mother love, I'll let you see for yourself. Check out both of her websites at www.cynthiaforcongress.com and www.house.gov/mckinney and look at what she stands for and has accomplished.

You would think that the Congressional members who go up to D.C. and actually do what they are paid to, would be portrayed in a positive light, but this is not the case and is where my confusion begins. After September 11th, you would expect the Members of Congress to start asking how and why did this happen? Did they? Surprisingly, no. They just went along with the memo from the White House saying that we were attacked because we were free. Now, I am only 20 years old and do not consider myself to be any sort of a genius, but I can already tell you that that statement does not make any sense. I cannot think of a single war that was started because one side was "free" and the other was not. This explanation is not good enough for me, should not be good enough for you, and definitely should not have been good enough for any of the Members of Congress. But I suppose it's always easier to go with the flow rather than against the current. And so began my mom's quest for the truth. I would have been willing to cut some of the other members of Congress some slack if they had come out in support of asking questions of what happened on 9/11, after my mom made the first initial approach, but this didn't happen, and so they get no sympathy from me. The exact opposite happened. Republicans as well as Democrats came out blasting my mom about her questioning of the events of 9/11. The word "unpatriotic" was used as a description of her as freely as liberals are labeled "flip-floppers" on Fox News!

Someone has yet to explain to me how it is un-patriotic to ask about the events of 9/11. I was getting fed up with all the unnecessary bashing my mom was receiving in the media. Story after story, insult after insult. I had been over to Italy for a summer camp, the summer before, and figured that the environment there would be a lot more enjoyable, and so I finished up high school in Italy. All this happened the same year she was up for election. All the media outrage inspired Republicans to cross over and vote as Democrats just to get her out of office. The whole idea of cross over voting sounds mighty illegal to me, and probably to you too. Well, that is because it probably is illegal in your state! Well, my mom resides from the great state of Georgia, where things are still a little bit back-wards. There was a similar case of cross over voting in California, but there, the case went to the Supreme Court where they found it unconstitutional for cross over voting to happen. Well, Georgia has kept to its old southern roots and has refused to change. The whole idea of crossover voting was masterminded by a guy by the name of Mark Davis, the creator of goodbyecynthia.com. In the film, American Blackout (definitely a film worth checking out, because it shows how my mom was unfairly portrayed in the media and does an in depth look at voter disfranchisement), he brags about how he orchestrates the cross over, and how happy he was that it was successful. Well, Mark Davis has reappeared this campaign. After looking at some of the contributors to Mr. Johnson's campaign and who they have contributed to in their past, it is clear that Mr. Johnson's campaign is being run mostly by Republican money! Please don't take my word for it, you can see for yourself. I'll walk you through it:

1) Go to http://www.fec.gov/finance/disclosure/dis-closure_data_search.shtml and click on "Candidate Search"
2) Type in "Johnson, Henry C" and click "Get Listing"
3) When his name pops up, click on it and then click on "Individuals Who Gave To This Candidate"
4) When this page pops up, print it off.
5) Now, go back to http://www.fec.gov/finance/dis-closure/disclosure_data_search.shtml and click on

"Individual Search" and then click "Advanced Search"
6) Find someone on the list that you want to look for (for example: David Flint). Type in Flint then David. Then choose the state Georgia. Then choose date range (For example: 01/01/2004 to 06/30/2006)
7) This creates a list of all the people David Flint has contributed from January 1, 2004 to June 30, 2006.

The only way to combat all this Republican money is by having money of our own and warm bodies who will volunteer and help us. After you have done your research on my mom, I am sure that you will agree with me that she needs to stay in Congress! Do not allow people who jump into races just to justify business deals to go up to Washington D.C. and blend in with the rest of the bland and boring crowd. Reward someone who has delivered for her district, who stands up for not only her local constituents but for Americans in general. Do not allow a minority of Republicans to decide who should represent a majority Democratic district! Do not allow big business companies or rich lobbying groups to decide who should represent the average worker and average family. Do not allow corruption and scandals to tarnish the principles that America is built on! It's up to people like you, who do not pay attention to CNN or Fox News, to help put the right people in office. In closing, I would like to strongly urge everyone who reads this to check out the following movies and websites:

- American Blackout (a beautifully done movie about voter disfranchisement in Ohio and Florida, and my mom, www.americanblackout.com)
- Loose Change (a movie that does an investigation of 9/11 better than CNN, Fox, ABC, CBS, NBC, or any other formation of the alphabet has ever done, www.loosechange911.com)
- OutFOXed (a movie that shows how much of a joke Fox News is)
- www.gnn.tv (an alternative news site, where you can get REAL news)
- www.fromthewilderness.com (another alternative news web site, created by Michael Ruppert, a former LAPD narcotics investigator)

- www.gregpalast.com (a New York times best selling author and journalist for the BBC)

The media is another component that adds to my confusion. Everyone complains about how liberal or conservative different media corporations are. Personally, I don't care if Fox News is conservative and are promoting their own views on the world. I just will not watch it. It only disturbs me when Fox News tries to disguise their coverage as "fair and balanced" or have the audacity to have something called the "no spin zone." Good grief. I don't mean to pick on Fox News, but they are the most obvious culprit of out-right lying. Here in my hometown of Atlanta, the major newspaper is the Atlanta Journal Constitution. People who believe they are educated read the Constitution and believe everything that is printed as facts. I see nothing wrong with reading the Constitution, but don't take everything that you read as facts. How can you when the newspaper is endorsing candidates? How can an organization claim to be fair and neutral, when they are trying to choose who should represent you?

*Coy McKinney*

**Isaac Hayes loves Cynthia. Cynthia loves Isaac Hayes. Rest in peace, Isaac Hayes.**

The online situation has then worsened in that starting in 2009, the State of Israel Foreign Ministry announced the hiring of tens of thousands of soldier warriors for its "internet warfare" squad. According to Ynetnews.com, "Foreign Ministry officials are fighting what they see as a terrible and scary monster: the Palestinian public relations monster." Their job is to post pro-Israel propaganda all over the internet. Having read these terribly obvious and extremely mean-spirited posts all over the internet wherever my name is mentioned over the last fewtwo years, I can truly say that much of what they post is vile, ugly, mean, and also poisonous. Here's just a sample:

> "Ms. McKinney is a racist and anti-Semite of the first rank. If she were white and male, she would be David Duke." -- Peter Swartz, Professor Emeritus, Cornell University*

Watch for it on the internet, but forewarned is forearmed. Neutralize it by knowing what it is. wherever my name appears.

In addition, it is clear that the "corporate-stream"mainstream media have done their job well of stoking antagonism. But, because I am well steeped in the methods of COINTELPRO, I understand what is happening. It doesn't make it pleasant, but it does help to understand what is being done. The interesting and sad fact is that if the people who wrote the foregoing messages were to talk to me, they would likely find that they have more in common with me than with the people whose ends are served by their behavior.

**Despite the venom that is hurled at me, I'll tell you one thing: I continue to have faith in the goodness of people. And I will continue to do the work that I do because it is necessary work, and I will admit that I am motivated by my love for the community of people out there who want and expect more for this country, Mother Nature, and our world.**

I've shielded my son, my colleagues, and most of my staff from what I have to see when I go through my inbox. But for those who delude themselves that there's no hatred out there, you just got a good dose of my reality. Despite the venom that is hurled at me, I'll tell you one thing: I continue to have faith in the goodness of people. And I will continue to do the work that I do because it is necessary work, and . I will admit that I am motivated by my love for the community of people out there who want and expect more for this country, Mother

---

*See http://www.discoverthenetworks.org/individualProfile.asp?indid=1508 for more of the same.

Nature, and our world. I'm motivated to find a better way. I hope those of you reading this book will also find the motivation and the courage to to do the work that will make our country what we and the world need it to be. With that having been said, let me hasten to add that on the night of the theft of my 2006 election, whose election data have, to this day, never been released to the public, I sang (and everyone who knows me knows that I absolutely love karaoke, but cannot sing one bit) a song by PINK whose lyrics were so moving to me: "Dear Mr. President." Here are those lyrics from PINK that I sang for George W. Bush:

"DEAR MR. PRESIDENT"
(featuring Indigo Girls)

Dear Mr. President,
Come take a walk with me.
Let's pretend we're just two people and
You're not better than me.
I'd like to ask you some questions if we can speak
honestly . . .
What do you feel when you see all the homeless on
the street?
Who do you pray for at night before you go to sleep?
What do you feel when you look in the mirror
Are you proud?

How do you sleep while the rest of us cry?
How do you dream when a mother has no chance to
say goodbye?
How do you walk with your head held high?
Can you even look me in the eye?
And tell me why?

Dear Mr. President,
Were you a lonely boy?
Are you a lonely boy?
Are you a lonely boy?
How can you say
No child is left behind?
We're not dumb and we're not blind,
They're all sitting in your cells,
While you pave the road to hell!

What kind of father would take his own daughter's
rights away?

And what kind of father might hate his own daughter
    if she were gay?
I can only imagine what the first lady has to say . . .
You've come a long way from whiskey and cocaine!

How do you sleep while the rest of us cry?
How do you dream when a mother has no chance to
    say goodbye?
How do you walk with your head held high?
Can you even look me in the eye?

Let me tell you 'bout hard work:
Minimum wage with a baby on the way!
Let me tell you 'bout hard work:
Rebuilding your house after the bombs took them
    away!
Let me tell you 'bout hard work:
Building a bed out of a cardboard box!
Let me tell you 'bout hard work!
Hard work!
Hard work!
You don't know nothing bout hard work!
Hard work!
Hard work!
Oh . . .

How do you sleep at night?
How do you walk with your head held high?
Dear Mr. President . . .
You'd never take a walk with me . . .
Would you?

And with that, I was off onto another chapter in my life as a former Member of Congress. The Democrats won a majority in both the U.S.
House of Representatives and the U.S. Senate. The country was hopeful
that attention would turn to a policy of peace and many in the peace
community awaited a followup to my impeachment resolution against
President George W. Bush for violating his oath of office, U.S. laws against
torture, and eviscerating the Bill of Rights and the U.S. Constitution.

# CHAPTER 11

# ELECTION PROTECTION

When men and women introduce me at functions, sometimes they refer to me as the Harriet Tubman of my day; the Rosa Parks of our day; many times, the Sojourner Truth of today. And here recently, especially from my New York supporters, I've heard myself being compared to Ida B. Wells-Barnett. But, interestingly, more than that quartet of committed and dedicated women of color, I find that in introductions of me or references to me, an overwhelming number of people pull three women from the Bible to use as a comparison.

Anyone who knows me knows that, despite going to Catholic elementary and high schools, and almost going to a Catholic university (Notre Dame), I'm not a biblical scholar. I've been told too many times to study the roles of Esther, Deborah, and Naomi, because in so many ways, I am told, I am like them. So, for this writing, I thought I'd find out about these women so I could know what it is about me that reminds so many people of them. And I decided to include my findings in this book.

I came to know Bishop Felton Hawkins of the Full Gospel Kingdom Church in Virginia through Carol Gould, and the three of us engaged in deep conversation about this. Included in that conversation was another Pastor, Kermit Jones, also of Virginia, and it was there that the significance of these comparisons matured. I asked Bishop Hawkins, Pastor Jones, and Carol Gould to share with me their thoughts on these three women, to school me as it were, on why these comparisons are made. Their eyes got big and wide. I could tell that this was something they, too, had probably given some thought to.

The normally quiet and reserved Pastor Jones became animated, bringing a big smile to his wife's face. We ended up talking all night. What you're about to read is a combination of their thoughts, on each of these Biblical women and how they relate to me. That is, why I think so many people refer to me in the same breath as they refer to these three women. I will start with Esther.

Before I tell Esther's story, I must clarify something about Israel's President, Bibi Netanyahu, giving "The Book of Esther" to President Obama. Netanyahu's act took place in an environment in which Israel was pressing the U.S. to go to war or to allow it to go to war against Iran. Esther's story takes place in Iran. I am certain that in comparing me to Esther, there is no intention whatsoever to encourage any war against Iran.

There are very few women in the world's history we are taught that are powerful examples of courage, humility, and commitment to the liberation of their people. Esther is one of many women down through the history of time that took a risk in order to benefit the people that she loved and cared about. Unselfishly, she, like others, dared to do something that would shake up political powers in order to help those who were in need--those who were downtrodden and outcast, and had been neglected and abused by the system.

Now, the interesting thing is that I can see why some people would draw parallels between Esther and me. Because, like Esther, I did use my opportunity inside the "King's Court" to alert the people to the devious plans being devised at the "Palace." Unfortunately for me, I did not win the favor of the king. I'm not yet able to see my country or my community saved from the malevolence of spiritual wickedness in high places. And because I now know what that comparison means, I must, right here, say that I am truly indebted to you all for the high esteem in which I am held. For I know that you truly understand the great sacrifices that I've endured to tell the American people, and the Black community in particular, the truth.

Esther used her favor to save her people. And I can guarantee one thing, that I will use whatever gifts and talents I have been blessed to have, to advance the values that we all have been taught, but that too few of us in such positions truly act on. Of one thing, the people can be sure: I will never use my position to sell out--not my community, not my country, not our shared values.

That's why I undertook the investigation of the Florida 2000 Presidential Election. And of course, I remain aghast that the Democrats not only failed to protect the black electorate in that election, but then repeated the transgression in the 2004 Presidential election. The result of the Democrats' failure to fight back has cost us our country.

While most of the entire world believes that George Bush was fairly elected and reelected, those of us who cared enough to do the investigations, know otherwise.

My bet is that Democratic Party leaders mad
that they didn't want to appear to be supporting black
strongly—?

**I remain aghast that the Democrats not only failed to protect the black electorate in that election, but then repeated the transgression in the 2004 Presidential election. The result of the Democrats' failure to fight back has cost us our country.**

of where our co.
is on the issue of race—
their failure to stand up has
cost us all so much.

Many no doubt
have wondered what a
different United States we
might have had with either
Al Gore or John Kerry as our
President. We shouldn't spend a lot of time in La-La Land on this one because the Bush - Obama transition holds some lessons for us in this regard. But that's foresight, and we didn't know that at the time. It was just a disaster having George Bush unelected and in the White House.

In any event, we will never know because the Democrats basically acquiesced to a Republican takeover of all the levers of government with all that that now means. The Democratic National Committee propaganda on what happened in Florida 2000 was that the Republican win was due to an "excess of democracy," and that the Green Party participation in the process had cost them twenty-five Presidential Electors. The truth was that their loss was due to their own failure to fight back against the "dearth of democracy" represented by election day police road blocks and pre-election voter scrub lists, both engineered by the Republicans.

The Democratic leadership did this so effectively that progressive rank-and-file Democrats and Greens, natural allies on so many issues, were pitted against each other at the polls going into the 2002 and 2004 cycles. Then, when the polls closed in 2004, while Kerry sat on a campaign war chest still filled with millions of dollars, it was the Green Party's Cobb-LaMarche campaign that raised hundreds of thousands of dollars to mount the challenge to election fraud in Ohio and New Mexico, demanding a recount. In the next sitting of Congress, Congressman John Conyers reported on misallocated voting machines, long lines, and frustrated voters. The swindle perpetrated in Ohio was so egregious that Senator Barbara Boxer and several Members of the Congressional Black Caucus objected to the Ohio Electors and on the Floor of the House of Representatives, winning two hours of debate so the story, as understood at that time, could be told. Now, of course, we know so much more of the mechanics of how the Ohio election was stolen.

In my own home state, the Green Party leadership pointed out that it wasn't the Bush shenanigans in Florida, or Gore's failure to carry Tennessee, which doomed the Democrats' chances in the 2000

Presidential election. It was the Georgia Democratic Party's leadership in the Legislature that sealed the result. Georgia Greens went in 1999, 2000, and again in 2001 to the Democratic leadership in both the State House and the State Senate, to the Lieutenant Governor, the Speaker, the Majority Leaders and Whips and Caucus Chairmen, and to Governor Barnes' Floor Leaders as well. They pointed out that Democrats had delivered Georgia's Electoral votes in only three Presidential races since Adlai Stephenson won Georgia, but lost the Electoral College to Dwight Eisenhower in 1956: Carter '76, Carter 80' and Clinton '92.

The Greens explained how the Democrats could use their existing control of both chambers and the Governor's Mansion to require proportional representation in the allocation of the Presidential Electors. Those six votes in 2000 would have made a twelve-vote difference, sufficient to overcome the ten-vote deficit Gore suffered with the theft of Florida and the loss of Tennessee.

So you could say that the moral imperative of today requires a sense of urgency attendant with whatever risks are necessary to save our country's soul. It is, indeed, our country's soul that is on the line.

As a result of my work around election protection, I have made some invaluable partnerships. Partnerships with lawyers, activists, journalists, academicians, scholars, whistleblowers, bloggers—true American Patriots--that I believe have the potential to transform and save the U.S.

# CHAPTER 12

# NO RAINBOWS
# WITHOUT
# RAIN

My 2006 reelection campaign had all the hallmarks of a stolen election. But what could I do about it? My situation was just like that of Blacks during the Civil Rights Movement and pre-Civil Rights Movement era: unsympathetic Whites were the judge, jury, and executioner. And very few people recognized the massive manipulation that had taken place. As far as the pro-Israel Lobby operating through the Democratic Party was concerned: one less vote against war. And as fate would have it, they would need that one vote more than ever very soon.

It rained for about one month. It was unreal. I had never experienced so much rain as occurred in 2006 after I lost my bid for reelection. The ruling from Georgia's judiciary that the election data belonged to Diebold and that the people of Georgia had no recourse other than to believe that the winner of my election (and any other election, for that matter) was who they said was the winner, still stands. I was told that I lost the election and was never given the election data to confirm that loss.

And it kept raining.

But the harsh reality that I faced was unemployment. With a kid in college. I was determined not to allow him to suffer for my politics. He graduated and took a year off to decide what he wanted to do. I thought about taking a year off, too, but there was a war going on and I wanted to be in the fight to stop it. Although I was the only incumbent Democrat to lose reelection, in January 2007 when the new Congress was sworn in, Democrats controlled both the House and the Senate. Even though I couldn't be there to vote "no" on war funding, the Democrats had campaigned on ending George Bush's war, so the anti-war Democrats and anti-war Republicans joined the rest of the world and waited for the first war-funding vote to end George W. Bush's war against the people of Iraq that had been sold to the U.S. public on a foundation of lies.

I traveled around the country making antiwar speeches before any audience that would have me. When I showed up at churches, people burst out in tears. I didn't understand it. My ordeal to represent my constituents and my values had been played out like a drama in front of the world. I didn't realize it, but despite the many instances of betrayal that had accompanied that journey, there were many people who supported me and my struggle. I remember meeting one Jewish young man who identified himself that way. He was in tears when I hugged him. He apologized for the cumulative ordeal that I had been through at the hands of the pro-Israel Lobby. I was so moved by him. I remember him to this day. He will recognize himself when he reads these words. And at that moment, it was only the power of human connection. He knew that my heart was filled with pain and at that moment, I knew that he knew. Amazingly, at that moment, I also knew that his heart was filled with pain. And he knew that I knew. It was an amazing moment.

Honestly, I've been really blessed to have experienced many such moments. I can feel our humanity. And with each connection, I become more convinced that we are all made of the same stuff. That we can get past what others might do to divide us in order to reaffirm our oneness with each other. I remember feeling that same way when I met Afghani refugees in Pakistan's refugee camps. One woman invited me in for a cup of tea although she had nothing to her name. She and thousands of others had been there for years because the United States decided to fight the Soviet Union in Afghanistan. But, they didn't do it with thousands of U.S. troops, they did it by hooking Soviet soldiers on heroin and demoralizing them. They did it by recruiting fighters from all over the Islamic World to go to Afghanistan to fight the godless Communists. This rolodex of fighters is what Robin Cook referred to when he wrote in the July 8, 2005 Guardian that Al Qaeda was nothing more than the CIA's rolodex. He wrote:

> Bin Laden was, though, a product of a monumental miscalculation by western security agencies. Throughout the 80s he was armed by the CIA and funded by the Saudis to wage jihad against the Russian occupation of Afghanistan. Al-Qaida, literally "the database", was originally the computer file of the thousands of mujahideen who were recruited and trained with help from the CIA to defeat the Russians.

I honestly believe that many of the "wars" that are being fought today are totally unnecessary. If so, Administration after Administration in the U.S. wouldn't have to lie to gain favor of the U.S. public.

Let me count the lies.

Well, actually I don't have to because other media fairness organizations did that for us. The Center for Public Integrity and the Fund for Independence in Journalism counted the lies in the run-up to the Iraq War and their tally came to 935. Colin Powell told the biggest lie at the United Nations in front of the biggest audience at the most critical time--when war could have been averted. Condoleezza Rice repeated the lies over and over and over again. She and Colin weren't alone in their perfidy, however. All in all, the world was lied to, according to the estimate, 935 times. According to the study, Bush lied 259 times and Colin Powell came in second with 244 lies. Ari Fleischer, who had said that I was asking my questions about 9/11 from "the Grassy Knoll," also was named in the study as a liar as well as Donald Rumsfeld and Paul Wolfowitz.

Iraq has been destroyed, U.S.soldiers killed and maimed and with the benefit of hindsight, we now know that the U.S. Administration lied to us. If they would lie to us about war and Saddam Hussein, what else are they lying to us about?

At any rate, we knew much of this by January 2007 when the Congress was sworn in without me. And when the war-funding vote came up, it was supposed to fail.

Well, when the vote actually came up in the U.S. House of Representatives, the roll call was taken and the war-funding bill passed by the exact number of votes it would take to pass any bill in the House--218.

What?

I couldn't believe it! The Democrats had said "Vote for us" and the people did that but the peace people who had voted for them didn't matter to them. And I would have provided the deciding vote: my replacement did what he was recruited to do and voted for the war funding then lied to his constituents, my constituents, and told them he was against the war and they believed him. My former District, Stone Mountain and Lithonia in Georgia, had provided the deciding vote in favor of more money for war--even while the local school system was combating a better than 40% dropout rate for its Black students and the County's infrastructure was in need of repair. County residents on occasion have since even been told to boil their water. Yet, instead of securing and providing a "peace dividend" to the people of Georgia, my replacement did what he was told by the War Party and cast the deciding vote to fund the Iraq War.

Realizing that the War Party had done a darn good job of vote-counting and that the war-funding bill was going to pass a Democratic

Congress and be signed into law by President Bush, I decided to do more than complain and give antiwar speeches. So, I gave one of the best speeches that I have ever written, I believe. Because I had only three minutes to say everything that was in my heart and on my mind. Here's what I wrote as my birthday gift to myself—independence from the War Party.

Here are my remarks:

Cynthia McKinney
Remarks in front of the Pentagon
"Voting for Complicity"
March 17, 2007

Well, it seems that George Bush and Democratic Leaders were right.

They confidently told us that not only would Democrats fund the surge, but that the Democrats would not stop action in Iran, too.

Now, we are not surprised when the unelected, illegitimate Administration of George Bush ignores us, but we are shocked that the Democratic majority in Congress chose war over us as we say Bring our troops home now!

The answer is clear: Our country has been hijacked.

What about a livable wage for America's workers?

What about the right of return for Katrina survivors?

What about repealing the Patriot Act, the Secret Evidence Act, and the Military Tribunals Act?

Why is impeachment "off the table"?

Our country is bankrupt yet this institution, the Pentagon, has "lost" 2.3 trillion dollars!

I want that money back . . .

For jobs . . . for health care . . . for education . . . for our veterans!

The Democrats have become so timid they won't even repeal the Bush tax cuts as a strategy to deal with a bankrupt nation.

Seems the story is the same: more money for war, but we can't feed the poor.

It's hard to believe, but now the Democrats are full partners in George Bush's wars.

And by funding his wars, the Democratic Congress is explicitly complicit.

Complicit in war crimes!

Complicit in torture!

Complicit in crimes against humanity!

Complicit in crimes against peace!

The FBI spied on us;

Condoleezza, Dick, and George lied to us.

In 1957, Dr. King observed that "Both political parties have betrayed the cause of justice."

And so it must be repeated today.

Our beloved America is dividing again into two Americas. Our struggle is for nothing less than the soul of our country.

We want an America that is respected in the commonwealth of man; we want our values to shine like a beacon throughout the world.

As an American of conscience, I hereby declare my independence from every bomb dropped, every threat leveled, every civil liberties rollback, every child killed, every veteran maimed, every man tortured.

And I sadly declare my independence from the leaders who let it happen.

We will not stop. We will win. We will take our country back!

To be honest, my declaration of independence was exhilarating. For so long, I had been wandering in the wilderness. Wondering why it was so hard to get the Democratic Party to live up to its pronouncements. Wondering why Black people seemed unwilling to ask hard questions about the nature of politics in the U.S. and their place in it; seemed unwilling to demand more of a government that had innumerable times demonstrated what it was capable of doing. Wondering why people accepted so much less than they should from those with positional authority and power over their tax dollars. Wondering . . . I am a peace person. My shocking realization was that the political rhetoric was just that. It was time for a break—a clean break—from the War Party and its leaders who purported to also be my leaders.

I felt as free as those women must have felt at Seneca Falls, NY in 1848 when they declared their independence from the political order of their day that denied them the right to vote. It was time.

All of a sudden, I noticed. The rain had stopped. The sun was shining. Hey, was that a rainbow over the way?

**Make war obsolete.**

**McKinney for President**
**runcynthiarun.org**

# CHAPTER 13

# RUNNING FOR PRESIDENT IN 2008

Pastor Driver had told me that when one door closes, another one opens. When we leave one vehicle, we just pop into another vehicle to get us where we want to go. And sure enough, another vehicle pulled into my driveway and I was invited to jump right in.

Members of the Green Party had long supported my Congressional campaigns—even as a Democrat. I was proud always that my campaigns were like the rainbow in the sky—multicolor and full of primary colors, too! Primary colors, side by side, not a clash, just beautiful. Wow! Why couldn't real life be that way!

And in 2004, they made their presence around me known to me. By the time 2006 rolled around and the unfortunate election results were in, they called me again. I knew that the Greens were environmentalists. Some of my very first political friends in Georgia were Greens and they would visit me at my office down at the Legislative Office Building of the Georgia Legislature. But, of course, the Greens weren't on the ballot in Georgia and so there was no legislative history of them winning elections and their Party representatives speaking their values in public spaces, so I decided to read up on them and see what they were about as a Party.

When I read their platform, I wondered where had I been for so long? The Green Party platform read like everything that I had said myself. I could see my own values in their platform. They wrote what many Democrats said they believed, but those Democrats probably knew nothing about the Green Party, and the Democratic Party would never even write what the Greens had written in their platform.

The Greens had labor rights, immigration rights, of course environmental rights, reparations, human rights. They openly discussed White skin privilege. They were actually the Party that fought for election integrity in Ohio when it was clear that the election had been stolen again by the Republicans by denying Black people their right to vote and to have their votes counted, it wasn't the Democratic Party that was there to defend their votes, it was the 99.9% White Green Party that was there, fighting for election integrity.

Bob Fitrakis is a leading member of the U.S. Green Party and an Ohio treasure. It was his research that revealed the means by which the Republicans were able to implement their dastardly deed. As it turned out, Republicans had manipulated the number of election machines per precinct so that majority Black precincts had fewer voting machines and longer lines.

The Green Party was known all over the world, but very little was known about the Party in my home state of Georgia. I decided to get to know the Greens and myself in the process. The Greens asked me to stand as their national leader and I agreed to do so.

The following are my Acceptance Remarks to the Green Party Convention in Chicago, Illinois on July 12, 2008, following my nomination to run for President:

> Let me introduce to you my family and your Power to the People Committee!
>
> My mother and father, Billy and Leola McKinney.
>
> My son, Coy, who just graduated from college in Canada!
>
> I want you to know that there is no way I could do this without their love and support.
>
> Your Power to the People Committee members who are with us today:
>
> You've all shared e-mails with her and heard her lovely voice on the telephone: Lucy Grider-Bradley, the campaign manager of my 2004 comeback campaign and FEC Compliance team leader for the Power to the People Committee!
>
> I've known him all of my political life. You've known him for years if you're a Green party member. Hugh Esco, website man with the Power to the People Committee!
>
> In two long road trips from Georgia to Maine, one trip through California, Oregon, and Washington,

Mckinney *for* PRESIDENT 2008

HOPES, VISIONS, POLITICS
with a Heart

Mckinney *for* PRESIDENT 2008

»be the change you want to see«

VOTE GREEN

»you can be part of the solution«

and by way of numerous e-mails, you all have come to know my friend, personal assistant, proud Haitian-American activist, et aussi, l'homme avec qui je pratique mon français, David Josué, standing firm against the occupation of Haiti.

John Judge is my friend. He shared U.S. government COINTELPRO documents with me that few except researchers have ever seen. John Judge is an expert on the murders of Malcolm X, John Kennedy, Martin Luther King, Jr., Bobby Kennedy, COINTELPRO, other government covert operations directed at certain U.S. citizens, and what really happened on 9/11. Maybe John can tell me how our military and intelligence infrastructures failed four times in one day after the taxpayers invested trillions of dollars in them.

Janet Young, proud accountant for the Power to the People Committee! Learned the true meaning of politics when she saw what happened to me after I put impeachment on the table.

I am also joined on the platform by members of the Reconstruction Movement who have come into the Green Party to support our Power to the People campaign! The Reconstruction Movement came into being as a result of dissatisfaction around government failures and unmet needs of Hurricanes Katrina and Rita survivors and the many communities across our country in need of reconstruction.

The RunCynthiaRun visionaries from California who are responsible for bringing me to the Party's Presidential process!

All of the Green Party candidates who are running for election in 2008!

And Rosa Clemente, your Vice Presidential nominee!

Thank you all for being here and standing with me today.

165

McKinney *for* PRESIDENT 2008

HOPES, VISIONS, POLITICS with a Heart

McKinney *for* PRESIDENT 2008

»be the change you want to see«

LIVING GREEN

»you can be part of the solution«

In 1851, in Akron, Ohio a former slave woman, abolitionist, and woman's rights activist by the name of Sojourner Truth gave a speech now known as "Ain't I a Woman." Sojourner Truth began her remarks, "Well children, where there is so much racket, there must be something out of kilter." She then went on to say that even though she was a woman, no one had ever helped her out of carriages or lifted her over ditches or given her a seat of honor in any place. Instead, she acknowledged, that as a former slave and as a black woman, she had had to bear the lash as well as any man; and that she had borne "thirteen children, and seen most all sold off to slavery, and when I cried out with my mother's grief, none but Jesus heard me! And Ain't I a woman?" Finally, Sojourner Truth says, "If the first woman God ever made was strong enough to turn the world upside down all alone, these women together ought to be able to turn it back, and get it right side up again!"

As it was in 1851, so too it is in 2008. There is so much racket that we, too, know something is out of kilter. In 1851, the racket was about a woman's right to vote. In 1848, just a few years before Sojourner uttered those now famous words, "Ain't I a Woman?" suffragists met in Seneca Falls, New York and issued a declaration.

That declaration began:

We hold these truths to be self-evident: that all men and women are created equal; that they are endowed by their Creator with certain inalienable rights; that among these are life, liberty, and the pursuit of happiness; that to secure these rights governments are instituted, deriving their just powers from the consent of the governed. Whenever any form of government becomes destructive of these ends, it is the right of those who suffer from it to refuse allegiance to it, and to insist upon the institution of a new government . . . But when a long train of abuses and usurpations, pursuing invariably the same object evinces a design to reduce them under absolute despotism, it is their duty to throw off such government, and to provide new guards for their future security. Such has been the patient sufferance of the women under this government, and such is now the necessity which constrains them to demand the equal station to which they are entitled.

Two hundred sixty women and forty men gathered in Seneca Falls, NY and declared their independence from the politics of their present and embarked upon a struggle to create a politics for the future. That bold move by a handful of people in one relatively small room laid the groundwork and is the precedent for what we do today. The Seneca Falls Declaration represented a clean break from the past: Freedom, at last, from mental slavery. The Seneca Falls Declaration and the Akron, Ohio meeting inaugurated 72 years of struggle that ended with the passage of the 19th Amendment in August of 1920, granting women the right to vote. And 88 years later, with the Green Party as its conductor, the History Train is rolling down the tracks.

The Green Party is making history today. According to one source, 45 women have run for President in primary elections in the United States in the 20th Century; 22 have made it on the ballot in at least one state in November. Thank you, Green Party, for pulling this history train from the station.

But we make history today only because we must. In 2008, after two stolen Presidential elections and eight years of George W. Bush, and at least two years of Democratic Party complicity, the racket is about war crimes, torture, crimes against the peace; the racket is about crimes against the Constitution, crimes against the American people, and crimes against the global community. The racket is even about values that we thought were long settled as reasonable to pursue, like liberty and justice, and economic opportunity, for all. Yes, Sojourner, there's a lot out of kilter now, but these two women, Rosa and me, joined by all the men and women in this room, are going to do our best to turn this country right side up again.

And just like the women and men at the Seneca Falls Convention in 1848 who declared their independence from the Old Order, I celebrated my birthday last year by doing something I had done a dozen times in my head, but had never done publicly: I declared my independence from every bomb dropped, every threat leveled, every civil liberties rollback, every child killed, every veteran maimed, every man tortured, and the national leadership that let this happen. At that pro-peace rally in front of the Pentagon, I noted that nowhere on the Democratic Party's Congressional Agenda for their first 100 days in the majority was any mention at all of a livable wage, the right of return for Katrina survivors, repealing the Patriot Acts, the Secret Evidence Act, the Military Commissions Act, or bringing our troops home now. Nowhere on the Congressional Democrats' agenda was an investigation into the Pentagon's "loss" of $2.3 trillion that Rumsfeld admitted to just before September 11th. And nowhere was there any plan to get that money back for jobs, health care, education, and for veterans. Not even repeal of the Bush tax cuts that have helped to usher in, according to some, levels of income inequality not experienced in this country since the Great Depression. And instead of Articles of Impeachment to hold the criminals accountable, impeachment was taken "off the table."

And so, taking these words directly from our own Declaration of Independence, and from the Seneca Falls document "it is the right of those who suffer from it to refuse allegiance to it."

There is no doubt that the people of this country and in the global community are suffering from Washington, D.C.'s policies today.

Even as the ice in the Arctic Ocean reportedly was melting, the United States was obstructing an international discussion of climate change goals-setting for 2020 at the recently-concluded G-8 Summit. Even while George Bush has made himself an international climate change villain by not signing onto the Kyoto Protocol, his own scientists at the U.S. Climate Change Science Program have predicted more heat waves, intense rains, increased drought, and stronger hurricanes to affect the U.S. due to the worsening effects of climate change.

Public policy can be our friend or it can be our foe in understanding and working through the immense changes our planet is undergoing. We the voters, the activists, the policy wonks, the candidates, and the elected officials all have a role to play in making public policy. As I have said so many times during this campaign for the Green Party nomination, politics is not a beauty contest; it is not a fashion show; it is not a horse race. Politics is the authoritative allocation of values in a society. Politics is about values being reflected in public policy. It is about having power over public policy. And we engage in the political process because we want our values reflected in public policy.

Had the Green Party's values been reflected in public policy since the beginnings of the Green Party in this country, the United States would have long ago implemented a livable wage; there would be no civil liberties erosion; diversity would be respected, appreciated and welcomed; education would be interesting and relevant to students' lives and no student would graduate from college $100,000 in debt in a Green Party USA because education, not incarceration and militarization, would be subsidized by the state. In a Green Party USA, health care would be provided for everyone here through a single payer, Medicare-for-all type health care system. We would have no homeless men and women sleeping on our streets and everyone who could work would have work. Rebuilding our infrastructure, manufacturing green technology, retooling our economy so that those who protect us, train us, heal us and prepare us for tomorrow are compensated in what is their true value to our culture and our society, based on their contribution to our civilization. Vietnam War-era veterans would be our last war veterans because we would never have been engaged in war and occupation against Afghanistan and Iraq. We would forego imperial designs on our neighbors to the north and south, never building any wall of division, not ever encroaching on their geographic or cultural sovereignty. In fact, if Green Party values were now reflected in U.S. public policy, our country not only would not be engaged in war and occupation, there would be peace in the Middle East based on self-determination, respect for human rights, and justice. We would strive to perfect our democracy at home through election integrity and no one would be denied their rightful place in our Union due to discrimination. Our neighbors in the global community would look up to us for our cultural and technological accomplishments. We would have apologized for genocide against the indigenous peoples of this land and the abomination of chattel slavery. Our country would have dignity on the world stage and in every international forum, and no one in this country would be made to live in fear.

Oh, if it could be true: that the values of the Green Party were reflected in the Federal Government's public policy. Let me wake up and snap out of my reverie. Yes, today's reality is harsh. Abu Ghraib, torture, rendition, lying, spying, war, stolen elections, Hurricanes Katrina and Rita, New Orleans, poverty, racial profiling, Sean Bell, the San Francisco 8, Benton Harbor's Reverend Pinkney, the Holy Land Foundation, 9/11/01.

Embargo, blockade, friendly fire, depleted uranium, white phosphorus, cluster bombs, bunker busters, shock and awe.

Predatory lending, mortgage crisis, foreclosures, a country $53 trillion in debt. And while Bear Stearns gets a bailout, you and I sink or swim.

Harsh? Today's reality is harsh. But what's even harder for many to accept and admit is that our quality of life today is the making of the Democratic and Republican Parties.

What our country has become through their public policy is reflective of their values.

We will never get a United States that is reflective of different values if we continue to do the same thing. Those who delivered us into this mess cannot be trusted to get us out of it.

That's why I signed up to do something I've never done before so I can have something I've never had before: My country, made in the likeness of the values of the Green Party.

When my father first started out in the world of politics in Georgia, he began as a Republican, because Georgia Democrats would not allow blacks to vote in their primaries. Some of my father's closest friends today are still Republicans because of that history.

My father served 30 years in the Georgia Legislature as a Democrat. Because of him, I served 4 years in the Georgia Legislature, where we were the country's only father daughter legislative team. And then I went to Congress and served 12 years working with the Democratic Party and its current leadership representing the State of Georgia.

My son grew up playing on the Floor underneath my desk in the Chamber of the Georgia House of Representatives. His buddies were the legislators down there, under the Gold Dome, who were my and my father's colleagues.

My mother is the genteel Southern lady who keeps our family glued together. A nurse by profession, a nurturer by instinct, she could patch over all the times I had a political disagreements with my Dad and it ended up being discussed, not only at the family dinner table, but also on the evening news.

My father and I stumped for candidates, and helped keep Georgia in the Democratic Party fold, until on my election night in 2002, I was forced to admit that the Republicans wanted to beat me more than the Democrats wanted to keep me. Both my father and I were put out of office after being targeted by a convergence of special interests operating in both the Democratic and Republican parties. In November of 2002, after the Primary Election losses of my father and me, Georgia went Republican: the first time since Reconstruction. With all kinds of certainty, I can say that my father and I—we McKinneys—we know too well how both the Republican and Democratic Parties operate.

And that's why I know we need an opposition party in this country. With 200 elected officials already, the Green Party can become this country's premier opposition Party. One thing is clear, Democratic and

Republican values are not Green Party values. And honestly, I believe, Green Party values are the values held by the majority in this country. And through our vigorous Power to the People campaign, we will proclaim our presence to every nook and cranny of this country. We are needed now, more than ever and here's an example of why.

It is hard to not hear the warning signs of a new war: a war against Iran. Dick Cheney told us to expect war for the next generation. The Republicans launched this war economy and their presumptive nominee said that we could stay in Iraq for the next 100 years and even sang a song for the bombing of Iran. The Democratic majority in Congress just voted to fund the war into 2009 and has 200 sponsors on a bill that declares war on Iran by calling for a naval blockade. A naval blockade is a declaration of war. The Democratic presumptive nominee wants to increase the size of the overused military and the budget for an already-bloated and wasteful Pentagon. I am the only candidate who has consistently voted against the Pentagon budget, voted against the war in Iraq, and I voted against the bills that funded it. The Green Party was against the war when it started, is against the war now, and is against any military action against Iran that might take place tomorrow. The Green Party is a peace party. A Green vote is a peace vote.

Not a word has been mentioned in this political season about the disparities that exist within our country with the recognition that public policy can erase them. And even though for the first time a woman and an African-American were being taken seriously in national primaries, a real discussion of race and gender has been studiously avoided on all sides. At a time when the United States is under review, itself, by the United Nations for its poor record on domestic respect for human rights, particularly in the aftermath of Hurricanes Katrina and Rita, a real discussion of race and gender is needed now more than ever. On some indices, according to United for a Fair Economy, the racial disparities that exist today are worse than at the time of the murder of Dr. Martin Luther King, Jr. Right here in Chicago, Hull House reported that it would take

200 years, without a public policy intervention from elected leadership, for the quality of life experienced by black Chicagoans to equal that of white Chicagoans.

Women are still the overwhelming profile of the minimum wage worker in this country. 65% of all minimum wage workers are women, according to 2005 statistics. Despite the law, women still go to work every day, performing the same tasks as men, yet bring home less pay than their male counterparts. Asian-American and Pacific Island women make 88 cents for every dollar earned by men, but African-American women earn only 72 cents and my Latina sisters earn only 60 cents for every dollar earned by men. Overall, according to 2007 statistics, women with similar education, skills, and experience are paid 77 cents for every dollar a man makes. Equal pay for equal work is not yet a reality for working women in this country. And the glass ceiling is all too real.

I'm very proud of my second cousin, Shonté, whose mother, a divorcée, raised her pretty much as a single mother. Shonté's mother, Shara, understood the value of her child getting a good education and helped her as much as she could with university tuition. The rest Shonté was able to secure by working on campus and in student loans. Shonté graduated from college, and then took a one-year Master's program in Social Work, and now wants to get her Ph.D. But she's already over $90,000 in debt. It doesn't have to be this way and we don't have to accept it. In other countries around the world, higher education is valued and is made affordable to all who want it. Only a sick government would place a banker in-between a student and her teacher.

An insurance lobbyist in-between a patient and his doctor.

Lying and spying before 9/11 Truth and the Constitution.

Only a sick government would place a wealthy family and their huge corporation and its genetically-modified frankenfood peddled by force in-between us and the organic food that's healthy for us to eat and that farmers would prefer to grow.

Only a sick government would do this.

And I am no longer willing to trust the ones who

are responsible for getting us into this mess to provide the solution to get us out of it.

The Green Party long ago took a stand for racial justice: against profiling, against police brutality, against discrimination of any sort, and for reparations stemming from the trans-Atlantic slave trade.

The Green Party long ago took a stand for gender equity.

The Green Party long ago took a stand against all discrimination.

The Green Party is a justice party. A Green vote is a justice vote.

And the day after the election, if voters have been disfranchised and don't believe the announced election results, it will be the Green Party that will be there, as it was in 2004, to demand election integrity.

It is for all these reasons and more that I redeclare my goals in the language of my sisters who convened at Seneca Falls, NY 160 years ago. They wrote:

It is their duty to throw off such government, and to provide new guards for their future security.

That declaration not only avoids the politics of the past, it contains a kernel for the future. How can those new guards for the future be won?

Here's how:

When I was first running for Congress and it was the year of the woman, women all over the country were saying, "We want our seat at the table." And when I got to Washington, I saw that policy was really made in a room, at a table. There were real seats at the table. Well, imagine what has happened to public policy making now.

There is a real room, with a window and a door and there's two seats at the table. The window is for us to look through while our representatives make policy for us so we can see what they're doing. At the table, one seat is for the Democrats and one seat is for the Republicans. Now, we don't know who did it, but one of them put a lock on the door and slipped a key to the corporate lobbyists who can come and go at will and whisper what they want to the Democrats, and then whisper what they want to the Republicans, and the result is that we the people, who pay for those seats and determine who sits in them, want one thing, but because the corporate lobbyists can come and go at will, our values get overridden and our representatives give us something else.

That's how we end up with everyone saying they're against the war and occupation, but war and occupation still gets funding.

That's how we end up with everyone saying they're against illegal spying on innocent people, yet end up with a telecom immunity bill being signed into law.

That's how we end up with everyone saying they're in favor of universal access to health care and no one implementing what the physicians, nurses, and health care providers support, and that's a single payer health care system in this country.

That's why my cousin and so many other students in this country face staggering personal debt just to get an education, yet our elected representatives keep voting to spend 720 million dollars a day on war and occupation, war crimes, and crimes against the peace.

Now, if we can entice people who have stopped voting because they see the system as rigged, to become active again, and to vote Green . . .

If we can convince those first-time voters from the previous two Presidential elections, though they might be discouraged because they saw their vote obstructed and then not counted while neither of the big parties fought to protect them, if we can convince them to vote Green . . .

If we can convince those who see two parties, but only one political agenda, to vote Green, then it is possible for the Green Party to get 5% of the national vote.

5% of the vote makes the Green Party, not a minor party in the eyes of the federal government, but a major party.

5% confers on the Green Party major party status. And with that 5%, we can pull up another chair at the table of public policy making. It only takes 5% of those who vote, including the near majority who don't vote, to come out for a Green Party President and then we will have an official third party in this country, and public policy that truly reflects our values.

Now, I'm known for taking bold positions, based on my own research, that have put me ahead of the curve. I was there on private militaries hired by the Pentagon and our State Department long before Blackwater began patrolling the streets of New Orleans in the aftermath of Hurricane Katrina.

I was there on corporate accountability and military contracting scandals before Iraq and Afghanistan.

I was there on enlisted members' and veterans' rights and health issues, like forced vaccinations and conscientious objection.

I was there on Hurricanes Katrina and Rita recovery and detoxification, restoration, and return issues.

I was there on 9/11 foreknowledge.

And I put impeachment "on the table."

I'm not afraid to address the issues that no one else will dare to talk about.

I'm not afraid to speak truth to empower.

Let me close with this.

Don't expect me to keep a count of the major party flip flops from now to November. I'm sure there will be many. But, in the end, that's not the important issue to understand. What is more fundamental to understand is this: the other political parties find themselves in this flip-flop predicament because they have to appear to share our values while they serve someone else's.

The Green Party doesn't have to engage in shape-shifting because the Green Party is funded by and belongs to you.

All over the world, Green Party members are working as elected leaders in government to make public policy reflect our Green values. Wangari Mathai, former Parliamentarian from Kenya, Nobel Peace Prize Laureate. Green Party member. Ingrid Betancourt, recently released hostage in Colombia, former Senator and Presidential candidate. Green Party member. Green Party members make public policy at the national level on every Continent, but not yet in our country.

Twenty years ago, Green party activists saw through this two-party box that voters have been put into in this country and started the Green Party here. And what we have to remember is this: whatever it is that we want in the realm of public policy, we can get if we have the right elected officials in office. Nothing for us is impossible. Politics is about shared values being reflected in public policy. And these Green party candidates standing with me are the right kind of people who will implement the right kind of public policy that reflects our shared values.

Voters in this country are scared into not voting their hopes, their dreams, their aspirations. But in Bolivia and Ecuador and Argentina and Chile and Nicaragua and Spain, and India and Cote d'Ivoire and Haiti, voters were not afraid to vote their hopes and dreams and guess, what. Their dreams came true. Ours can, too.

Every one of you in this room today and each of the individuals I've met and communicated with online across our country has made a difference in my life. And moreover, the 5% who will vote for us, will help us make a positive difference in the lives of people around the world. Who we are makes a difference. What we do makes a difference.

We are in this to build a movement. We are willing to struggle for as long as it takes to have our values prevail in public policy. A vote for the Green Party is a vote for the movement that will turn this country right side up again.

I want to invite everyone who shares our values to join our Power to the People campaign. C-Span viewers can learn more about us at www.runcynthiarun.org. I want to work with the nominees of the other small political parties so we can form a united front. I'm asking for your vote because in reality the only "wasted" vote is a vote against conscience, a vote against our dreams. Vote your dreams, Vote your conscience. Vote our future. Vote Green.

Thank you, Green Party, for granting Rosa and me this supreme honor. Now let's go out there and get busier. We've got a lot of work to do.

Power to the People!

## MONEY FOR PEOPLE, NOT FOR BANKS

Cynthia McKinney believes that our current banking system was designed to serve private banks rather than the public. As President, she will urge that the power to create money be taken from private hands and restored to the Congress. Help Cynthia ensure that "the full faith and credit of the United States" is used to fund public works directly, without interest owed to financial middlemen.

## YOUR HELP IS NEEDED.
www.runcynthiarun.org

**Donate.**

**Volunteer.**

**Vote.**

 VOTE GREEN.

Federal regulations require contributions from only US adult citizens or legal residents. Corporate contributions are not accepted. Contributions are not tax deductible. Paid for by the Power to the People Committee · Cynthia McKinney for President · Joan Christian, Treasurer · P.O. Box 311759 · Atlanta, Georgia 31131-1759

As the nominee of the Green Party on the Presidential ticket, I traveled around the country. I stopped in the hamlets of America; I visited the hills and molehills of Alabama and Tennessee. I traveled far and wide and got to know how vast and how grand, how scenic and how beautiful; how honest and how true are the people of this country. I stayed in the homes of the people and learned what Green Hospitality is. I stayed in Maine along a river, I bathed outside in northern California with the trees, hiked in Oregon, and came to know the other side of life.

People all over the world know more about the Green Party; it has won elections and has at least one Member of Parliament in France, Canada, Austria, Italy, Ireland, and Germany. Eventually, the U.S. will be counted in that number. Independent voters will eventually have their voices heard and their votes counted and not channeled into the two-party system. What is a candidate to do when independent or third parties are not reasonably allowed even on that candidate's state ballot? The U.S. has a long way to go. And even when Greens win in court, they still don't necessarily get on the ballot: The state of Georgia is a case in point. As of this writing, Judge Story has not even bothered to rule on a Georgia case for ballot access filed by the Georgia Green and Constitution Parties even though the State of Georgia technically has defaulted in the lawsuit that was based on a Tennessee court victory for the Green and Constitution Parties.

Despite the fact that the Greens are a peace party, somehow the Greens in Germany decided to support the war against the people of Iraq. Later, I met other Greens, like Swedish Greens, who supported the bombing of Libya. This leads me back to my question—the same question that Dr. Martin Luther King, Jr. posed about White "Liberals." Because these wars are being carried out by White countries against people of color countries. And why is it so easy for "principles" to be broken when it comes to Whites standing up for people of color? I know that is a very broad brush and I don't intend to paint it over those who do not merit the whitewash. There are many, many Whites in my life who live their principles in the deepest most meaningful way. We meld. This is not meant to reflect on them in any way. However, I have to wonder why the antiwar movement is so impotent. Is the answer that when faced with the prospect of losing one's White skin privilege, vast numbers of otherwise principled people become otherwise?

I raise this point because of a very important lecture given by Dr. Jeffrey B. Perry on the writings of Theodore W. Allen and his opus, *The Invention of the White Race* that examines exactly these questions. Allen traces U.S. history back to discover exactly when "White" was used to describe European Americans. According to Perry, Allen believed that the "White" race was invented by the U.S. political and economic elites as a means of social control. Particularly when African and European laborers came together to forge a new economic order, a better one for them, then the elites created "White" and awarded privileges on that basis. While watching a video of one of Dr. Perry's lectures on Allen, I wrote:

> the white race was invented as a result of labor solidarity in Bacon's Rebellion; a system of racial privileges was deliberately established that defined the white race and established racial oppression against Blacks; the system of racial privilege was disastrous for European American workers and for Black laborers; white skin privilege weakened white labor position vis a vis the ruling class.
>
> In St. Croix: the 5% couldn't control the 95% so they recruited the 15% colored to do their bidding. Didn't work because the 15% sided with the 80% Black and they all got emancipation. In the U.S. the 5% enlist the 15% through the extension of white skin privilege.

While I watched Dr. Perry's lecture on Hubert Harrison and Theodore Allen, I couldn't help but think that I had finally found the missing puzzle piece to explain things. The antiwar movement is impotent because it is meant to be impotent. The social justice movement is impotent because it is structured and financed to be that way. In order to effect the deep structural change that is needed to achieve peace and dignity based on truth will take all of us doing a little bit more, but some will have to dig deep and ask more of themselves than they have grown accustomed to giving. I want change so badly, I decided to start with myself. And I know others can do it, too. And we must create the environment around us to foster the kind of questioning and personal reflection that it will take for us to move from where we are now to where we know we need to be. Dr. Perry and Theodore W. Allen have a thesis that is definitely worth exploring and I intend to explore it. We never know where we will find allies along the way and who would ever have thought that it would come from Dr. Perry, a scholar with Princeton, Harvard, Rutgers, and Columbia in his background.

The Green Party gave me a grassroots foundation that I did not have before my 2008 Presidential nomination. My travels across the U.S. brought me into contact with some of the best people this country has to offer. If their voices were heard in the political process, this country would also have much better policies. Our work has got to be to make that happen. And at the same time, to open our field of vision to see what the real impediments are to the alignment between professed values and behavior: between our professed national values and our public policy.

My academic training is really helping me in the wisdom department and teaching me how to take sustained tiny steps in order to arrive at the big change that will save this country from its current political course. It is teaching me to help others arrive at that same place, too, so that we can make that big change together.

Horace Mann once said, "Be ashamed to die until you have won some victory for humanity."

With strong words like that, my path can be nothing if not clear.

From rain to rainbows.

While a Congresswoman, Cynthia invited Uri Avnery, Israeli writer and founder of the Gush Shalom peace movement, and his wife to Capitol Hill—his first visit to the U.S. Capitol invited by a Member of Congress.

CHAPTER 14

# STONE MOUNTAIN, ISRAEL, AND GAZA

As I've said before, my father would always ask while shaking his head, "What does Stone Mountain have to do with Israel; what does Israel have to do with Stone Mountain?" I had been trying to represent my constituents and people who didn't even care about my constituents were upset with me because I didn't put the residents of another country first, before my own constituents. It was one of those Churchillian "riddles wrapped in a mystery inside an enigma." I had never taken one of those American Israel Public Affairs Committee trips to Israel, and I had never been to Palestine, either. So, I decided to go during Operation Cast Lead when Israel chose to use U.S.-supplied weapons against the people of Gaza, Palestine and see for myself what was going on in that part of the world, with the use of U.S. weapons technology. The only catch was that we were going by boat through international waters. On my way to the airport, I stopped by my parents' home to let them know what I was about to do, and my father's last words to me before I left was, "You all will be sitting ducks."

At 5:21 am eastern time, I sent out the message, "On my way to Gaza" with very little elaboration except to mention that I would be with a group of activists and doctors who would deliver medical supplies and perform needed surgery for the sick and wounded in Gaza. In that message, I also complained that I had been blocked from flying to Damascus, Syria to participate in a "Right of Return" Human Rights Conference.

That was the first time that I felt the power of the internet. It was amazing. Everywhere, I could see the busy chatter back and forth, Cynthia is going to Gaza.

And my dad was right: just like the *U.S.S. Liberty,* we were sitting ducks as we came under attack by the Israeli military while we were in international waters. Of course, we activists were armed with medical supplies for the sick and wounded and were accompanied by surgeons and pediatricians. One of those surgeons has become a dear friend, David XX.

While world attention was raptly following Israel's bombing of Gaza that lit up the night sky like the decorations on a Christmas tree, the news was interrupted for a special very important break: Israel was reporting that a small group of activist provocateurs had intentionally rammed one of its warships inside Israeli territorial waters. Well, this was the story after several concoctions but not a single word of it was true. And were it not for the journalistic integrity of a veteran CNN journalist— with emphasis on the word journalist—the true facts would never have been publicly disclosed or widely disseminated. Imagine a journalist being told to lie while he's in the middle of a very dangerous situation and he, arguing back to his bosses that what Israel was saying was a lie, and that he was not going to report a lie. And imagine us, wet, seasick-- not me, though--and scared, having to endure listening to CNN and Karl wrangle back and forth, but with Karl standing his ground for the truth.

Here's the first message I sent out by e-mail after our unfortunate encounter with the Israeli warship:

December 30, 2008: Oh What a Day!

I'm so glad that my father told me to buy a special notebook and to write everything down because that's exactly what I did.

When we left from Cyprus, one reporter asked me, "Are you afraid?" And I had to respond that Malcolm X wasn't afraid; Dr. Martin Luther King, Jr. wasn't afraid. But little did I know that just a few hours later, I would be recollecting my life and mentally preparing myself for death.

When we left Cyprus, the Mediterranean was beautiful. I remember the time when it might have been beautiful to look at, but it was also filthy. The Europeans have taken great strides to clean it up and yesterday, it was beautiful. And the way the sunlight hit the sea, I remember thinking to myself that's why they call it azure. It was the most beautiful blue.

But sometimes it was rough, and we got behind on our schedule. We stayed on course, however, despite the roughness of the water and due to our exquisite captain.

There were no other ships or boats around us and night descended upon us all rather quickly. It was the darkest black and suddenly, out of nowhere, came searchlights disturbing our peace. The searchlights stayed with us for about half an hour or so. We knew they were Israeli ships. Who else would they be?

They were fast, and they would come close and then drop back. And then, they'd come close again. And then, all of a sudden there was complete blackness once again and all seemed right. The cat and mouse game went on for at least one half hour. What were they doing? And why?

Calm again. Black sky, black sea. Peace. And then, at that very moment, when all seemed right, out of nowhere we were rammed and rammed again and rammed again, the last one throwing me off the couch, sending all our food up in the air; and all the plastic bags and tubs—evidence of sea sicknesses among the crew and passengers—flew all over the cabin and all over us. We'd been rammed by the Israelis. How did we know? Because they called us on the phone afterwards to tell us that we were engaging in subversive, terroristic activity. And that if we didn't turn around right then and return to Larnaca, Cyprus, we would be fired upon. We quickly grabbed our life vests and put them on. Then the captain announced that the boat was taking on water. We might have to evacuate. One of my mates told me to prepare to die. And I reflected that I have lived a good and full life. I have tasted freedom and know what it is. I was right with myself and my decision to join the Free Gaza movement.

I remembered my father's parting words, "You all will be sitting ducks." Just like the U.S.S. Liberty. We were engaged in peaceful activity, a harmless pleasure boat, carrying a load of hospital supplies for the people of Gaza, who, too are sitting ducks, currently being bombarded in aerial assault by the Israeli military.

It's been a long day for us. The captain was outstanding. Throughout it all, he remained stoic and calm, effective in every way. I didn't know how to put my life jacket on. One of the passengers kindly assisted me. Another of the passengers pointed out that the Israeli motors for those huge, fast boats were U.S. made--a gift to them from the U.S. And now they were using those motors to damage a pleasure boat outfitted with three tons of hospital supplies, one pediatrician, and two surgeons.

I have called for President-elect Obama to say something. The Palestinian people in the Gaza strip are seeing the worst violence in 60 years, it is being reported. To date, President-elect Obama has remained silent. The Israelis are using weapons supplied to them by the U.S. government. Strict enforcement of U.S. law would require the cessation of all weapons transfers to Israel. Adherence to international law would require the same. As we are about to celebrate Dr. Martin Luther King, Jr.'s birthday, let us remember that he said:

1. The United States is the greatest purveyor of violence in the world, and
2. Our lives begin to end the day we remain silent about things that matter.

I implore the President-elect not to send Congress a budget that contains more weapons for Israel. We have so much more to offer. And I implore the Congress to vote "no" on any budget and appropriation bills that provide more weapons transfers, period.

Israel is able to carry out these intense military maneuvers because taxpayers in the U.S. give their hard-earned money to our Representatives in Congress and our Congress chooses to spend that money in this way. Let's stop it and stop it now. There's been too much bloodshed. And while we still walk among the living, let us not remain silent about the things that matter.

We really can promote peace and have it if we demand it of our leaders.

Well, despite all of the media hoopla, the two-step jig that Israel forced upon itself because it chose to deceive rather than tell the truth, blew an already big story up even bigger when Israel's lies were rebuked live and on the air by the CNN Reporter who was onboard with us. (Al Jazeera's reporter was allowed to tell the truth unfettered.)

On New Year's Day, I sent the following e-mail message out to my list and I was suddenly at the center of an international drama. The word, "Gaza" rolled off the lips of people who had never heard of Gaza.

To this day, I am amazed at how deeply the story of my efforts in Gaza are known in the community. Here's that message I sent out after our boat had been rammed and CNN and Al Jazeera reported our situation accurately:

**January 1, 2009**
**We Lived to Tell the Story: Lebanon Rescued Us**

Yesterday, we met with the President of Lebanon, the Chief of the Military, and the Interior Minister who all thanked us for responding [to the needs of the people of Gaza] and risking our lives on a mission of mercy; we profusely thanked them for rescuing us.

What would we have done, stranded out at sea, prohibited from reaching our destination, low on fuel, with a badly damaged boat if Lebanon had not accepted us? Lebanon sent their ships to find us. Lebanon rescued us. Lebanon welcomed us. And we are truly thankful.

It's official now. We've been told that the sturdy, wood construction of our boat, *Dignity*, is the reason we are still alive. Fiberglass would probably not have withstood the impact of the Israeli attack and

The Free Gaza 21 and land crew.

under different circumstances, we might not be here to tell the story. Even at that, the report that came to us yesterday after the Captain and First Mate went back to Sour (Tyre) to inspect the boat was that it was sinking, the damage is extensive, and the boat will take, in their estimation, at least one month to repair. Tomorrow, we will bring the *Dignity* from Sour to Beirut. And now, we must decide what to do and from where we will do it and how we are to get back to wherever that might be.

My personal, and I know the group's, thanks must go to Al Jazeera, that allowed three of their reporters to be onboard with us on our voyage. As a result, Al Jazeera carried the story of the *Dignity* live, from castoff in Cyprus when our spirits were high, right up through the menacing maneuvers of the huge, super fast Israeli ships before they rammed us, the Israeli calls on the ship phone after the ramming calling us terrorists and subversives and telling us to return to Cyprus (even though the Israelis later claimed that they didn't know who we were, they knew enough about us to tell us where we had come from), and the fact that we didn't have enough fuel to follow their instructions, right up to their threat to fire at us if we didn't turn around, ending with our beaten-up boat limping into Sour harbor in Lebanon. Al Jazeera carried our story as "breaking news" and performed a real service to its audience and to us. Al Jazeera called the Israelis to inquire about the incident right as it was happening and I am sure the Israelis were prepared to leave none to tell the story. Al Jazeera told the story and documented it as it was happening.

One of those Al Jazeera reporters with us was Sami El-Haj, who was detained in Guantanamo by the United States for six incredibly long years. What an honor to even exchange glances with such a humble man who had endured so much pain at the hands of the U.S. government. I apologized to him that my tax dollars were being used in such a despicable way. And Sami's crime according to the U.S.? Born in Sudan, and reporting for Al Jazeera in Afghanistan, Sami was the wrong color, the wrong nationality, the wrong religion, reporting for the wrong news outfit, telling us the truth about a wrong war. And for that he survived incarceration for six long years. Sami El-Haj, Guantanamo prisoner number 345.

Another incredibly committed journalist who was with us was CNN's Karl Penhaul. Karl reported the truth even when his own station was repeating Israeli disinformation. The fact that we were traveling with these alert journalists added to the flat-footedness and obvious crudeness of the Israeli response. Sadly, Israel has changed its story too many times to count, and that's because they are not telling the truth.

We lived to tell the story. Karl's incredible reporting, just a portion of our story, can be seen on CNN at <http://www.cnn.com/2008/WORLD/meast/12/30/gaza.aid.boat/index.html> where there's also video and a photo of our damaged boat. A little more of the story and film of the extensive damage can be seen at <http://www.cnn.com/2008/

WORLD/meast/12/30/gaza.aid.boat/index.html#cnnSTCVideo>

This video and the photos of Karl's report is particularly interesting given that Israel claims that our boat was only scratched and that, in actuality, our captain, while trying to outmaneuver them, damaged their warship.

I'm told that CNN only played my full statement once--and that's the time that it aired live. Of course, they cut the reference to the U.S.S. Liberty. What are they afraid of? [The U.S.S. Liberty was a United States technical research ship, attacked by both Israeli jet fighters and torpedo boats during the Six Day War in 1967, killing 34 crew members and wounding 171 crew members. Israel claimed it had attacked by mistake due to confusion about the ship's identity. While a subsequent U.S. investigation bought the claim, many others, including survivors of the attack, have argued that it was deliberate.]

Last night I was on PressTV.com, along with others who were on the *Dignity*, and we debated a representative from WINEP, the Washington Institute for Near East Policy. I reminded the audience that the Palestinians don't have nuclear weapons, depleted uranium munitions, white phosphorous, or F-16s, but the Israelis do. The facts, however, tend to get garbled after being processed by the "Grand Wurlitzer" organ of state-sponsored disinformation utilizing the world's press.

With the truth clearly on our side, Israel has been reduced to releasing the ridiculous bombast below, given to me by a reporter who came to our hotel in Beirut for a visit. With their multiple, conflicting stories, it is clear that the Israelis did not expect us to live to tell the truth.

On the drive from Sour through Saida to Beirut, we were welcomed like heroes because our ordeal had been seen by everyone on Al Jazeera. The mayor of Sour came to welcome us. The mayor of Saida insisted that we stop there, on our way to Beirut, for a special ceremony. But there was something else that was visible along our drive, and that is the devastation that Lebanon, itself, has received as a result of the Israeli war machine. The scars of the war are still evident everywhere. I will write more on that tomorrow.

And one final note, President-elect Obama roared like a mighty lion onto the political scene, but now he is as silent as a lamb in the face of the death and destruction that is happening in Gaza. As we approach the birthday celebration of Dr. Martin Luther King, Jr. let us remember what Dr. King said:

In the end, we will remember not the words of our enemies, but the silence of our friends.

And after five days of aerial bombardment by Israel, the carnage in Gaza continues.

Here is the palaver that the Israelis put out for public consumption. It is pitiful that a powerful and mighty country like Israel would be reduced to publishing something so petty and weak as the following press release dated December 30, 2008:

[seal]
Consulate General of Israel to the Southeast
Press Release
Office of Media Affairs

FOR IMMEDIATE RELEASE
12.30.2008

Israel continues to take its humanitarian relief efforts in Gaza seriously. Border crossings into Gaza remain open, and every effort is being made to deliver aid to the Palestinian people. Nearly 100 trucks carrying relief supplies entered Gaza on the 28th & 29th of December and additional shipments are arriving. Israel is working closely with UNSCO, UNRWA, the Red Cross, and WHO to ensure the entry of the required aid, especially food and medical equipment.

Unfortunately, former Congresswoman Cynthia McKinney has taken it upon herself to commit an act of provocation, leading a small boat of supposed assistants into the conflict zone. She endangered herself, her assistants, and the vessel's crew. The Israeli navy hailed Ms. McKinney but the former Congresswoman failed to respond, thereby leading to the incident. We regret that during this time of crisis, while Israel is battling with the terrorist organization of Hamas and defending its citizens, that we are forced to deal with Ms. McKinney's irresponsible behavior.

Consulate General of Israel
to the Southeast
1100 Spring St NW, Ste 440
Atlanta, GA 30309-2823

Michael Printy Arthur
Director of Media Affairs
404.487.6511
media@atlanta.mfa.gov.il
For additional information, please visit our website.

Well, there you have it. The Israeli press release rings so hollow and so petty because, as they say, the emperor has no clothes and we all can see his nakedness. A lot has happened since Israel's Operation Cast Lead. And just as it would have been better for them to leave Gaza alone, it would have been better for them to have left us alone. On January 5, 2009 at 8:59 am Eastern Time, I sent a message with the title, "Home With My Parents." Israel's attack on the *Dignity* blew up in Israel's face. But I still had not reached Gaza, so the Palestine episode of my life journey was still not done. After I made it back home to Georgia and my parents, I climbed onto another boat and attempted to get into Gaza again.

But, the political landscape inside the U.S. significantly changed with the Israeli ramming of the *Dignity*. I had never seen a press release like the one below issued from the Black church:

National Black Church Initiative
P.O. Box 65177
Washington, DC 20035

dcbci2002@yahoo.com
www.naltblackchurch.com

Contact Person
For immediate release
Rev. Anthony Evans
Media Advisory

NATIONAL BLACK CHURCH INITIATIVE COMDEMNS
ISRAELIS FOR THE KILLING OF 500 PALESTINIANS
IN THE GAZA
ISRAEL HAS BLOOD ON THEIR HANDS
AND THEIR SOUL

Washington, DC- The National Black Church Initiative (NBCI) morally condemns the Israeli Government military action into the Sovereign State of Palestine Gaza killing an estimate of 500 Palestinians. Eighty percent of the deaths are innocent-women and children according to reports. Israel's indiscriminate use of American made bombers on the densely populated Gaza territory is morally unconscionable and reprehensible. As religious leaders, we cannot idly stand by and accept immoral excuses as Israel uses sophisticated weaponry to alienate the Palestinian people. Israel will have the Christian church to believe that it is holy and we are biblically mandated to agree with Israel as they systematically persecute and indiscriminately kill the Palestinian people. We see Israel's evil very clearly. Israel is causing a humanitarian nightmare in Gaza.

CNN reported that the Israeli Navy deliberately damaged the relief vessel – the Dignity, carrying medicine and food for the residents of Gaza. They wanted to prevent this humanitarian relief supply from reaching those who have been hurt and wounded from the bombing. This is one of the most despicable acts in all of humanity. This was verified because CNN correspondent Karl Penhaul was on board at the time of the incident. Former Honorable U.S. Representative Cynthia McKinney was also on board to witness this despicable incident. They wanted to stop her for witnessing the destruction that is raining down on the people of Gaza.

Therefore as President of 34,000 African American churches, I have issued a directive to stop traveling to the Holy Land for the next five years and for every church to condemn Israel's vicious assault on humanity. Israel does not have a monopoly on what is good and merciful and does not in any way carry favor with God anymore than their Palestine brothers and sisters.

NBCI strongly rejects the notion held by a large majority of white evangelical conservative churches that the Christian church has a moral obligation to protect the State of Israel. We believe strongly that this is a narrow and self serving biblical interpretation of the scriptures. The correct biblical interpretation compels us to condemn Palestinian or Israelis who innocently take the lives of others and wrap themselves up in the name of God, the Torah or the Koran. Any religious tradition that argues that they have a monopoly on righteous, godliness and mercy is not only wrong, but evil.

"I guess now that the Jewish community around the world will consider NBCI as anti-Jewish because we are not supporting the extermination of the Palestinian people, says the Rev. Paul Sewell, Southeastern faith command leader. We will let them think what they want to. We are going to call it like we see it. If the Jews have committed evil, we will denounce it. If the Palestinians have committed evil, we will denounce it as well.

The Rev. Anthony Evans, President of NBCI says that the response by the Israeli Government to the few rockets that landed in Israel proper is disproportionately and morally unfair of the amount of death that has occurred, and the use of the most sophisticated and advanced weaponry on a densely population like Gaza is just an unspeakable crime against humanity. It should be condemned and that's why we are doing it. We are not afraid to be called anti-Jewish because we know it is a lie because we are on record of condemning the Palestinians as well and we can prove it because the Israeli Ambassador has written me in the past. In this case, the Israeli Government is guilty of murder.

About NBCI

The National Black Church Initiative (NBCI), a coalition of 16,000 African-American and Latino member churches works to eradicate racial disparities in healthcare. In addition to our member churches, we have 18,000 sister churches. NBCI is a faith-based health organization dedicated to providing critical wellness information and preventive health screening to all of its members. The African-American community ranks first in eleven different health risk categories. NBCI's purpose is to partner with national health officials to provide health education, reduce racial health disparities, and increase access to quality healthcare.

Rev. Anthony Evans
President
National Black Church Initiative
Baby Fund Project
P.O. Box 65177
Washington, DC 20035

I hope that no discomfiture came to the Initiative or to Reverend Evans because of his outspoken rejection of silence in the face of Israeli atrocities being committed against the people of Gaza. Thousands marched in every major city across the U.S. against Israel's bombing of Gaza. I spoke at the ANSWER Coalition's Washington, D.C. "Let Gaza Live" protest that took place on January 10, 2009.

Here is what I said:

Cynthia McKinney
"Let Gaza Live"
Washington, D.C.
January 10, 2009

We don't see the images. They are neatly censored from our view in this country. But everywhere else around the world the carnage that is Gaza is being seen and the people are revolted by what they see.

They see dead babies, decapitated bodies, defenceless relief workers killed. Maimed men, makeshift morgues, mortified mothers.

They see exploding white phosphorus shells, cluster bombs, depleted uranium munitions.

They see what is reportedly the world's fourth most powerful military using all of its power against a defenseless people.

In fact, they are witnesses to 15 days of war crimes, crimes against humanity, ethnic cleansing, and genocide.

They see Hugo Chavez expel Venezuela's Israeli Ambassador and they see lawmakers in Ecuador condemn Israel's actions, calling for an investigation into Israel's crimes against humanity.

And despite the obvious facts of an Israeli-sponsored terror campaign against Palestinians in Gaza, a piece of territory roughly twice the size of the District of Columbia, they see the U.S. Congress support a resolution totally supporting Israel, even though Israel is in violation of U.S. and international law.

They see Senate Majority Leader Harry Reid, swaggering in insult to black America by initially refusing to seat Roland Burris from Illinois in the Senate, yet that same Reid cowers before the pro-Israel lobby, and they wonder why.

And sadly, they see the U.S. President-elect, who roared onto the scene like a lion, remain as quiet as a lamb in the face of the utter inhumanity of Israel's actions, and they wonder why.

And then, they see us. Gathered here in front of the White House, reaffirming our own humanity. The tears of the Palestinians roll down our cheeks, even as we bury our own victims of police murder.

A new day is coming in U.S. politics. We will use the power of our vote to change U.S. policy. We will no longer check our values at the door and support politicians and political parties that fail to deliver.

Not one more bomb to Israel.

In defense of humanity, we will not give up and we will win.

On January 26, 2009, after Israel had completed Operation Cast Lead and killed untold numbers of Palestinians and had leveled many of Gaza's office buildings, including schools and police stations, I sent a letter to President Obama and issued the following statement that, had it been heeded, could have put the United States in a much stronger position to broker peace between the Israelis and the Palestinians:

**Cynthia McKinney**
**Statement on Obama Actions Thus Far re Gaza**

"Mr. President: Give Us a Clean Break from War"

In a message to President Obama today, former Congresswoman Cynthia McKinney wrote:

It is time that the United States negotiates in good faith with Hamas, the legitimate representative of the Palestinian people. It is also time that the U.S. government tells Israel to release the Hamas Parliamentarians it illegally arrested. President Obama, please say something about Gaza. You have been roundly condemned for your continued silence in the face of war crimes and crimes against humanity committed by Israel in Gaza. Silence is complicity. Not one more bomb for Israel.

Israeli action in Gaza has outraged the world. Starting with Israel's inhumane blockade of Gaza when it didn't like the 2006 election results that put Hamas officially into power. In September 2007, Israel declared Gaza an "enemy entity." Of course, Israeli efforts to isolate the

Gaza Strip can be traced back to Ariel Sharon as early as 2005. In carrying out its military Operation Cast Lead, Israel not only committed war crimes and crimes against humanity, it also carried out a long-standing goal of Gaza isolation. The President's continued silence on Gaza and the Palestinian right of self-determination is unacceptable.

I would like to commend President Obama for recognizing that peace is the imperative and that the United States can play a constructive role in its attainment. However, placing a phone call to an irrelevant "leader" in an attempt to revive his political standing is not a route to peace: it is a journey down the same road that we're already on, that is massacres, genocide, war crimes, crimes against humanity, torture--all with U.S. weapons, paid for by U.S. taxpayers.

The President must call the elected representatives of the Palestinian people and that means dealing with Hamas.

President Obama has already spoken with Israeli Prime Minister Ehud Olmert. George Mitchell, the President's Middle East Envoy, is reportedly scheduled to visit the region, but is expected to meet only with Egyptian, Israeli, Saudi, and Jordanian leaders, and the West Bank's Abbas. Unfortunately, despite worldwide revulsion and United Nations outrage at Israeli actions in Gaza, Gaza has not been reported to be one of the Presidential Envoy's destinations.

Even worse, one of the first officials that Obama called on his first day in office was Palestinian Mahmood Abbas. Abbas, however, is no longer President, heading a government that has no opportunity to govern, from a state that exists only as a construct not made by the Palestinian people. For the United States to embark upon the path of peace, it must recognize and act on the fact that Mahmood Abbas is now irrelevant.

I believe that the call to Abbas occurred because of pressure on President Obama from outraged activists around the country and around the world calling for him to do something. But Abbas is irrelevant if the goal is peace.

If the goal, however, is to appear to be doing something while all the time doing nothing but allowing the violence of U.S.-sponsored military action to spread including saber rattling against Syria and Iran, then the President is on the right path. The American people voted for change and peace. President Obama's current path will produce neither.

I have implored President Obama to say something about Gaza. He has been roundly condemned for his continued silence in the face of war crimes and crimes against humanity committed by Israel in Gaza. Silence in the face of such criminal behavior is complicity.

President Obama must urgently place a call to the elected government of the Palestinian people. President Obama can send a strong message to the warmongers inside his own party and present them with "a clean break" from war. I encourage him to do so. We will not be fooled by actions that have the appearance of putting us on a path for peace, but that are public relations projects that buy time for more war.

To activists and human rights lawyers around the world I say: Now is not the time to let up. We must be unrelenting in our pressure for justice and recognition of the rights of all peoples embodied in the Universal Declaration of Human Rights. Those rights include the right not to be occupied. And the right to resist occupation. This is the embodiment of self-determination. And the Palestinian people are holders of these rights.

It is time that the United States negotiates in good faith with Hamas, because it is the legitimate representative of the Palestinian people. It is also time that the U.S. government tells Israel to release the Hamas Parliamentarians it illegally arrested.

While the United States Government spends precious resources to imprison Palestinians in the United States who attempted to ameliorate the humanitarian disaster in Gaza, I will attempt another trip to Gaza to assess the depth of the worsened humanitarian catastrophe now there.

I have repeatedly called on the President to ask for and the Congress to vote not one more bomb, not one more dime for the Israeli war machine.

The tectonic shift in public opinion that was underway would later acquire cataclysmic proportions after my second attempt to get into Gaza and Israel's reaction to it. I sent this message to the President which set things off:

> Mr. President, Please ask the Israelis to not harm our boats and to let us proceed to Gaza. The Israelis are paying attention and have printed stories about our boats in both the Jerusalem Post and Ha'aretz. We are doing nothing more than what you have already requested the Israelis to do: ease up on the Gaza blockade. Please ask the Israelis to allow us to proceed to Gaza without harm.

> Sincerely,

> Cynthia McKinney

The Associated Press wrote an article saying that we planned to defy the illegal Israeli blockade of Gaza again and Heddy Epstein a wonderful holocaust survivor who had planned to go to Gaza with us was brutally attacked just steps from her home rendering her too ill to make the trip with us. Sadly, she had received threatening phone calls calling her names. She transcribed one of the messages that said, "We will find a way to deal with protesters of your type." Although Heddy wasn't able to travel with us on the *Spirit of Humanity*, I was so fortunate to later meet up with her in London at a fundraiser for an Afghani girls school hosted by journalist Yvonne Ridley. Heddy told a newspaper that reported on her pre-voyage attack: "I know what it means to be discriminated against and to suffer; I care profoundly about issues of justice and fairness and peace. And I care about people—not just Jewish people. I care about everybody."

And then, as we set off for Gaza again, the unthinkable happened. Israel escalated its attack on my efforts, along with other activists, by kidnapping us from international waters in our ferry, *Spirit of Humanity,* forcing us to go to Israel instead of to Gaza, arresting us upon arrival in Israel, and putting us in jail for seven days in Ramle Prison in Israel.

**Israel escalated its attack by kidnapping us from international waters in our ferry, forcing us to go to Israel instead of to Gaza, arresting us upon arrival in Israel and putting us in jail for seven days in Ramle Prison in Israel.**

One of our prisoners was able to smuggle the video of the ferry being captured by the Israelis and take it with us into prison. A talented activist/videographer onboard and in prison with us posted it on the internet after his release--which provided more coverage of the unfortunate and illegal actions of the Israelis against us.

Another of our activists was able to smuggle a cell phone off the ferry--the Israelis took possession of all of our possessions, especially any electronic equipment. The cell phone allowed us to make recordings while we were in prison and among the first messages we recorded were our observations of racism inside Israeli prisons--the one we were in was filled with people of color--Asians and Africans. Don Debar, formerly of Pacifica News at New York's WBAI, now with CPRMetro.org, would take our recordings that we would leave on his telephone voice mail and upload them to youtube. Dissemination of our daily messages proved too popular to ignore and the corporate-stream media were forced to cover my incarceration. We also made pubic our findings about racist Israeli prisons and sparked controversy inside Israel to the point that Israeli newspapers later reported that Israelis did not like that they were being called racists, sparking a conversation about whether or not our observations were on target.

While incarcerated, I wrote "Letter from an Israeli Prison," along the lines of the treatise put out by Dr. Martin Luther King, Jr. upon his Civil Rights Movement era incarceration in the Birmingham, Alabama jail.

I spent July 4th in prison in Israel. I was held the longest of any of the U.S. prisoners. On the evening of July 7, 2009, I finally made it home and sent the following message to my e-mailing list:

Hello,
Well, all I can say is "Thank you!" Your calls, faxes, protests, and prayers all made a huge difference and helped to secure our protection and our release. I would also like to thank those at the Tel Aviv Embassy for their work on behalf of the three U.S. citizens held by the Israelis. For those of you who missed it, here is the statement I put out from the Israeli prison. Please forgive the undone, but needed edits. I have tried twice, now, to get into Gaza. I just got off the phone with George Galloway who extended a personal invitation to me to join him and the US convoy in Viva Palestina! I'm certainly excited about that. Maybe I will finally make it to Gaza.

Here's my "Letter from an Israeli Prison:"
Original audio message available here:
http://freegaza.org/it/home/56-news/984-a-message-from-cynthia-from-a-cell-block-in-israel

A funny thing happened to me on my way to Gaza. Before I left for Gaza, I was giddy with excitement. The children needed school supplies. It was a last-minute, but urgent request. Please bring crayons for the children. And so I accepted contributions of crayola crayons, #2 pencils, pencil sharpeners, paint brushes, and crayola watercolors.

When I told people that I was going shopping to buy crayons for the children of Gaza, everyone wanted to donate. By the time I left, my suitcase could hold no more. So, full of expectation, I entered the airport in the U.S. headed once again to Larnaca, Cyprus where the Hope Flotilla, consisting of the "Free Gaza" and the *Spirit of Humanity* were to embark to Gaza.

The "Free Gaza" was to be donated to the people of Gaza so they could replace some of the boats confiscated or bombed by the Israelis during Operation Cast Lead.

It was a beautiful dream. And dream it had to be because I had tried to get to Gaza before. At the

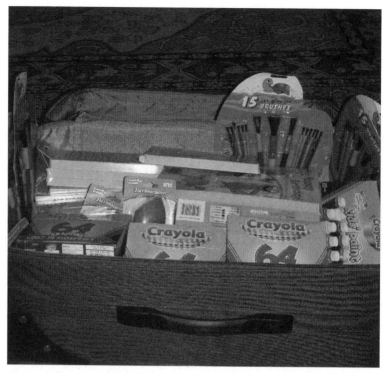

Our incendiary cargo bound for Gaza: crayola crayons, pencils, paint brushes...

outbreak of Israel's Operation Cast Lead, I boarded a
Free Gaza boat, with one day's notice, and tried, as
the U.S. representative in a multinational delegation,
to deliver three tons of medical supplies to an already-
besieged and ravaged Gaza. But, during Operation Cast
Lead, U.S.-supplied F-16s raised hell fire on a trapped
people. Ethnic cleansing became full-scale, outright
genocide.

U.S.-supplied white phosphorus, depleted
uranium, robotic technology, DIME weapons, and
cluster bombs - new weapons creating injuries never
treated before by Jordanian and Norwegian doctors.
I was later told by doctors who were there in Gaza
during Israel's onslaught that Gaza had become Israel's
veritable weapons testing laboratory; and its people
used to test and improve the kill ratio of their weapons.

The world saw Israel's despicable violence thanks
to Al-Jazeera Arabic and Press TV that broadcast in

English. I saw those broadcasts live and around the clock, not from the USA but from Lebanon, where my first attempt to get into Gaza had ended because in international waters the Israeli military rammed the boat I was on that carried medical supplies. That boat, the *Dignity*, was completely destroyed in its encounter with the Israeli military.

Again, on a humanitarian mission aborted by the Israeli military. I am now known as Israeli Prisoner #88794. I am in cell number 5, Ramle Prison. How could I be in prison for collecting crayons for kids and trying to get the crayons to them?

The Israeli authorities have tried to get us to confess that we committed a crime. And while in the cellblock, I have no access to my clothes and a cell phone, not the crayons or any clothing that has the word "Gaza" on it. Zionism has surely run out of its last legitimacy if this is what it does to people who believe so deeply in human rights for all that they put their own lives on the line for someone else's children. Israel is the fullest expression of Zionism, but if Israel fears for its security because Gaza's children have crayons then not only has Israel lost its last shred of legitimacy, but Israel must be declared a failed state.

I am facing deportation from the state that brought me here at gunpoint after commandeering our boat. I was brought to Israel against my will. I am being held in this prison because I had a dream that Gaza's children could color & paint, that Gaza's wounded could be healed, and that Gaza's bombed-out houses could be rebuilt.

But I've learned an interesting thing by being inside this prison. First of all, it's incredibly Black: populated mostly by Ethiopians who also had a dream. My five cellmates have been here for about six months each. One is pregnant; they are all in their twenties. They thought they were coming to the Holy Land. They had a dream that their lives would be better. The CIA-installed puppet in Addis Ababa, President Meles, whom I have met, has put the once-proud, never-colonized Ethiopia into the back pocket of the United States, where it has become a place of torture, rendition, and occupation. Ethiopians must flee their country because superpower politics became more important than human rights and self-determination.

My cellmates came to the Holy Land so they could be free from the exigencies of superpower politics. They committed no crime except to have a dream. They came to Israel because they thought that Israel held promise for them. Their journey to Israel through Sudan and Egypt was arduous. I can only imagine what it must have been like for them. And it wasn't cheap. Many of them represent their family's best collective efforts for self-fulfillment. They made their way to the United Nations High Commission for Refugees. They got their yellow paper of identification. They got their certificate for police protection. They are refugees from tragedy, and they made it to Israel. Only after they arrived, Israel told them "There is no UN in Israel."

The police have license to pick them up and suck them into the black hole of a farce for a justice system. These beautiful, industrious, proud young women represent the hopes of entire families. The idea of Israel tricked them and the rest of us. In a widely propagandized slick marketing campaign, Israel represented itself as a place of refuge and safety for the world's first Jews and Christians. I, too, believed that marketing and failed to look deeper. The truth is that Israel lied to the world. Israel lied to the families of these young women. Israel lied to the women themselves who are now trapped at Ramle.

And what are we to do? One of my cellmates cried today. She has been here for six months. As an American, crying with them is not enough. The policy of the United States must be better, and while we watch President Obama give 12.8 trillion dollars to the financial elite of the United States it ought now be clear that "hope," "change," and "yes we can" were powerfully presented images of dignity and self-fulfillment, individually and nationally, that besieged people everywhere truly believed in.

It was a slick marketing campaign, as slickly put to the world and to the voters of America as was Israel's marketing to the world. It tricked all of us but, more tragically, these young women.

We must cast an informed vote about better

candidates seeking to represent us. I have read and re-read Dr. Martin Luther King Jr.'s Letter from a Birmingham Jail. Never in my wildest dreams would I have ever imagined that I, too, would one day have to do so. It is clear that taxpayers in Europe and the U.S. have a lot to atone for, for what they've done to others around the world.

What an irony! My son begins his law school program without me because I am in prison, in my own way trying to do my best, again, for other people's children. Forgive me, my son. I guess I'm experiencing the harsh reality which is why people need dreams. I'm lucky. I will leave this place. Has Israel become the place where dreams die?

Ask the people of Palestine. Ask the stream of black and Asian men whom I've seen being processed at Ramle. Ask the women on my cellblock. [Ask yourself:] what are you willing to do?

Let's change the world together and reclaim what we all need as human beings: Dignity.

I appeal to the United Nations to get these women of Ramle, who have done nothing wrong other than to believe in Israel as the guardian of the Holy Land, resettled in safe homes.

I appeal to the United States Department of State to include the plight of detained UNHCR-certified refugees in the Israel Country Report in its annual Human Rights Report.

I appeal, once again, to President Obama to go to Gaza: send your special envoy, George Mitchell there, and to engage Hamas as the elected choice of the Palestinian people.

I dedicate this message to those who struggle to achieve a free Palestine, and to the women I've met at Ramle.

Cynthia McKinney, July 2nd 2009, also known as Ramle prisoner number 88794.

Cindy Sheehan responded, headlines reading "Cindy Sheehan demands the immediate release by Israel of 2008 Green Party Presidential Candidate Cynthia McKinney and other kidnapped aid workers on the boat: The *Spirit of Humanity.*"

June 30, 2009
By James Lane

Nobel Peace Prize Nominee, Human Rights' Activist and Gold Star Mother, Cindy Sheehan, calls on the Israeli government to immediately release the members and crew of the boat The Spirit of Humanity that was attempting to deliver humanitarian aid to the devastated peoples of Gaza.

Speaking from Newton, Mass, Ms. Sheehan commented: "The detention of the crew and human rights' workers on The Spirit of Humanity is a clear violation of international law, as the blockade of Gaza is a clear violation of not only international law but the human rights of the people of Gaza. Not only must the Israeli government immediately release and recompense the captives, but it must allow the humanitarian aid to penetrate the blockade."

She continued: "I not only call on the Israeli government to do the right thing, but I call on our own President, who has claimed that he is an advocate for human rights, to condemn this act of international piracy by the rogue state of Israel and also demand the release of the kidnapped aid workers. This condemnation must be as strong and clear as the condemnation for the Somali "pirates" was. A very courageous and dear friend of mine, Cynthia McKinney, was on that boat and the captives must all be treated with dignity and respect and speedily released."

Israeli prisoner number 88794 was deported from Israel, thereby barring her from entering that country for ten years. Although I embarked on a journey whose destination was not Israel, because I was kidnapped and taken there, the deportation means that I will never be allowed to visit the West Bank--which I would like to do--as long as Israel controls ingress and egress, instead of the Palestinian state. Perhaps one measure of the Arab Spring will be the extent to which these policies change in the countries surrounding Israel so that individuals wanting to visit Palestine can do so unfettered by the Israeli state.

I continued the fight for Palestinian rights, taking part in the Bertrand Russell Tribunal on Palestine held in Cape Town, South Africa in 2011, and again in New York City in 2012. The Tribunal will announce its Final Report in Brussels in March 2013.

Cynthia McKinney with Mairead Corrigan MaGuire at the Bertrand Russell Tribunal on Palestine held in Cape Town, South Africa in 2011.

# CHAPTER 15

# RACISM WHERE YOU LEAST EXPECT IT

There were two Blacks among the 21 Free Gaza Movement activists onboard the ferry "Spirit of Humanity." We all were so dedicated and were able to meld into a unit so smooth, it was as if we all ha reached a state of "flow." Everybody was in synch and everything was rolling along so well. Until we hit a bump that left a smarting bruise on our experience.

One of the activist leaders was worried. Terribly uncomfortable. It wasn't the dangerous nature of our mission; it wasn't that something had happened back home and we were thousands of miles away from any of our loved ones. It wasn't that we had cold feet. Our mission leader had just been hit with a two-ton brick: one of our key activists--a team leader--had just reported that one of our volunteer activists had been caught smoking marijuana. That's a huge no-no! And our mission leader was in a quandary. The person who was reportedly caught smoking marijuana was the only Black person--other than me--on the trip. This was a mighty awkward situation.

I could feel it in the air. I could feel the tension in the room. I could feel the strain in the room. I just happened to have been in the room while our leader was dealing with this report. Our leader was clearly anguished. With all of the bad stuff going on already, the last thing we needed to deal with was indiscipline among the ranks. But it was there and so there was no choice for our leader, but to deal with the issue. But given the multiple delicacies that were involved, I volunteered to approach our gentleman activist and see what was up.

So, I went to him and told him that it was reported that he had been seen rolling a marijuana cigarette and smoking it.

Talk about Vesuvius erupting! No, not Vesuvius, Krakatoa--an even worse volcanic explosion that killed more than 30,000 people! A destructive stereotype had just been unfairly dropped on a volunteer who had paid his way to become a Free Gaza Movement activist struggling for Palestinian freedom when Black people aren't even free. And what's more, it was a Palestinian who had leveled the charge without even talking to him to clarify what it was thought had been seen. These are exactly the sentiments that the Black male Free Gaza volunteer expressed to me after he showed me the remnants of his tobacco. Moreover, he had been joined in a smoke by at least one of the other men, but of course nothing was even said about anyone but him.

It was an ugly scene. Not because it was just an innocent matter of mistaken activity; but because it was laden with so much of what White stereotypes have created of Black men that this very strong Black man was immediately reduced to a caricature of himself in the instant that a presumption was made and then reported without even talking directly to the Black man to see what was up.

That someone struggling for dignity would rob a cohort of his dignity so cavalierly is sad but not amazing or surprising to me. When I look at the reports coming from Libya today--and I do mean today--even as you read this, of the wanton slaughter of Black-skinned Libyans, by their lighter-skinned African brothers, I become outraged. While I was in Tunisia, I experienced something very strange, but perhaps indicative of how sick a colonized mind can be. I was riding in a taxi and the taxi careened, it appeared intentionally, into a woman on the street begging. I objected to the driver who objected to my objection. So there we were, both indignant: me over his behavior and he over the lady's behavior. I told him that he was not going to hit poor women while I was in his car. His response to me was that she is always there and she is always begging. And then I said, you are both African and you should show some compassion to your sister. He snapped his head around to me and told me that he wasn't African. Stunned, I asked him if he was born in Tunisia and he said yes, and reiterated that he was not an African.

I took a lot away from that exchange, but the kernel of it being that colonialism has done a job on people of color. White supremacy has to be tackled all over the world and has inculcated a sense of inferiority of people based on skin color; if one can escape the scourge of being "of color" and become "White" even if only for a moment, it is a powerful elixir that will cause people to betray their own country in pursuit of acceptance by Whites It seems that people so afflicted believe that the White self is considered the better or even the best self. What won't some folks of color do in pursuit of Whiteness? That's another book. But, interestingly, I've had more than one Southern White come to me and express outrage at these light-skinned Libyans being able to get away with genocide and how perplexing it is that very few Black "leaders" [misleaders] are speaking out and attempting to stop U.S. support for its Libyan allies that are carrying out this African genocide.

In the end, when our Palestinian leader was told how hurtful those inaccurate conclusions were to the person about whom they were made, it all made for a very sad and unfortunate situation. I think everyone involved learned something. Including me.

At any rate, I finally made it into Gaza, not by sea but by land, with George Galloway and Viva Palestina USA. On July 16, 2009 I sent out an e-mail message with the title, "No Wonder the Israelis Didn't Want Photos Taken." We went through the gates late at night because it took the Egyptians so long to process us at Rafah.

## CHAPTER 16

# I'M STILL GRIEVING

These were my remarks at my Father's HomeGoing Ceremony. July 19, 2010, at the Jackson Memorial Baptist Church in Atlanta, Georgia.

Reverend Creecy, Reverend Sutton, Reverend Rice, Elected Officials, and all of you:

Thank you all for being here with us today to honor my father and to *help* all of us who knew and loved him manage our collective grief. It's funny how I never believed that it would come to this. You all know that Billy was larger than life. He was honest, smart, street-wise, pensive, yet playful. That's why I can say without a doubt that Billy taught me how to live.

After I came back from a humanitarian mission to Gaza, but instead having spent 7 days in an Israeli prison, I went on a nationwide tour to tell interested communities what had happened to me. At the Seattle airport, a supporter who has now become my friend, paid me the highest compliment: she told me that I was "alive."

I thought long and hard about that. Because, honestly, much to my father's chagrin, there are so many people in our community who pass their days just marking time instead of making a difference. Billy knew that it was within our capacity to materially change our conditions, if we would only do what is required. He knew *that* because he *did* that. And somehow, he transmitted that faith in our fellow human beings to me and taught me to be free.

My father also taught me how to love. I've learned from my own personal experiences that it's easy for us Americans to think that we can just order love and pick it up at the drive-through window. But through this journey with my father, I've learned to appreciate the African and Asian views of love--that its touch is so deep to our core as human beings, that it is unquantifiable, it is undefinable, and it is what helps to give us core and value and depth and meaning--when we find it.

Billy taught me love on two levels. He taught me the kind of love that would risk his job to challenge police brutality; that would challenge racism and discrimination; that would give away my Christmas "Etch-a-Sketch" the day after Christmas to a needy child in Bowen Homes. I never forgot that.

And so, I learned to love my community because every action in my father's being showed me how to do that. I learned to love humanity because I saw my father grow in his own attitudes and admit that he was wrong about gays and apologize to them in 1996 when he saw their dedication to me after I was forced into a bruising legal battle to remain in Congress and it was only the white gay community in Atlanta that would cross the racial "Maginot" line that is Candler Road out in Decatur and come into my campaign headquarters and fold letters and stuff envelopes and answer phones and do whatever was necessary to help me win reelection in a vastly redrawn district. And I did win in a hotly contested race.

My father loved people. He sacrificed too much in the way of personal wants and his family sacrificed, too, because his focus wasn't on only us, it was on his beloved community, too.

But he has been unfairly smeared by special interests in this town who want to preserve *their* interests at the expense of yours. And my father was not about to sacrifice your interests. In my father, you had a protector and I know you all know that.

And so, when the American Israel Public Affairs Committee and other aspects of the pro-Israel Lobby in this country, including their supporters right here in Georgia, targeted me for defeat, my father came to my rescue by telling the truth. I was targeted by the pro-Israel Lobby because I dared to question the Bush Administration about what happened on September 11, 2001 and because I have the audacity to believe that no group of people, including Palestinians who *are* the Semitic people in this discussion, by the way, should suffer as Blacks in the United States have suffered. Billy McKinney called them out and let you know the truth about what was going on and who was doing it in the midst of intentionally-created confusion and campaign chaos.

That chaos included acts of political sabotage, including both my father and I being abandoned by some of our closest personal and political friends. The attack on us was total. And the battle was for your mind so that you would lose respect for someone unafraid of speaking truth to power. My father came to my defense because I rightly questioned how George Bush could "win" an election in which he lost the vote; why Africa's diamonds, oil, cobalt, copper, uranium, coltan, timber, and fisheries enriched economies in Europe, the United States, and Israel while Africa remained broke and broken. What I was doing went to the core of the existing power configuration in this country and I began to expose its method of finance.

Afterall, I was sent to Washington to represent you. Only thing was that when I got attacked, Billy came to my defense. And he was punished for doing so. Every bad word you read or hear in the special interest press about either one of us, just know that the powerful individuals who operate in the shadows of power, pulling the strings of your elected officials, the U.S. military, government contracts--they all want to keep things in your life exactly as they are now and Billy McKinney understood fully that we need change, but that we are not going to get the deep, structural kind of change we need--we can't get it on the cheap.

Billy McKinney made the kind of principled sacrifices that allow us to sleep better at night.

Lord, what are we going to do now?

Billy McKinney was all about love. And Billy McKinney loved Leola. During his illness, he would just sit and stare at my mother. And she would ask him what he's looking at. And he would say "I'm admiring how beautiful you are."

Billy and Leola were the definition of love. And in these last months, they have shown me how devoid my life is of that kind of undefinable, unquantifiable love. In that regard, I have a lot of introspection to do.

Billy McKinney also taught me how to cry. Over these past few months, I didn't know my body could create so many tears. I have never in my life known this kind of sadness. But Billy taught me to understand that even at the depth of my grief, I must never forget the grief of others: that mothers are crying all over the world because of U.S. policy.

My father was such a strong black man. It would make me cry just to watch him endure his illness with such grace and dignity. He never complained. No matter how much discomfort my father was in, his universal response was "it's all good." And one day at the hospital he was so uncomfortable, he was really uncomfortable, but I heard him say aloud to himself, "It's gonna be alright, *anyway.*"

One day he wanted the nurse to reposition him. He was getting his medicine in a way that prevented him from being moved, but he was uncomfortable. So he begged the nurse to please reposition him. Then, as the nurse was about to leave the room, Billy turned to me and asked, "Did she give in?"

Billy McKinney taught me how to live and how to love, how to cry and how to die. My father, BIlly McKinney, was a hell of a man.

On behalf of the family, I'd like to thank all of you for the love you gave my father during his life and the support you give to us now.

**A Glimpse into the life of
Honorable James Edward "Billy" McKinney,
Sunrise February 23, 1927 -- Sunset July 15, 2010**

James Edward "Billy" McKinney was born to the late Ann Lewis in Atlanta, Georgia. He was raised by his loving grandmother, Annie Bell Dixon. Billy joined the U.S. Army in 1945. Upon his return to Georgia from the European war theatre, while still wearing his U.S. Army uniform, Billy was arrested for drinking from the "White Only" water fountain. He attended Clark Atlanta, University and joined the fraternity Phi Beta Sigma.

In his younger days, Billy was an avid tennis player. He also spent a lot of time reading and researching, turning himself into a "walking encyclopedia." His unique view of the world sometimes found him at odds with so-called conventional wisdom, but Billy McKinney was true to his principles, regardless.

"Billy," as he is fondly known by family, friends and colleagues grew up to become a socially and politically conscious young man; always fighting for justice and equality. This mind-set led him to join the Atlanta Police Department in 1947. Billy was one of the first black policemen in the City of Atlanta. He often reflected on walking the streets of Atlanta being allowed to police only "colored" folk, since Black policemen were not allowed to arrest Whites. He readily recognized this injustice and formed a one-man protest, picketing the Atlanta Police Department headquarters on his off days, often in his police uniform and much to the ire of his fellow officers.

It was on his Grady Hospital "beat" that he met and married his loving wife of 56 years, Leola Christion McKinney. To this union, was born a daughter, Cynthia Ann McKinney. Billy also had 2 sons, Gregory and James, from a previous marriage.

Billy made a conscious decision that picketing from the outside was not as effective as being on the inside as a part of the law-making body, helping to make laws that made sense. He ran unsuccessfully for Alderman, County Commissioner, as well as U.S. Congress as an Independent Candidate in 1982, against Wyche Fowler.

Billy McKinney was NOT a quitter, and in 1970, was elected to the Georgia State Legislature after the passage of the 1965 Voting rights Act mandated election law changes in the State of Georgia. His position in the Legislature was accompanied by that of his daughter in 1989, as she too was elected to the Georgia State Legislature. Thus, Billy and Cynthia served as the first father-daughter team of lawmakers in the history of the State of Georgia. Billy served as an elected official in the State where he was born and raised for more than 30 years.

Many bills were enacted during his years as a public servant that changed the legislative landscape of the State of Georgia. In tribute to his service, a stretch of Interstate 285, from I-20 to the Cobb County line is named in his honor; Representative James E. "Billy" McKinney Highway.

Billy was one of the forgotten Civil Rights advocates and activists. He often joined causes for justice and equality with his then-young daughter on his shoulders. He marched with the more recognized leaders and fought just as hard with the less recognized, but just as important people in the neighborhoods and communities in Atlanta.

His political prowess was recognized across the nation and the world, and his advice and counsel were sought from elected officials and candidates for elected office near and far. He was requested to tell his life story annually for a period of time to students from California State University at Pomona, as the group toured the South on their Civil Rights Tour; and he often spoke at events of socially conscious organizations. Billy served on numerous boards and was active in many organizations.

He leaves to cherish his memory his wife, Leola; daughter, former Congresswoman Cynthia Ann; 2 sons, James and Gregory; one grandson, Coy and 2 granddaughters, Morgan and Lauren; sisters-in-law Joan Christian (Thurman), Atlanta, GA, Virginia Christion, (Roosevelt "Fat"), Birmingham, AL; brothers-in-law Ernest Christion (Luvenia), Birmingham, AL, Haywood Christion (Wylean), Birmingham, AL Eugene Christion (Cassandra) Atlanta, GA; and many loving nieces, nephews, cousins, neighbors, and friends.

## CINDY SHEEHAN SAYS
## CYNTHIA MCKINNEY SHOULD HAVE RECEIVED
## THE NOBEL PEACE PRIZE

*"I wonder if the Nobel Committee looked at the videos of the G20 protests in Pittsburgh a couple of weeks ago when the US stormtroopers were hunting down protesters like dogs and beating them and teargassing grandmas (me) without provocation. If any American 'politician' got the NPP [Nobel Peace Prize], it should have been Cynthia McKinney."* Cindy Sheehan from Facebook.

CHAPTER 17

# THE POWER OF ORGANIZING

The Bush Administration admitted to torture, renditions, secret prisons, illegal and unconstitutional wiretapping, misleading and false intelligence that led to war in Iraq. How much more will the American people accept? How much more will the American people tolerate?

Apparently a lot, because now the Obama Administration is following in Bush's footsteps defending the Bush Administration in U.S. Courts, expanding the U.S. war machine into Afghanistan, Yemen, Somalia, Pakistan, and extending the U.S. mandate in Iraq, despite promising to bring our troops home. Whistleblowers who told the truth about illegal U.S. government behavior are sentenced to prison or are tortured while in prison and this is during the golden age of President Obama.

I spoke out against the Bush Administration because I was morally compelled to. And I continue to speak out today on important issues where I must. Yes, I've been punished for it; made an example of. But, in the end, the message is getting out. I do believe that many will see through the hate that is directed at me to the truth in my message. As a result, I hope fundamental change can be made in the way we conduct our political business here in this country, because it affects so many people, not just here in the United States, but around the world in our global community.

So, whether it was U.S. payments to the bin Laden family for their services in Afghanistan or the Pentagon's breaking of its promise to provide pre-deployment health screenings to our service men and women on their way to Iraq; whether it was the anthrax and smallpox vaccines for our troops administered by a company that tolerated sexual slavery and trafficking among its employees or the theft of a Presidential election; whether it was fighting for the sacred lands of the U'wa people in Colombia or of the Aboriginal Australians; whether it was blood diamonds or enforcement of the Convention for the Elimination of Racial

Discrimination, I was one of the American people's canaries in the mine-shaft. And although one mineshaft has been temporarily shut down, this canary intends to continue to sing. After all, I come from Atlanta, whose symbol is the phoenix, the mythical bird that rises from its own ashes. And with the phoenix as my symbol, my spirit too shall continue to rise.

I remain an optimist about the possibilities for promoting justice in America and in the world. But, I have to admit that I am much more sobered than I have been in a very long while. I must also admit that things are getting worse, not better. And that our beloved community is coming apart even as I sling glue every which way I can. I have tried to be resourceful when things haven't quite worked out as I would have liked and I've learned to make a lot of lemonade. My commitment to myself and to all of you is that I will continue the search for a winning formula so that we can have a government that actually proselytizes for peace.

Therefore, so long as the boat needs rocking, I will rock on.

We can beat down the mightiest walls of conformity, if we are united. And we can change the dialogue, and even the outcome of events, if our cause is right and is clearly explained to the people. That's why the failure of "The Left" to challenge President Obama today is so disappointing. I do believe that a united front standing for peace, human rights, dignity, and justice can achieve those goals within a titanic struggle. I do believe that the majority of people in the United States want these values reflected in U.S. public policy. I do believe the old adage made popular by Frederick Douglass that power concedes nothing without a demand and that it is our responsibility to demand that our values be reflected somewhere in U.S. policy--especially in U.S. foreign policy that now is defined by belligerence and war. We do not have to accept losing when our cause is just: we must engage even more and be willing to reach out to others who might also share our views, but remain silent. In short, we must grow our movement. And I believe that we can because I believe that most people in the U.S. feel exactly as I do.

However, in light of the very obvious discrepancies between our values and U.S. policy, it is clear that our strategies to achieve peace and ensure dignity must also change. And if the "acceptable" leaders of The Left" refuse to accept the need for a change in tactics to achieve these worthy objectives, then our only recourse is to change our notion of who these "acceptable leaders" are and exchange them for "unacceptable or inconvenient" leaders. The movement's failure to do that will lead me to the only conclusion remaining that I can make from this failure and that is that "The Left" isn't really "objectively left:" that is, the values its acceptable leadership professes are only as good as the context within which those values reside. Or even worse, just more partisan opportunism without a real desire to resolve nagging issues harmful to the U.S. people and the U.S. national interest. Hmmm.

I think that's what gets me into trouble, why I'm regarded by the power brokers as "inconvenient" or "unruly:" I do my own research and am in full possession of the facts when I venture into an issue area. And I am confident that, despite the hatred and the negative propaganda, to "COINTELPRO" me (in the words of the F.B.I. "to expose, disrupt, misdirect, discredit, or otherwise neutralize"me), time has already proven me right on so many issues.

And I guess that's why I'm so resilient. I've read the COINTELPRO script, and it's still being followed. I know what the game plan is. After all, from Marcus Garvey to Fred Hampton and beyond, the same script has been followed. It's not rocket science. The only reason I know it, though, is because they were dumb enough to write it down and I'm smart enough to read it. That's why I highly recommend that all high school and college students write at least one research paper on COINTELPRO, so that they can understand the extent to which a self-professed "democratic" government will go to limit dissent and silence courageous, but inconvenient, truth tellers.

The COINTELPRO papers put into context everything the government of the United States is capable of doing in both its domestic and foreign policies. And after having read them, I'm sure that social justice activists, informed and united, can prevail. The United States and the countries it calls the "coalition of the willing" or its allies, including its NATO allies, do not have to be at war; our Presidents do not have to be war criminals. And they do not have to cajole other heads of government to become war criminals, too. There is another way and as soon as we have connected that critical mass of people in the United States who feel this way, too, U.S. policy will undergo a fundamental change—as fundamental a change as occurred after the murder of President John F. Kennedy and after the September 11, 2001 attacks in New York City and the Pentagon near Washington, D.C. But, this time, the change will be for the better. When the people are sick and tired of being sick and tired, the people will demand better. I sure hope it doesn't take too long!

I remember. The civil rights movement in the United States was driven by people who had no money—but they used what little money they had, in the form of an economic boycott—to change their political conditions of the day. They did not have the right to vote, but they used what political currency they had to change the laws of their day.

When people come together, I believe, we really can change things—and if we have honest, incorruptible leadership.

That's why maligning authentic Black leaders is so important inside the United States. The COINTELPRO Papers exposed that thinking. The FBI sought to divide Blacks from Whites and Blacks from Blacks by calling pliable, malleable Blacks "responsible." Imagine if we could replicate what I did in the Old 11th District of Georgia; imagine White Americans actually liking the message of a Black man or woman who has not been pre-filtered by the very ones who want to keep us all divided! It can happen! That's why some folks keep an "enemies list." Martin Luther King, Jr. was on the F.B.I.'s enemies list. Everywhere I go now, my supporters and friends are fearful that I might be on one, too--now.

The United States and the global community are in their current predicaments because one group decided to organize itself very well and to finance its organization. I consistently ask the question, "Whose Revolution gets financed?" The swing to the extreme right in the United States is happening because the Revolution to the right is very well financed. The swing in U.S. policy toward Israel, no matter how many U.S. laws are broken by Israel or Palestinians killed, is because the pro-Israel Lobby inside the United States has extremely robust financing, and so their Revolution gets successfully translated into U.S. policy. So it could be with us, too.

But now, is it possible to overcome the pro-war and other special interests that are playing and winning in U.S. electoral politics today? My answer is an emphatic yes. Even though, in many cases, the pro-justice, pro-peace political forces have not even put a team together to send onto the field of play, and even though its present leadership is sleeping with the enemy or just plain asleep. Incredibly, its grassroots supporters either don't know that; I can't believe they wouldn't care about that.. The result on the pro-peace side is an ineffectual amalgam of many forces obtaining shoestring finance from one or two single forces. Therefore, the team that is fielded reflects the values of this particular extant set of donors; this is as good as it goes--a few "Left" voices that sound increasingly" corporate-stream,", but this approach so far only seems to have bolstered the class of "misleaders" and doesn't go far enough to actually win policy changes. Therefore, the peace team doesn't even have a first-string team ready to challenge the political process on behalf of its own professed values, let alone a farm team waiting in the wings to get its turn on the field of play.

The announcement that just one family--two brothers, the Koch Brothers--were ready to raise $88 million for the Republican Party for the 2012 elections just lets us know that we must have someone(s) to help us finance the organization and mobilization necessary to stop this machine in the making. We don't even need as much as the war machine needs because our values reflect a majority view. As I have said so often, "We don't need to match them dollar for dollar; we just have to have enough.".

Progressive forces in the United States have had glimmers of success: Abolition (an end to slavery), Women's Suffrage, Labor Rights, the Civil Rights Movement, Women's Rights, the Environmental Movement, and Gay, Lesbian and Transgender Rights, to name a few. In an interview for another manuscript, Dr. Peter Dale Scott told me emphatically that he believed in the resilience of U.S. civil society and its ability to make the necessary changes to turn this country around.

Internationally, we have seen that Freedom Revolutions can be won when organized and financed properly, starting in 1804 with the Haitian Revolution. And, today, all over Latin America, people power is pushing itself into the forefront. Such that, not only is there currently an effort to protect human rights, but also to assert nature's rights! Cuba, Venezuela, Nicaragua, Bolivia, Ecuador, and Paraguay (all members of the Bolivarian Association for the Peoples of Our America, or ALBA) are standing classical economics on its head by recognizing nature's rights.

I am calling for a "Freedom Revolution" in the United States so that we, too, can join the community of humanity where dignity, peace, justice, and truth are valued and reflected in U.S. public policy. This could begin with the simple act of protecting the U.S. Bill of Rights and restoring Constitutional government in the U.S. There ain't nothing like freedom and we've got to organize to protect our freedom from warmongers, corporate tax cheats, special interests, and other fanatics gone wild digging deep into the public purse by leveraging their political prowess. The other side is organized; there's power in organizing; we've got to get organized, too! And when we organize, we can win.

Ain't nothing like freedom!

Cynthia, Leola, Coy...

# CHAPTER 18

# IT DOESN'T END HERE

This book has been a long time coming. In it, I tried to give you a sense of the roller coaster that I've been on for much of my adult life. I asked my loved ones and friends to read it for accuracy, so that the many facets of one incident here and one incident there could be considered. I do understand that where you stand today might depend on where you sat the day before. Everyone who has read this book has told me that from their vantage point, everything portrayed is as it actually happened and was perceived by them. Some told me that I have been too kind given the harsh and unmerited treatment that I have received at the hands of a few.

It is true that many inside and outside of my extended community love me and are still hurt by the treatment that I have received in the mainstream press and from those who want to keep me out of Congress. I have met many who feel that they suffered a personal loss when I was ejected from the Congress. The United States does not have to be at war with the world. And this country does not have to be at war with itself. The discourse does not have to descend into vitriol; I am now trying to become my best self. And I am absolutely convinced that through conversation, understanding, and connection, it is possible for open people to come together to make our country its best self, too. We are together in our common struggle for Truth, Justice, Peace, and Dignity. And I know that when we work together, we win.

Wearing an orange jump suit, protesting Guantanamo Torture.

(Left) ANSWER anti-war protest. (Above) Brian Haw protested war in front of Parliament in a tent, died there, protesting war.

**Cynthia Motobiking in Paris.**

Cynthia with migrant workers in California.

Universidad
Santiago de Cali
Feb 15-16-17 2007

Cynthia with Afro-Colombians in Santiago de Cali.

Cynthia at the destroyed home of Qaddafi's son, Tripoli, Libya, 2011.

Members of the DIGNITY Delegation who accompanied Cynthia to Tripoli, LIbya during the 2011 NATO bombing.

Cynthia with Dr. Fowzia Siddiqui and Sarah Flounders in Peshawar, Pakistan seeking Justice for Dr. Aafia Siddiqui.

Opening speaker at 2012 Chicago Conference, "From Civil Rights to Human Rights and Self-Determination?" sponsored by the International Human Rights Association of American Minorities (IHRAAM), an international NGO in Consultative Status with the UN.

Jurors of the Final Session of the Bertrand Russell Tribunal on Palestine, Brussels, Belgium.

# FOR THE RECORD

# LETTER TO CLINTON ON THE CONGO

CYNTHIA A. McKINNEY
4TH DISTRICT, GEORGIA

COMMITTEE ON INTERNATIONAL
RELATIONS

INTERNATIONAL OPERATIONS AND HUMAN RIGHTS

COMMITTEE ON
ARMED SERVICES

MILITARY PROCUREMENT
MILITARY PERSONNEL

### Congress of the United States
#### House of Representatives
#### Washington, DC 20515–1011

WASHINGTON OFFICE:
☐   124 CANNON BUILDING
WASHINGTON, DC 20515
(202) 225–1605
FAX (202) 225–0691

DISTRICT OFFICE:
☐   246 SYCAMORE STREET
SUITE 110
DECATUR, GA 30030
(404) 377–6900
FAX (404) 377–6909

INTERNET ADDRESS:
cymck@hr.house.gov

August 31, 1999

Honorable William Jefferson Clinton
President, United States of America
The White House
Washington, DC 20515

Mr. President:

I have just returned from the Democratic Republic of Congo, meeting with committed individuals from myriad walks of life. Unfortunately, I feel compelled to report to you that crimes against humanity are being committed in the Democratic Republic of Congo and throughout Africa, seemingly with the help and support of your Administration. I would suggest to you that U.S. policy in the Democratic Republic of Congo has failed and it is another example of our policy failures across the Continent. One only has to point to diplomatic duality in Ethiopia and Eritrea, indecisiveness and ambivalence in Angola, indifference in Democratic Republic of Congo, the destruction of democracy in Sierra Leone, and inflexibility elsewhere on the Continent. The result is an Africa policy in disarray, a Continent on fire, and U.S. complicity in crimes against humanity.

Mr. President, everywhere people whisper it, but are too "polite" to say it out loud: your Africa policy has not only NOT helped to usher in the so-called "African Renaissance," but has contributed to the continued pain and suffering of the African peoples.

Meanwhile, thousands of people die unnoticed across the entire Continent each day from poverty, disease, and war. This is not the legacy that you want to leave for all of us who have supported you and who also care very deeply for Africa. And I am convinced that you don't want the "drift" of your Africa policy to inflict more suffering among the world's most vulnerable people as you wind down your last days in the White House.

In addition, your failure to intervene and stop the illegal invasion of Democratic Republic of Congo by your allies, Uganda and Rwanda, has directly led to the commission of crimes against humanity by their troops in the Democratic Republic of Congo.

Even now, you ask the world to "shadow kiss" this outrageous policy by calling these two countries "uninvited" when the world knows that both Uganda and Rwanda are military aggressors deep in the territory of the Democratic Republic of Congo, far away from their borders. The atrocities being suffered daily by all the people of this region are outrageous and are compounded by bad U.S. policy and indifferent U.S. leadership.

The world laughs at U.S. arrogance in constructing this fiction: and Africans are outraged by it. That is why the policy to destabilize and topple President Kabila took such an unexpected turn.

You still have time to act. Uganda and Rwanda must not only sign on Tuesday the Lusaka peace accord—along with their proxies, the so-called rebels—they must also begin an immediate withdrawal from Congolese territory. Give meaning to the mantra of late that the territorial integrity of the Democratic of Congo should be maintained. The United Nations must be given adequate resources and the mandate to keep this peace. The Democratic Republic of Congo must be helped affirmatively on the road to transparency, respect for human rights, and democracy. Your personal involvement and leadership is critical now. You should endeavor to ensure this outcome.

Enforcement of sanctions against UNITA, alone, will not solve Angola's critical problem now that Savimbi has demonstrated his willingness to kill and maim even the very people he purports to lead. However, the United Nations has put forward serious proposals to tighten and enforce sanctions against UNITA that need our energetic support. Savimbi remains unrepentant as the death toll attributable to him continues to climb and poor Angolans should not have to suffer because of an individual movement largely created and secretly funded for years by the United States.

Moreover, the United States should now focus on how to help the Angolan government defeat Jonas Savimbi and the armed wing of UNITA. Despite recent rumblings from Savimbi's envoys suggesting that he wants a political solution, this new political offensive should be seen as nothing more than a twisted, insincere, sarcastic, and insulting ruse. Over the past decade he has had two political solutions and destroyed them both (Bicesse in 1991, Lusaka in 1994). Jonas Savimbi has amply demonstrated that he cannot be trusted. And while he talks, poor Angolans continue to be crippled by his bombs. The only talk we should entertain from Savimbi now is how he is going to disarm his troops.

As a first step, our Angola policy should include the defeat of UNITA as its cornerstone; secondly we should make clear to the MPLA that sliding back to a one party regime (and the vicious suppression of freedom of the press) and rampant corruption are over; thirdly we must vigorously engage in substantial help for reconstruction; and fourthly, Savimbi should be indicted as a war criminal. We should not turn away from this responsibility, as we have done before, to demonstrate that Savimbi and his kind are enemies of all mankind and that grave crimes do not go unnoticed.

Lastly, the Organization of African Unity has spoken on the Eritrean Ethiopian conflict and has put forward a solid peace proposal. While the OAU position is supported by the European Parliament, the United Nations, and many governments, we seem to be frustrating the peace process by adding additional stipulations. Unfortunately, while U.S. policy equivocates, thousands of people have been killed, hundreds of thousands of innocent civilians have been displaced, and the war is spreading to neighboring countries. The entire Horn of Africa is at risk and could suffer the same tragic fate as the Great Lakes region. Your personal engagement could bring these warring sides to a quick, just, and lasting peace.

Finally, Mr. President, you must take personal charge of our policy in Africa. The current policies have boomeranged against us and have bankrupted us in the eyes of our victims and the world. How can you justify leaving Africa in flames as you leave the White House?

It is now time for you to personally engage on these important issues. I stand ready to be your ally on the Hill for all these important issues. We all know that when you get involved in a concerted push for peace it does make a difference. The time for your personal engagement is now.

Thank you, Mr. President, for your consideration of this request. Now, more than ever, your attention is needed to help Africa climb out of this vicious downward cycle.

Sincerely,

Cynthia McKinney
Member of Congress

# LETTER TO
# GEORGE W. BUSH
# ON THE CONGO

March 28, 2001

The Honorable George W. Bush
President
The United States of America
The White House
1600 Pennsylvania Avenue, NW
Washington, D.C.  20500

Dear President Bush:

I am writing to express my great concern that public comments and policy statements in recent years by your new appointee for Assistant Secretary of State for Africa, Walter H. Kansteiner III, could be a harbinger of a nightmarish U.S. foreign policy for the resolution of the tragic war in the Democratic Republic of Congo. I hope that this is not the case and I respectfully request your immediate and most forceful assurances that these statements do not reflect your view on the resolution of the current crisis in Congo.

As you, no doubt, know Mr. President, the United Nations Security Council has found that the international crisis in the Great Lakes region has been brought about by the illegal invasion of eastern Congo by the armed forces of Rwanda and Uganda, who are the real powers behind various armed Congolese rebel groups. The United Nations has resolved that all parties to the conflict should cease fighting and that Rwanda and Uganda should unilaterally withdraw from the Congo.

Mr. Kansteiner's first statement regarding this crisis in Democratic Republic of Congo which causes me concern was a written view in an Eastern Zaire Issue Brief (10/15/96) for The Forum for International Policy. In this issue he posited an idea for the resolution of the war in Congo that he himself characterized as "radical." Mr. Kansteiner wrote:

"A more radical approach would be to divide territory between the two primary ethnic groups. Creating homogenous ethnic lands would probably necessitate redrawing international boundaries and would require massive 'voluntary' relocation efforts, shifting Tutsis to a newly created Tutsi state and likewise for Hutus."

Mr. Kansteiner's second statement of concern to me was made on August 23, 1998 in a "Pittsburgh Post Gazette" article in which Mr. Kansteiner was quoted as saying that "the breakup of the Congo is more likely now than it has been in 20 or 30 years."

Not only are Mr. Kansteiner's ideas "radical," I find them shocking and even reprehensible. I cannot agree with him that the vest best and only prescription for peace in Congo should come at the expense of the territorial sovereignty of the Democratic Republic of Congo. The partitioning of Congo in the way prescribed by Mr. Kansteiner would amount to a reward to Rwanda, Uganda and their allies whose combined invasion has now cost the lives of two million Congolese men, women and children and the displacement of an estimated 500,000 civilians in eastern Congo. In my view Mr. Kansteiner, and indeed all persons of good conscience, should be demanding that at a minimum and as a prerequisite to any peace in Congo, the armed forces of Rwanda and Uganda completely withdraw from the territory of the Democratic Republic of Congo and that all persons responsible for the commission of grave crimes against civilians in eastern Congo be prosecuted to the full extent of the law.

I never cease to be amazed by the fact that a man who kills another can be prosecuted for murder in a domestic court but a man who orders the killing of 200,000 or more men, women and children won't be prosecuted but instead would be invited for peace talks. Mr. Kansteiner's prescription for Congo only reinforces my perception that international diplomacy has very little regard for the violations of international law and widespread abuse of the world's civilian populations.

As I write this letter, I'm reminded of your father's steadfast and much celebrated defense of Kuwaiti sovereignty after the illegal invasion by Iraq. Surely, your Administration is not now ready to allow or perhaps even reward the invasion, occupation, and dismantling of Congo or indeed any other country on the African Continent.

Mr. President, the scale and nature of the crimes which have been and are still being committed in eastern Congo rival anything being committed in the world today and they warrant our nation's strongest condemnation and firm action. Human Rights Watch has consistently reported on the widespread torture and murder of civilians in eastern Congo. Incidents of women being raped and tortured in front of their children abound. Even reports of women being raped with branches and then being buried alive have been documented. Human Rights Watch even reported on a case of a Congolese woman being raped and then forced to stand in a pit full of water in which a dead infant was already floating from another woman who had miscarried earlier during her torture.

Just this week on March 22, 2001 the Rome based Catholic missionary news agency, MISNA, reported that Rwanda was now operating concentration camps in eastern Congo in which slave laborers brought from Rwandan prisons are being forced to work in underground mines to gather Congo's precious resources for sale to U.S. and other foreign corporations. This is clearly a grave violation of international law and is evidence of the fact that Rwanda and its conspirators may be about to reduce African human rights to a whole new low by following Nazi and Japanese precedents of enslaving civilian populations to produce wealth.

As you well know, far too many foreign business interests behave like screwworms eating out the healthy flesh of Africa's body politic. Unfortunately, they sate themselves on Africa's minerals while leaving only rot behind.

I have a long-standing and deep commitment to human rights worldwide and Africa in particular. This commitment transcends partisan politics. I have publicly stated my hope for the success of your Administration and the improvements in Africa policy that I hoped you would implement. I have met with leaders on your foreign policy team and I have great respect for them.

The United States has much to offer the world. Our values are a beacon around this planet. Our foreign policy should be consistently and fairly applied and make the American people proud. I hope and pray that your Africa policy will uphold international law and put an end to Congo's pain.

I respectfully request a briefing on your Africa policy in general and your Great Lakes policy in particular.

I await your thoughtful response to my concerns.

Sincerely,


Cynthia McKinney
Member of Congress

# STATEMENT
# JOINT SUB-COMMITTEE
# HEARING ON SUDAN

April 3, 2001

Statement
Congresswoman Cynthia McKinney

Joint Subcommittee on International Operations and Human Rights and Subcommittee of Africa Hearing on Sudan

I want to thank our Chairwoman Ileana Ros-Lehtinen and the Africa Subcommittee Chairman Ed Royce and Ranking Member Donald Payne for calling this important hearing.

I am happy to see that the theme for today's hearing on the Sudan is "America's Sudan Policy: A New Direction."

Why?

Because a number of UN Special Rapporteurs, Human Rights Watch, Amnesty International and numerous other organizations and news reporters have all confirmed that during Sudan's bloody 18-year civil war, massive human rights violations have occurred against the Sudanese civilian population.  And that at the heart of the suffering is oil from the oil rich southern regions of Sudan which is being pumped out of Sudan through the Port of Khartoum for consumption by the West.

Sudan, is not a new crisis.  It has been with us for years and the United States and western nations have been negligent with respect to tending this crisis for almost two decades by formulating weak and impotent policies, one after the other.  The war in Sudan is as brutal today as it ever was.

The civilian populations living on or near oil fields and the NGO's that courageously support them have for years been targeted by both the Government of Sudan armed forces and various opposition rebel groups. Clear evidence now exists of massive forced displacements, enslavement, aerial bombardments, low level strafing of villages, hospitals, schools and churches from helicopter gunships armed with heavy machine guns, and thousands upon thousands of individual acts of murder, torture, and rape. The violence against women has been particularly brutal and includes allegations that women have been raped and their infants nailed to trees with iron spikes.

And all the while western oil companies continue to operate within the human rights disaster that we call Sudan and pump their precious black gold. We in the West might as well be filling our gas tanks with blood from the hundreds of thousands of poor souls who have lost their lives in the Sudan.

Perhaps Mark Curtis of the organization Christian Aid put it best in a recent issue of the British-based Guardian in an article "Boom time for few signals misery and death for many."

Amnesty International reported that a shipment of Polish battle tanks arrived in Sudan on the day the first export of oil left the Port of Khartoum. There is no doubt that Sudan's oil shipments are being reinvested in their ongoing war in the south.

It is as if we really don't want the warring to end and that we are deliberately unwilling to fashion a policy that really will produce the stated desired results.

For example, we all know that the United States has placed certain trade restrictions on Sudan. Yet, gum Arabic is exempted and it is the number one export of Sudan. Coca Cola and the other major soft drink conglomerates need gum Arabic. So, what do we do? We proudly proclaim that we've got sanctions on Sudan, but we exempt gum Arabic.

Worse still we allow Talisman Energy, a corporation from Calgary which has a number of U.S. citizens in high level leadership positions, to be listed on the New York Stock Exchange. And there we allow them to raise vast amounts of capital from U.S. Fund Groups and individual investors in order that those funds can then be immediately used in their operations in Sudan, such as the building of roads, airstrips and other facilities on the oil fields.

Let me tell you why permitting Talisman Energy or any other corporation for that matter to raise funds in the U.S. for use in their Sudan operations is bad.

The Canadian Special Envoy John Harker and his investigations team confirmed that during 1999, Talisman Energy was permitting the Government of Sudan to arm, refuel and then fly helicopter gunships and Antinov bombers from their Heglig airstrip. Those same helicopters then flew off and bombed and strafed nearby villages, schools, hospitals, and churches. And to show the knowledge and complicity of Talisman Energy in the great crimes being committed by these aircraft John Harker reported disturbing evidence that these Sudanese aircraft mysteriously left the Heglig airstrip just before his team's arrival, and once he had completed his investigations and had left the airstrip, the Sudanese aircraft then magically reappeared.

John Harker even reported on disturbing evidence that fourteen Nuer men seeking work at the Heglig oil compound were taken inside the Talisman compound and there murdered by Sudanese troops.

How can this type of atrocity occur right inside Talisman's own compound and yet nothing be said?

When I hear reports that the Talisman Energy CEO Wayne Buckee and his corporation is committed to an International Corporate Code of Conduct and the ending of violence in Sudan I can only laugh. The evidence that Talisman is complicit in the great crimes being committed in Sudan is irrefutable and has been reported on endlessly for years.

Talisman's press statements defending their actions in Sudan are hollow and have now become a bright shining lie.

But Talisman is not alone in Sudan there are many others trading in the blood oil of Sudan—Lundin Oil (Sweden), Petronas (Malaysia), OMV-Sudan (Austria), Sudapet (Sudan), Agip (Italy), Elf-Aquitaine (France), Gulf Petroleum (Qatar), Total Fina (France), Royal Dutch Shell (Holland), National Iranian Gas Comp (Iran), China National Petroleum (China), Denim Pipeline Construction (Canada), Weir Pumps & Allen Power Engineering (England), and Europipe (a consortium of European pipe building (corporations) and pipe builder Mannesmann (Germany).

All these major international corporations are trading in Sudan and generating billions of dollars of oil revenue. Many of them are among the world's most powerful and influential corporations in the oil industry. If they all acted together with the international community and genuinely sought consensus to end the suffering in Sudan, then I am sure that much, much more could be done to end the suffering in Sudan.

Either we, the United States Congress and the Bush Administration are serious about Sudan's suffering or we are not. How much longer will we allow it to go on.

How much more time will we continue to grant major international corporations to actively trade here in the United States and take those funds into Sudan and in so doing worsen the human rights situation for millions of innocent Sudanese people?

When will we demand accountability from these corporations?

When will we demand an end to their complicity in the slaughter in Sudan?

Does Africa exist for the Bush Administration?

Where does human rights fit in the foreign policy of the Bush Administration?

Where are the State Department representatives today?

I fear that because Sudan is so big and bountiful, that it will suffer the same fate as the Democratic Republic of Congo—in that it will continue to be preyed upon by outside forces and subjected to wars, fueled by foreign governments and other greedy outsiders, for their own purposes and their own gain.

I look forward to hearing from today's witnesses who I know really care about the people who are affected by this continuing saga of death, genocide, and ineffective policy.

Thank you.

Cynthia McKinney

# STATEMENT: UN COMMISSION ON HUMAN RIGHTS

June 6, 2001
Statement
Congresswoman Cynthia McKinney

### Oppressors at the Rein:
### Has the UN Commission on Human Rights Lost its Course?
### A Review of its Mission, Operations, and Structure

### International Operations and Human Rights Subcommittee
### of the House International Relations Committee

Thank you Madam Chair:

We are here today to question whether or not the United Nations Commission on Human Rights has lost its course.

Too many times I have found myself bound by conscience to speak out against the United Nations and the countries that set its policies. Too many times, those policies with which I have been forced to disagree, have sadly been set by Washington, D.C.

The fact that Argentina and France have both issued subpoenas for the attendance in court of former Secretary of State Henry Kissinger for the U.S. role in the murder and disappearance of their citizens is only a harbinger of things to come.

As a matter of policy, our government seems to have routinely done to the poor and people of color abroad what it has done to the poor and people of color at home.

We know too little about decisions that were made in the name of the United States, decisions that were made for me and for you, yet are now shaken off as merely responses to the exigencies of the Cold War.

Decisions that in some instances led to the overthrow of elected governments, but in all instances to U.S. support of heinous dictatorships with U.S. taxpayer dollars: like in Indonesia, South Korea, Argentina, Chile, Guatemala, Ghana, and Congo Zaire. The Pan-African News Agency cites a report on an alleged plan by the U.S. and other European countries to dump 29 million tons of toxic waste in 11 African countries. The materials to be dumped included industrial and chemical wastes, pesticides, sludge, radioactive wastes, as well as other hazardous wastes. I ask you, how can this country dump toxic waste on the poor and consider itself to be a champion of human rights across the globe?

On the U.S. Defense Intelligence Agency website is a document uncovered by Professor Thomas J. Nagy which discusses how allied forces could block Iraqi efforts to purify its contaminated drinking water and so lead to the full degradation of the Iraqi water treatment system within six months. Attacking the Iraqi public drinking water supply flagrantly targets civilians and is a violation of the Geneva Convention and of the fundamentals laws of civilized nations.

In contravention of even our own laws, U.S. weapons are used around the world in human rights abuses as states suppress their own people or their neighbors. Only a few days ago, Dick Cheney states that Israel should stop using U.S.-built F-16 warplanes against Palestinian targets.

In its conduct of foreign policy, my government has not always taken the high road. The actions launched against Henry Kissinger suggest that other countries will no longer tolerate the failure of the United States to consider human rights in its action abroad.

But human rights is not only about foreign policy.

Human rights is about domestic policy, too.

When we in this country talk about human rights, those words are usually intoned with an outward vision. We speak of human rights around the world.

However, today, for just a few moments, I want to talk about human rights at home.

On too many occasions, blacks in the United States have felt compelled to step outside of the political and judicial system in this country and appeal to the global community for the protection of their human rights. On too many occasions, the United States has failed to protect the human rights of black Americans.

And until this issue is addressed and addressed appropriately, when we speak to others about the failures in their human rights, they see hypocrisy dripping from our lips as we berate them about their treatment of their citizens.

In 1947, at the dawn of the United Nations organizations, W.E.B. DuBois registered the UN's first such complaint in an address entitled, "Petition on Behalf of Negroes." Julian Bond, Chairman of the Board of the NAACP, along with dozens of civil rights groups and activists during the UN's Jubilee Conference recognized the need still to petition on behalf of black suffering in the U.S. today.

And then again in 1951 Paul Robeson returned to the United Nations with the first call for reparations entitled, "We Call Genocide," which demanded compensatory damages over the slave trade.

In 1967, in response to approximately 150 uprisings—some chose to call them riots—in this country, the United States Government called on a national commission to conduct a study to determine the cause of this phenomenon and how to prevent it from continuing. The resulting report is popularly known as the "Kerner Report," which stated that the cause of these uprisings was white racism, racism being defined as a belief that race is the primary determinant of human traits and capacities and that racial differences produce an inherent superiority of a particular race.

One of the recommendations resulting from this report was that the United States government needed highly trained intelligence officers to counter the effects and stop the continuance of these uprisings.

In the FBI's own words, its counterintelligence program, then known as COINTELPRO, had as a goal, "to expose, disrupt, misdirect, discredit, or otherwise neutralize" the activities of black organizations and to prevent black leaders from "gaining respectability."

Why is it that today, in 2001, I can read a headline that states, "Citizens Group Sues Pentagon for the Release of Surveillance Files on the Assassination of Dr. Martin Luther King, Jr.?"

What does our Pentagon have to hide?

Madam Chair, let me be clear when I say this: racism in this country is a human rights issue.

It is an issue that has permeated every crack and crevice of our society from our playgrounds to the highest levels of our government.

Today, black federal employees have filed discrimination lawsuits against the Departments of Agriculture, energy, State, Treasury, and EPA. Swift and commendable action on the part of then-Secretary of Education Richard Riley, prevented a full-blown demonstration on the part of that Department's black employees.

If blacks inside the U.S. government receive such treatment, how do you think blacks outside the government are treated.

I'll tell you.

Our Department of Justice admits that blacks are more likely than whites to be pulled over by police, imprisoned, and put to death. And though blacks and whites have about the same rate of drug use, blacks are more likely to be arrested than whites and are more likely to receive longer prison sentences than whites.

Can we ignore the fact that this country continues to counter the world trend against he death penalty, executing 85 prisoners in 2000, many of whom were mentally impaired as well as those who were under the age of 18 at the time they committed a crime? Twenty-six of those who were executed were black men.

We began this year by executing a retarded black woman.

The International Covenant on Civil and Political Rights, the American Convention on Human Rights and the Convention on the Rights of the child all have provisions that prohibit anyone under 18 years old at the time of the crime being sentenced to death, and yet we continue to stand in direct and clear violation of these international treaties.

Government studies on health disparities confirm that blacks are less likely to receive surgery, transplants, and prescription drugs than whites. Physicians are less likely to prescribe appropriate treatment for blacks than for whites and black scientists, physicians, and institutions that might prevent or change this are shut out of the funding stream.

A black baby boy born today in Harlem has less chance of reaching age 5 than a baby born in Bangladesh.

I watch every year as the Congressional Black Caucus shrinks while important sections of the Voting Rights Act will soon expire. And quite frankly, after crippling Supreme Court decisions, there is not much left of affirmative action to mend.

From August 31st to September 7th of this year, the United Nations will host the World Conference Against Racism, Racial Discrimination, Xenophobia and Related Intolerance in Durban, South Africa. The United States and Britain don't want to talk about slavery and its vestiges. Africans and African Americans do.

Even as Britain's streets light up with Asian rage, Britain and the United States would rather not talk about racism.

Recently, Human Rights Watch stated that the United States' being voted out of the UN Commission on Human Rights is a sign that "people are watching the U.S. very closely."

It is my belief that people are indeed watching and we certainly cannot and will not continue to command respect across the world on the issue of human rights if we do not attend to our human rights issues here at home.

Bobby Kennedy said that we used to be a force for good in the world. And, indeed we were. What has gone wrong?

On the Memorial of D-Day, June 6th, when we helped bring freedom to Europe, we have been thrown off the UN Human Rights Commission.

I hope this panel today can help to tell me what has gone wrong and what we can do to return our international standing. Thank you, Madam Chair.

# MCKINNEY vs. THE ATLANTA CONSTITUTION et al.

STATE COURT OF FULTON COUNTY  STATE OF GEORGIA

CYNTHIA MCKINNEY, Plaintiff

v.    Case No. _____

COX ENTERPRISES, INC., d/b/a THE ATLANTA CONSTITUTION and THE ATLANTA JOURNAL and THE ATLANTA JOURNAL-CONSTITUTION, CYNTHIA TUCKER, Editorial Page Editor HANK KLIBANOFF, Managing Editor JOHN MELLOTT, Publisher  Defendants

COMPLAINT

1. Plaintiff Cynthia McKinney is a 6 term Black Congresswoman from Georgia who resides in DeKalb County, Georgia.

2. Defendant Cox Enterprises, Inc., (hereinafter referred to as Defendant Cox) d/b/a The Atlanta Constitution and the Atlanta Journal and the Atlanta Journal-Constitution (hereinafter referred to as Defendant Atlanta Journal-Constitution) is a foreign corporation doing business and publishing that newspaper in the state of Georgia.

3. Defendant Cox is a global media conglomerate which owns and operates18 daily newspapers and owns over 22 cable tv stations, 14 radio stations and 6 tv stations.

4. Defendant Cox is subject to the jurisdiction of this Court with proper venue and may be served at CT Corporation System, its registered agent

**CYNTHIA MCKINNEY,**
Plaintiff

v.                                          Case No. _____

**COX ENTERPRISES, INC.,**
d/b/a THE ATLANTA CONSTITUTION
and THE ATLANTA JOURNAL and
THE ATLANTA JOURNAL-CONSTITUTION,
**CYNTHIA TUCKER,** Editorial Page Editor
**HANK KLIBANOFF,** Managing Editor
**JOHN MELLOTT,** Publisher
Defendants

## COMPLAINT

1. Plaintiff Cynthia McKinney is a 6 term Black Congresswoman from Georgia who resides in DeKalb County, Georgia.

2. Defendant Cox Enterprises, Inc., (hereinafter referred to as Defendant Cox) d/b/a The Atlanta Constitution and the Atlanta Journal and the Atlanta Journal-Constitution (hereinafter referred to as Defendant Atlanta Journal-Constitution) is a foreign corporation doing business and publishing that newspaper in the state of Georgia.

3. Defendant Cox is a global media conglomerate which owns and operates18 daily newspapers and owns over 22 cable tv stations, 14 radio stations and 6 tv stations.

4. Defendant Cox is subject to the jurisdiction of this Court with proper venue and may be served at CT Corporation System, its registered agent at: 1201 Peachtree Street NE, Atlanta, Fulton County, Georgia 30261.

5. Defendant Cynthia Tucker is the Editor of the Editorial Page for the Atlanta Journal-Constitution and wrote the false and defamatory material complained of herein in a column

at: 1201 Peachtree Street NE, Atlanta, Fulton County, Georgia 30261.

5. Defendant Cynthia Tucker is the Editor of the Editorial Page for the Atlanta Journal-Constitution and wrote the false and defamatory material complained of herein in a column published on or about July 30, 2006, and may be served at her place of business at 72 Marietta St. NW, Atlanta GA 30303.

6. Defendant Hank Klibanoff is the Managing Editor of the Atlanta Journal-Constitution who approved the offending column for publication, and may be served at his place of business at 72 Marietta St. NW, Atlanta GA 30303.

7. Defendant John Mellott is the Publisher of the Atlanta Journal-Constitution and may be served at his place of business at 72 Marietta St. NW, Atlanta GA 30303.

8. At all times material hereto the Defendants Cynthia Tucker, Klibanoff and Mellott were employed by Defendant Cox, were the agents and employees of Defendant Cox and were acting within the scope of their agency and employment relationship with Defendant Cox.

9. The acts and omissions of Defendants Tucker, Klibanoff and Mellott are imputed to Defendant Cox as a matter of law.

## THE LIBELOUS AND DEFAMATORY STATEMENTS

11. On July 30, 2006, the Defendants libeled Plaintiff by the publication of false and defamatory statements published in the column of Cynthia Tucker on page A-08, under the headline "Voters can see through McKinney."

12. Tucker wrote of the Congresswoman's interaction with the Capitol Hill policeman: "she slugged him with her cellphone." This false and libelous allegation is not supported by any witness or any other evidence.

13. Tucker maliciously attempted to spin this incident into a felony by falsely alleging that Cynthia McKinney assaulted the officer with a weapon.

14. Instead of admitting the fact that the officer used force against the Congresswoman, Tucker states only that the officer "stopped her," in an effort to falsely portray Cynthia McKinney as the wrongdoer and aggressor.

15. Tucker falsely attempted to attribute what she interprets as anti-Semitic statements from Cynthia McKinney's father to Cynthia McKinney

by stating that "her father, a spokesman for her campaign." Her father was not a spokesman for the campaign or for her. The attempted attribution was false, defamatory and libelous.

16. Tucker wrote of Congresswoman McKinney: "She suggested that President Bush had known in advance about the Sept. 11 attacks but did nothing to stop them so his friends could profit from the ensuing war." The 2006 award winning documentary film "American Blackout" had already definitively exposed this statement by Tucker as false, as the Congresswoman never made this connection even though Tucker continues to assert that she did.

17. Tucker falsely wrote: "She doesn't have the power or prestige to pass a resolution in support of sweetened ice tea." At the time she wrote this Tucker knew that the Power Rankings by Congress.Org ranked Cynthia McKinney 277 of 435 Congresspersons in legislative effectiveness, making her the highest in legislative effectiveness among the Democratic Georgia delegation.

18. The July 31, 2006 Cynthia Tucker column contained other false, malicious, defamatory and libelous matter.

19. Thereafter the Defendants published, republished and otherwise disseminated these false and libelous statements over and over, even after actual notice that they were false and libelous.

20. The Defendants, through its agents and employees, failed to properly employ reasonable procedures to investigate their false and libelous allegations before publication or after.

21. The false and defamatory words in the column in question were not supported by any objective facts or truthful information.

22. By letter dated July 31, 2006 counsel for Cynthia McKinney provided the Defendants with the statutory opportunity to correct and retract the libelous and defamatory statements set forth in the column.

23. By letter dated on or about August 15, 2006, counsel for Defendants conveyed their refusal to issue any correction or retraction and conveyed their insistence that the statements were true and accurate.

24. In fact, the Defendants submitted this false and defamatory column, along with nine others, for a Pulitzer Prize, and Defendant Cynthia Tucker won a Pulitzer even though her column in question was based on these

same false and defamatory matters.

25. Sadly, the truth is not a yardstick for measuring a columnist's Pulitzer worthiness. See Poynteronline.com, 4/5/2004, Pulitzer Juror's Tale: Do's, Don'ts and a Single Sad Surprise, By Keith M. Woods.

26. At the time Defendant Tucker wrote the column in question, a federal grand jury had already reviewed all the evidence relating to the incident involving the Capitol Hill Police incident, and on June 16, 2006 declined to charge Plaintiff with any offense; moreover there was never any evidence, or other basis in fact, that a cell phone was used in the incident. (Ex. E)

27. The Cynthia Tucker false and defamatory column was malicious, but was just part of the malicious campaign by the agents and employees of Defendant Cox Enterprises to bring down McKinney by whatever means were available to their media empire. BOMB THREATS AGAINST MCKIN-NEY FROM COX FACILITY

28. While Cox agent and employee Cynthia Tucker was dropping her bombshell libelous statements, actual bomb threats were being tele-phoned directly to Cynthia McKinney from the Cox Atlanta-Journal Constitution facility in Cobb County. These bomb threats were made on or about June 17, 2006 (Ex. A)

**COX RADIO JOINS IN LIBELOUS ATTACK**

29. During this same election cycle, Cox radio personality Neal Boortz, on or about March 31, 2006, blasted his slanderous "ghetto slut" slur against Congresswoman McKinney on his daily radio program broadcast in Atlanta on WSB 750 radio. (Ex. B)

**COX'S INDICTMENT BY ASSOCIATION**

30. Even though McKinney was not indicted in the Capitol Hill police incident, and the Defendants knew she would not be, Cox's Atlanta Journal-Constitution ran an article on August 3, 2006, just days before the Congressional primary runoff, under the headline "Gwinnett consultant indicted on election law charges" and "Associate to Bill McKinney also faces charges." The article on page 1 announced that "political consul-tant Bill McKinney" was indicted. (Ex. D) But the official indictment was actually for a person named William Dennis McKinney, a white political consultant operating in Gwinnett County, Georgia, essential facts omitted from the Cox story. Funny thing, Cynthia McKinney's father is the former

Fulton County state representative named Billy McKinney.

31. As a proximate result of the false and defamatory statements by the Defendants the members of the public were lead to believe that Cynthia McKinney unjustifiably attacked and slugged a policeman with a weapon, in fact a deadly weapon which is defined under Georgia law as an object, device and instrument which when used against a person is likely to result in serious bodily injury; that she was anti-Semitic; that she had accused the president of being a war-monger for profit; and that she was not the most influential, legislatively, of the Georgia Democratic congressional delegation.

32. As a proximate result of the false and defamatory statements by Defendants, Cynthia McKinney's reputation has been permanently damaged.

33. As the proximate result of the false and defamatory statements by Defendants, Cynthia McKinney has suffered physical consequences, from stress, emotional distress, mental pain and suffering and wounded feelings.

34. As the proximate result of the false and defamatory statements by Defendants, Cynthia McKinney has suffered public hatred, contempt and ridicule.

35. As the proximate result of the false and defamatory statements by Defendants, Cynthia McKinney has suffered permanent impairment to her ability to continue her livelihood and her office as Congresswoman.

36. Defendants possessed knowledge of the falsity of their statements about Plaintiff and acted with reckless disregard for the truth or falsity of their statements.

37. The false and defamatory statements of the Defendants demonstrate wilful misconduct and that entire want of care which raises a presumption of conscious indifference to consequences and gross negligence.

38. The Defendants' relentlessly defamatory campaign against Plaintiff shows that they acted maliciously.

39. The Plaintiff is entitled to an award of punitive damages from Defendants in order to deter, punish and penalize Defendants from repeating their unlawful conduct.

Wherefore, Plaintiff requests: A. Judgment against the Defendants; B. Damages in an amount to fairly compensate Plaintiff for the injuries and harm caused, on excess of $10 Million (ten million dollars);  C. Punitive damages to penalize and deter Defendants;  D. Costs;  E. A jury trial.

_____ J.M. Raffauf,  Attorney for Plaintiff

**Mike Raffauf, attorney.**

But it seems that the *Atlanta Journal-Constitution* doesn't just pick on me, but on anybody like me, as courageous State Representative Aisha Thomas Morgan discovered in 2005, when she voiced opposition to H.B. 244 requiring voters to show photo ID before voting, and found herself compared by AJC to "our Ambassador to Outer Space, Cynthia McKinney" in a discourse which itself might have been termed racist.

### At the heart of Friday's walkout

Published on: 03/13/05

It's too easy to say the past is never truly past. Every now and then, we must decide which past will stay with us — and for how long.

That was at the heart of last Friday's brief walkout by black legislators at the state Capitol. It was one of those startling, intense clashes of culture sure to help us define Georgia politics for the next generation or so.

The topic was a set of bills, one in the Senate and another in the House, to require that a voter present a photo ID before casting a ballot.

Republican heads were concerned about the Florida of November 2000, a time and place of butterfly ballots and razor-thin margins. Black Democrats had the Mississippi of 1960 on their minds — an era of literacy tests and other innocent-looking barriers to the ballot.

GOP lawmakers knew the bills would stir trouble — but not how much. "I didn't anticipate the depth of the emotion," admitted Sen. Cecil Staton (R-Macon), sponsor of the Senate bill.

"I looked at the current law and the things you can use for voter ID — I mean, you can walk in and vote with a power bill?" he said, not without some exasperation.

But the concern is more than just academic. There is a deep suspicion among many newly empowered Republicans that the voting process in many African-American communities is tainted. How else, many ask in private, to explain U.S. Rep. Cynthia McKinney?

Examples are hard to come by — voter fraud is a

difficult crime to prosecute, Staton said. "But I think we would be putting our heads in the sand if we did not recognize that voter fraud is going on in this state," he said.

African-American lawmakers say the Republicans well understand that voters on society's edges — the ones least likely to carry a driver's license or passport — are disproportionately black.

As the bills passed each chamber Friday, some of the anger expressed by black lawmakers was pure theater. State Sen. Emanuel Jones (D-Decatur), who wrapped himself in shackles as he walked out, owns three car dealerships.

But Sen. Kasim Reed's (D-Atlanta) tears of rage as he spoke from the Senate well were quite real. The normally soft-spoken Atlanta lawyer and many others came close to screaming in frustration at the Republican inability to see that, among many black Georgians, voting is as sacred a ritual as going to church, and should remain just as inviolate.

"It's not part of their life experience, so they don't think about it," said Rep. Carolyn Hugley (D-Columbus). "I'm just one generation removed. My mother was 40 years old before she could vote."

Senate Minority Leader Robert Brown (D-Macon) predicted that the evening would torpedo the GOP's current effort to woo black voters. "This is a defining moment for the relationship between Republicans and African-Americans," he declared.

Staton said his legislation is simply the finger of history moving on to other business. "This isn't about what happened 40 years ago, or about slavery," he said. "This is about 2005."

Ultimately, whose past is pertinent isn't a matter for the Legislature to decide. Georgia remains subject to the Voting Rights Act, and any change in election law must be approved by the federal government. That's who will decide whose past is truly past.

You may have read about H.B. 244. This Republican-backed bill would require registered voters to show some sort of photo identification before they step into the voting booth. The proposal enraged black legislators. I am with them on this issue. If I had to show poll workers my driver's license picture, they would fall down laughing and I would be too embarrassed to vote. My photo looks like Forrest Gump with a hangover.

What was interesting is how some of these legislators chose to register their displeasure. The best protest came on Family Day at the Capitol when legislators' families were supposed to see firsthand what Mommy and Daddy do all day beside scarf down free food. State Rep. Alisha Thomas Morgan, a young firebrand from Cobb County, used the festive occasion to go to the well of the House of Representatives and trash the bill by singing, "Ain't Nobody Gonna Turn Me Around." Despite House Speaker Glenn Richardson's insistence that she stop showboating in front of the visitors, she kept right on singing. Political observers disagree on whether Richardson's irritation was due to the fact that Morgan had gone past her allotted time or because her singing reminds one of a mortally wounded frog. Rep. Morgan's antics have led some in the media to compare her to our Ambassador to Outer Space, Cynthia McKinney. (If Morgan's lawyers are reading this, I think there is a libel suit just waiting to be filed.)

We could be witnessing an exciting new trend in political persuasion: Singing. Why make long-winded speeches? Why waste money on high-priced lobbyists? Why purchase advocacy ads? From now on, if you have a political ax to grind, just sing about it. Can you imagine how successful the flaggers would have been if instead of threatening anybody who disagreed with them, they had gathered at the Capitol, locked arms and sang to the tune of "Camptown Races": "We don't like the new state flag, doo-dah, doo-dah. And we're gonna be a constant nag, all the doo-dah day." It simply boggles the mind. Or, what if the Georgia Department of Industry, Trade and Tourism had formed a glee club and adapted "Georgia on my Mind" to sell the highly unpopular H.R. 218, which shields details of economic development negotiations from public view:

"Georgia, Georgia, no one needs to know the deals we must make if Georgia is to grow." There is no question that we would have a state-of-the-art toxic waste site up and running at this very moment if the tourism folks could have carried a tune in a bucket.

The Board of Regents is catching a lot of flak these days, thanks to the questionable public behavior of one of its members, along with efforts to hide donor information from the public. The board currently has a favorability rating slightly below that of syndicated newspaper columnists. Perhaps Georgia taxpayers would be more understanding of their high-handed methods if the regents would defend their actions with the help of Georgia Tech's "Rambling Wreck" fight song: "We're in charge of schools, we set the rules, And a helluva mess we've made. Rah! Rah! Rah!"

And then, there is the dysfunctional City of Atlanta, which couldn't manage a two-car funeral if you spotted them both vehicles. After much public debate, the Atlanta City Council recently gave firefighters and police officers a 4 percent pay raise, and while everybody was in a warm and fuzzy mood, awarded themselves a 22 percent increase. If there is a public backlash to the group's self-serving actions— or if anybody in Atlanta even cares anymore, which I doubt—council members can break out in song. Maybe an updated version of "Trees": "I think that you shall never see A better-paid incompetent than me."

Surely, no one can argue with that. If the trend of singing our political issues catches on, it will only be a matter of time before I begin furnishing you a weekly sing-along version of this column. Before I can do that, however, I will need to think of something that rhymes with "Liberal Weenie." Doo-dah. Doo-dah.

# GUS SAVAGE: AIPAC CAMPAIGN FUNDING TO DEFEAT CANDIDATES CRITICAL OF ISRAEL

LAYING OUT THE FACTS (House of Representatives - March 29, 1990) [Page: H1342]

The SPEAKER pro tempore. Under a previous order of the House, the gentleman from Illinois [Mr. Savage] is recognized for 60 minutes.

Mr. SAVAGE. Madam Speaker, I rise tonight to deal with the problem that occurred in my recent primary election, the one in which— let me just say that I was successful, despite this problem. However, I want to bring it to the attention of our Nation tonight. For while I mention it in reference to my own experience in the recent primary election, I am convinced that it constitutes a danger for all America and threatens to rip the fabric of our democracy.

I represent the Second Congressional District in Illinois. It is not an inner-city district. It consists mainly of bungalows, semi-professional, and blue collar workers, second and third generation families there. It is approximately 30 percent suburban, approximately 30 percent nonblack. It is an industrial district that has housed most of the heavy industry in Illinois—automobile assembly plants, stamping plants, three steel mills, at one time, four.

In this campaign a strange thing occurred. A column was written by a columnist in the *Sun-Times*, the *Chicago Sun-Times* newspaper, by the name of Vernon Jarrett, that raised questions about who really was my opponent, because of what appeared to be a strange tilt in the sources of his campaign funding.

I want to share some facts with Members here this evening, that perhaps could be shared by some others who have been targeted, apparently as I was in this primary, and unfortunately, they lost their reelection bid.

After seeing this column, I began to check the records in the Federal Election Commission report of my opponent for this year, which was available only for January and February, of course, and began to check the identities of those who had contributed to his campaign. I want to let Members know what I found.

It relates to an organization called the American-Israel Political Affairs Committee. So before I begin to give numbers, amounts, let me first familiarize Members with the American-Israel Political Affairs Committee, because it is not well-know beyond Capitol Hill in Washington, DC, and your elected representatives. It is indeed a rather shadowy operation, and I want to not just try to describe the American-Israel Political Affairs Committee, better known as AIPAC, and I will refer to it from the initials, A-I-P-A-C, AIPAC. This is not to be confused, incidentally, with the term `PAC'—referring to political action committees, as Members know, are those organizations under the Federal Election Commission that organize to contribute money to campaigns for Federal candidates and others. However, AIPAC means the American-Israel Political Affairs Committee, not a PAC—has no right to contribute money to candidates, therefore, but rather than to try to describe it myself, I want to just read excerpts to Members from newspapers reports that I discovered when I began to pursue this matter. In the process, I began to realize that I had been targeted for defeat by AIPAC.

First, *The Wall Street Journal,* June 24, 1987, an article by John J. Failka, and reads just in part, refers to the American-Israel Public Affairs Committee, or AIPAC, as `one of Washington's most powerful lobbying organizations.' He points out in the article that `According to a computer-aided analysis of 1986 Federal Election Reports, despite AIPAC's claims of noninvolvement in political spending, no fewer than 51 pro-Israel PAC's, most of which draw money from Jewish donors'—I am reading a quote from *The Wall Street Journal*—`Jewish donors and operate under obscure-sounding names are operated by AIPAC officials, or people who hold seats on AIPAC's two major policymaking bodies'. Continuing this article, `The analysis shows that three of seven regional chairpersons at AIPAC direct PACs'—meaning political action committees, those who can legally contribute money and do—`three of seven regional chairpersons of AIPAC direct PAC's, political action committee, and 26 more political action chairmen or treasurers sit on AIPAC's 131-member executive committee which meets four times a year and set overall lobbying strategy.

'Twenty-two more political action committee leaders hold seats on the second advisory body or AIPAC, a 200-member national council.'

[Page: H1343]

[TIME: 1950]

And it concludes: 'While the pro-Israel PACs'—that is political action committees, not AIPAC—'represent diverse and supposedly bipartisan Jewish committees in almost every major city and region in the country, their spending patterns are remarkably similar.'

I ask you to bear with me as I read from three or four clippings briefly to lay the ground work to understand this obscure operation, because however obscure and disguised, if you will bear with me you will learn what should be of great concern to us all. Here is the next clipping—and I am going to relate these down the line—is from the *Washington Times* newspaper, January 13, 1989.

It says in part: 'A group of prominent Americans concerned about Washington's diplomatic tilt toward Israel filed a complaint yesterday with the Federal Elections Commission charging in a 100-page complaint that AIPAC has worked so closely'—I am just reading—'with legally established PAC's to target political candidates on the basis of their positions toward Israel, that the PAC's'—political action committees—'are in effect affiliates of the lobby group.'

That would be illegal. That would be in violation of the Federal election laws. It would be in violation of what AIPAC contends are the limits of its own activities. And I continue from the same clipping: 'AIPAC's formidable ability to monopolize congressional support is based not upon an appeal to American national interests'—now, get this—'but upon threats by special interests that has resorted to conspiracy and colusion.' That is a quote.

That is Richard Curtis, formerly the Chief Inspector of the U.S. Information Agency and one of the plantiffs in this case.

'The complaint supported by more than two dozen exhibits'— this is not longer the quote; this is in the newspaper clipping or the report—'demands that the FEC force AIPAC to register as a political action committee and disclose its activities. Such a ruling would hamper the effectiveness of the lobby which operates behind the scenes to recruit support for Israel, the largest recipient of United Sstates aid, with $3 billion annually, and to oppose weapons sales to Arab foes of the Jewish state.'

Now, that is from the *Washington Times*, by Isaiah Poole.

I have just a couple more, because I will bet that most of you are not familiar with AIPAC nor any of this that I am reading. This is from the *Washington Post*, November 14, 1989, an aritcle by Charles R. Babcock. It says:

Internal AIPAC documents made available to the Washington Post, however, show that the group's top political operative was actively involved with pro-Israel political action committees--PACS--trying to help raise money for several condidates in the 1986 Senate races.

A memo from Elizabeth A. Schrayer, then AIPAC's deputy political director, five weeks before that election urged an assistant to call several pro-Israel PACs and `try' to get $500 to $1,000 donations for five specific Senate candidates.

In the Sept. 30, 1986, memo, Schrayer listed nine pro-Israel PACs and noted that some had not contributed to certain candidates.

Four other documents are 1985 letters from Schrayer to individuals in Massachusetts, California and Hawaii. In them, she offers to provide fund-raising ideas and arrange speakers for a new pro-Israel PAC, sends a sample solicitation letter and list of pro-Israel PACs to a fund-raiser for Evans, and volunteers to answer questions about starting a PAC.

AIPAC's major goal is maintaining the level of foreign aid to Israel, now $3 billion a year. * * * and defecting arms sales to Arab countries.

Now, what this is beginning to show you is that the interest or the purpose of AIPAC is to promote a foreign nation, not in America's interest, an organization operating within America composed of Americans, in the interest of a foreign nation interfering in the internal affairs and the elections of this Nation.

Let me go a little further now. Here, this is again from the Washington Post, dated October 7, 1988. Let us see what kind of interference this is. For what purpose, and who do they attack? Let us watch this. This article is written by the same Charles Babcock. It says this: Now listen closely.

The American-Israel Public Affairs Committee (AIPAC), the nation's chief pro-Israel lobby, has become a subject of attention twice in the past week because of reports of partisan involvement or personal attacks in the 1988 political campaign.

One case centers on a year-old internal AIPAC staff memo urging that Jewish reporters raise questions about Jesse L. Jackson's sex life and finances.

That is AIPAC pursuing the interests of a foreign government, beginning to try to develop surreptitious means of hurting and damaging a Presidential candidate in this Nation. This gets closer and closer, as you would notice, to something un-American.

Now, here in a special report of the Washington Report on Middle East Affairs of July 1989, it points out--and I am reading again--`70 active pro-Israel political action committees'--now, those are PAC's that give money to influence the outcome of elections--`spent $3,870,052 in direct contributions * * * in the 1988 elections.'

I am skipping over and just reading excerpts.

`There are several factors * * * that make pro-Israel PAC's unique. The first is their names.'

Now, you might ask, what is in a name? Why try to name something in a way as to not reveal its purpose and its function?

It continues in this article: `* * * Edward Roeder, whose Sunshine News Service publishes PAC's Americana--that is a book--`to draw this admission from Robert Golder, president of Delaware Valley PAC.'

That is Robert Golder, president of the Delaware Valley PAC. That is an innocent sounding name, Delaware Valley PAC. That could be about nature. It could be about streams or whatever else might attract people to the small State of Delaware. It could be about the headquarters, about the many corporations that are located there.

But what does Golder, the president of the Delaware Valley PAC say? This is from the article: `This PAC is a group of American Jewish people working for a strong American position on Israel * * * I don't know that it's necessary for outsiders to know who we are * * * it's a small group of Jewish fundraisers raising money from mostly Jewish contributors, and we can explain who we are to them.'

[Page: H1344]

[TIME: 2000]

The article, and I am no longer quoting Golder, but the article by Richard Curtis, continues that, `If 70 pro-Israel PAC's active in 1988 coordinated their giving,' and to do that through AIPAC would be illegal, `coordinated their giving, internal AIPAC documents instructing employees to contact named PACs and tell them to give designated amounts to named candidates which have fallen in the hands of both the Washington Post and the TV show, Sixty Minutes.'

Mr. Speaker, you may recall the show when Mike Wallace exposed AIPAC. They indicated that coordination involving at least 20 of the major pro-Israel PAC's took place in 1988 and that such coordination makes AIPAC and those PAC's into a single PAC, circumventing the law that limits donations to a single candidate.

Now let us, after I got through that, described a PAC to you and make you a bit more familiar with AIPAC; so now let me go back to where we started and relate it to my recent primary.

Here is a letter dated February 28, 1990, from a Robert H. Asher, 211 East Chicago Avenue, Chicago, IL. Now I am going to tell you, and I will identify for you, this Robert H. Asher later. Let me first read this letter that was mailed by Robert H. Asher.

Let me just tell you right now so I do not hold you in suspense. Robert H. Asher was the president of AIPAC. But let us read.

'Gus Savage has one of the worst attendance records in Congress.'

Well, now of course that is untrue. The records of how often one votes in Congress is a matter of public records in print, and though many of you may know that in newspapers and television for the past 8, 9 years, whenever—many times when they just mentioned my name they say, `Gus Savage who has such a poor attendance record,' and, if I say that is in print, then they can find out just what that record is, and they would discover that record was not poor except for the few months of bereavement when in 1981, I lost my wife of 34 years to a very excruciating ailment, that except for that, nowhere near poor. But yet he says this, and, as I said, I will explain later why it might be interesting to note that the press has been saying this for the past 8 or 9 years knowing that it was not true and knowing that you would have, perhaps, no interest enough to check to find out whether it was true or not and just accepted it.

And he says that, `Since he is consistently anti-Israel,' Gus Savage, `anti-Semitic, pro-PRO, pro-Farrakhan, his lack of attendance is probably a good thing.'

That is a bit scandalous, but let us see what his purpose of disseminating such falsehoods is.

`If Savage is not defeated this time, he'll be in Congress as long as he wants.'

Well, I hope he was correct in that regard at least.

Then he concludes, `Please send your check payable to the Committee to Elect Mel Reynolds in the enclosed envelope. The primary is less than a month away. Sincerely, Robert H. Asher.'

I wonder why he is so interested in AIPAC influencing the outcome of a primary election in the Second District of Chicago? The main issue in the Second District in Chicago is not Israel. It is about jobs. There are unemployed steelworkers, unemployed automobile workers. Jobs. Working conditions. Wage rates. Federal assistance to avoid mortgage foreclosures as a consequence of unemployment resulting from the structural economic changes in our country. Not Israel. Why then would he be so concerned about the outcome of that election? Let us see just how concerned he actually is.

Now what I am going to do is where I really feel the point I wanted to reach that makes this all relevant. I have here a list of the executive board of AIPAC, an executive board of AIPAC and its national council and officers. That is how I know who Robert H. Asher is. What I intend to do here now is to take the Federal Election Commission report filed by my then opponent, Mel Reynolds, filed here, his signature, for January and February of this year, the only one, the latest one that is available.

Now I am making this statement because I want my colleagues to conclude or agree with me that we need to strengthen the Federal election laws. We need to enforce that which now exists against AIPAC, and we need to be concerned about an agency whose main concern is the interest of a foreign government, taking advantage of the rights and privileges of American citizenship to influence your Congress.

Now, Reynolds had to file this, as all candidates do, and, incidentally, let me say that when I go to point out to you how much money he raised, you will find during that period, though they say incumbency is protected by our capacity to raise so much money; in that period I only raised $15,000, but Reynolds raised $51,000, more than three times as much.

Never held office before in his life. Did not live in the district until a couple of years ago.

What about all of this money? Well, I can tell you something about money. I was, during our break in January, taking a little time off. I play golf; at least I claim I do. Some of those who play with me deny that. But at least I try, and I enjoy it, find it relaxing.

So, there is a great golf course down in the Bahamas called Paradise Island. So, I went to Nassau to play golf. And, after you finish a round of golf, you go back to the hotel resort, as some of you have done, I hope, and you go outside because it is such a wonderful climate there, and there is an outside bar; a refreshment stand may be a better way of putting it. You go out, and you refresh yourself, and they have entertainment outdoors there by the bar, and in this instance there is calypso singing which is very common in this part of the world, and a fellow was singing a song, a calypso song. I had not heard it before, but I do remember the lyrics because it was so interesting, and they are applicable here.

As my colleagues know, calypso is like the blues to African Americans. It is their complaining about personal problems, and in this song that is what he was complaining about. According to the lyric of this song, this man was complaining about his woman, not uncharacteristic of calypso songs, nor of the blues. Apparently she had come home very late one night. In fact, she stayed out all night long, and, as they say, the sunshine had caught up with her. The song indicates that she came in, fell asleep, and the man was so concerned and distraught, a very poverty-stricken family, and he started checking to see was she all right. And he noticed her purse, which was usually bare, was just chock full of something, just bulging, a bulging purse, and he opened the purse, and money just fell out. All kinds of money, and that is what the song says, all kinds of money from all kinds of places.

Well, of course in a resort like Nassau people come from all over the world, and, as the song goes, he tried to awake her to ask her, 'Where did you get all of this money?' That is the title of the song. And

it goes, "Where did you get'—I cannot sing, unfortunately. Some people say I do not speak too well either, but let me just talk it.
[TIME: 2010]

It says, 'Where did you get this money, American money, German money, Japanese money, Jewish money, where did you get all of this money?' That was the question I asked myself when I saw that my opponent had raised so much more money than did I. Where did he get it, all of that money?

Well, fortunately, the FEC report requires that anyone who gives you $200 or more, any individual, must be listed by name and address and any PAC, that is a political action committee that gives you money, must also be listed by name and address and the name of its treasurer shown.

All right. Now, I was a journalist before I was ever elected to office for some 20 years, an award-winning journalist, learned a lot about how to do research and, of course, it was not hard to research this, so I took this list. I looked at his individual contributors, and let me give you these figures. Just bear with me, if you please.

Now, of that amount that he had raised, $8,250 of it was itemized as individual contributors, meaning people who gave him $200 or more. Of that $8,250 let us see how much came from where. To do that I refer back to this list from AIPAC, now blown up, so you can see listed under executive committee and national council and officers. I wanted to see how many people who contributed this money, the large sums, also are on the executive committee of the national council or as an officer of AIPAC. It is called cross-checking, you know.

Let us just go down and see. First of all, the contributor is that same Robert Asher. Now, the most an individual can give to a candidate is $1,000. The most that a PAC can give to a candidate, however, is $5,000. Private corporations cannot give money. Unions cannot give money out of a union fund.

Now, let us just check it. Robert Asher, as I told you, is the President of AIPAC. His address is 5100 Oakmont Road, Highland Park, IL. That is not in the second district, not even in Chicago, but he is interested in the second district to the tune of $1,000.

Let me just read this list.
Mary Jane Asher, $1,000, Highland Park, IL.
Daniel Asher, $1,000, Highland Park, IL.
Howard David Sterling, Beverly Hills, CA, $250.
Louis A. Morgan, $500, Highland Park, IL.
Susan Asher, $1,000, Highland Park, IL, and on and on. I will not read it all to you; but I took these names, the Ashers, Robert Adler, $500.
Louis Morgan.
Irvin Wein, $500.

I took all those names and found that they were all on the Executive Committee of AIPAC, not living in Chicago, let alone in the Second Congressional District, but board members of AIPAC who were not supposed to try to finance campaigns, not legally. They do not have the legal authority.

When I added it all up, as you can, if you would like to check this, because everything I have mentioned is relative to you. AIPAC is listed in the FEC report of my opponent. All this is available to you.

Add it up. It shows the sum of $8,250 from individual contributors, itemized contributors, $6,750 was from these.

In other words, 82 percent. I am not saying that he got a few contributors who like AIPAC or love Israel to give him some money, nothing unusual at all about that, but not 82 percent of all of those contributions for people affiliated with AIPAC, one organization, not in the Second District, the primary purpose concerned the interest of a foreign nation.

Now, from PAC's, political action committees, people organized to give money to campaigns, he received from those $20,500. So I wanted to check to see what PAC's. Well, you have again, all of this is easy if you know your research, and I hope you are following me so you can practice some of this yourself. It is surprising what you learn sometimes, just in a little time.

This is the almanac of Federal tax, published right here in Washington. This is a reference book. It lists all the PAC's and their officers; but more than that, it groups them by purpose. If you have a good labor record, such as I do, you would want naturally to solicit funds from the labor unions, so they list all the labor unions and you can go solicit your money.

It also groups them by whether they are pro-Israel or not in this almanac of Federal PAC's, 1990.

Let us see. It says, `The emergence of a network of pro-Israel PAC's as an important source of campaign funds for Federal candidates has become an issue of intense controversy even among American Jews who want to promote Israel's security, but don't want to be perceived as being driven by a single issue.'

I did not say that. That is what the book says.

It goes on, `There is little doubt that contribution decisions are centralized either through a formal or informal arrangement,' and then it proceeds to list these pro-Israel PAC's.

It says, `It is well-documented that many of the pro-Israel PAC's were created with AIPAC's encouragement.'

AIPAC, despite its name, is not a PAC, but a lobbying organization. Under Federal election law, PAC's are deemed to be affiliated if they are established, directed, or controlled by a common organization or if they have the same officers, vendors, or contributors. Then it lists these pro-Israel PAC's affiliated with AIPAC.

So I took this list, you see, and compared it to his list of PAC contributors. The total he received was $20,500. Let us see how much of that $20,500 came from these pro-Israel PAC's affiliated with AIPAC, AIPAC of which most of you have never heard, but which influences who represents you in this august body.

Now, let us go and take a look.

PAC's, $5,000 to candidate for Congress from the Joint Action Committee PAC. The Joint Action Committee PAC, listed right here. Let me get the list here. Listed right here. Joint Action Committee PAC, Highland Park, IL, affiliated with AIPAC, a pro-Israel PAC, according to this almanac, this reference work, rather, that I did not write.

Washington PAC, $1,000 to Reynolds for Congress, Morris Amitay, treasurer, Washington, DC, in this list.

Multi-issue PAC, $1,000 Highland Park, IL, in this list.

Citizens Organization PAC, $5,000, Los Angeles, CA, in this list, I haven't got to the Second District yet, you notice.

Look at these names. Nothing says anything about pro-Israel in these names, obscure names. Why?

Citizens Organization PAC, Los Angeles, CA, $5,000.

Hudson Valley PAC, Spring Valley, NY, not in the Second District of Illinois, Spring Valley, NY, no steelmills up there, $1,500 Reynolds for Congress.

Americans for Good Government, $1,000, Jasper, AL, in this list.

East Midwood PAC, $250; Garden State PAC, Union, NJ, $1,000, in this list; Desert Caucus PAC, Tucson, AZ, $1,500, in this list; Heartland PAC, Cleveland, OH, $2,500, in this list.

[Page: H1345]

[TIME: 2020]

What does it all mean? It means of the $20,500 that he received from PAC's, $19,750 came from PAC's with obscure names, affiliated with AIPAC, an organization whose main concern is the interests of Israel, not America, be that interest good or bad, right or wrong, but a foreign government. That amounts to 96 percent of all his receipts from PAC's. That means practically all of that money in that purse or his purse, practically all came indirectly from AIPAC, more than $9 of every $10 of the money for one to challenge me in the Second District of Illinois, where Israel's interests are far from being primary.

Now, let me say something about my position regarding Israel that may explain the concern, but certainly does not justify a body with no legal right to do so whose primary concern is a foreign nation rather than the interests of America, trying to determine the outcome of an

American election for Congress. That, my friends, Mr. and Mrs. America, is dangerous, indeed.

Israel receives almost one-third of all the United States' foreign assistance, $3 billion in the foreign assistance bill, and usually $400 million or $500 million more tacked on here and there, roughly $3.5 billion a year. That is not the Government's money. That is your money, your tax dollars.

We do not have enough money to maintain full funding for student grants and student loans for those in need to attend the colleges of their choice, for which they are qualified, not enough money to create jobs programs for those pockets of poverty in our Nation, not enough funds for long-term Medicare for our senior citizens in need, but $3 1/2 billion of your tax dollars to one little nation, Israel, a nation with only about 3 1/2 million citizens. That means then that you are giving $1,000 a year to every man, woman, and child citizen of Israel. Think about that.

Since I am particularly concerned about the welfare of the third world, since it is the poorest part of our Earth, one on which we are dependent and benefit greatly, this Nation; we benefit greatly from the natural resources of the 45 sub-Saharan African nations. Now, while Israel only has 3 1/2 million citizens roughly, there are some 350 million citizens in the 45 sub-Saharan African nations.

How much do we give them out of our foreign aid? A $550 million only, which comes to, compared to the $1,000 per Israeli, $1.57. Our resources are there, but our money goes to Israel. It seems to me we should drop some of the pollen where we get the honey. Even bees know that.

My position is that that is upside down. We should give the larger amount to the larger group of people who are in greater need and from whom we benefit the most materially in Africa, give the $3.5 billion to Africa, and let the $550 million go to Israel, but more than that, $1.8 billion of that $3.5 billion is for war, military aid. Well, my God, Military aid? To Israel? A nation that holds in prison presently some 9,000 Palestinians unfairly, unjustly, many without charges? Military aid to a nation that in the past 3 years has killed unarmed, defenseless 650 men, women, and children of Palestine?

Why not better take that military aid and take it over to Zambia in Africa, give it to the African National Congress so they can be sufficiently armed to chase off the face of the Earth the last remaining vestige of fascism, the apartheid regime of South Africa? That is my position.

Someone said, `Well, Gus, you receive money from PAC's, almost always labor PAC's, but PAC's, organized labor unions. The checks often come out of Washington, DC. That is not the Second District. Why is that not the same?'

It is not the same because American trade unions do not represent the interests of a foreign power. They represent the interests of American workers. That is an American interest. Some 40,000 citizens of the Second District of Illinois are members of trade unions, because I said that that is an industrial district, and PAC contributions, while maybe from Washington, come on the recommendation and request of their local affiliate, the United Automobile Workers. The United Automobile Workers give you a contribution from here, but it is because of the recommendation from its region 4 back in my district. So it has a right to be involved, and its interests are not un-American. It is not putting the interests of another nation above its own. No comparison, indeed.

If I may, before concluding, point out this connection between this interest, this insidious interest, and the mass media in this country. You may think you know something about mass media, because you are exposed to it so in television, but really it is, in many ways, as obscure and mysterious as AIPAC.

Ask yourself who owns CBS. Who is the president of ABC? Who are the board members of NBC? Where does Tom Brokaw live?

You know where I live. You know what is my salary. You know my marital stautus. You know where I went to school. You know my views. You know my children's names.

You know Tom Brokaw far better than you know Gus Savage, or you think you do. Is he married? What is his salary? What are his views? For all you know, he may be one of those running around with a hood burning crosses, because you do not know. Powerful man. Controls your airwaves, determines whether Gus Savage can go on the air or not, determines what is said about Gus Savage, good or bad, right or wrong, true or false, unaccountable to you.

[Page: H1346]

[TIME: 2030]

You cannot fire him, you cannot unelect him. You did not pick him.

I want to say something about the campaign coverage, because it was rather strange. It may not be correlated by AIPAC, but the apparent influence of a network of reporters across this country and the major daily newspapers and the television stations operating in the same way, telling the same lies simultaneously, makes one wonder.

My campaign, the *Chicago Tribune*, that is the major daily newspaper, largest circulation in Chicago, has a Pulitzer Prize columnist named Mike Royko, who wrote a column during this campaign strongly condemning me, and falsely so.

He said in the column that I had phoned him and told him that what appears to be my concerns are really false. I am not really concerned about civil rights, racism, and so forth in America. I just use that to help stir people up.

He said when I told him that on the phone that he felt this, and then he told me what he said to me and what I said back and what he said, and so on. But the problem is, I never talked to Mike Royko in my life, by phone or otherwise. In other words, he made up the column.

When I protested to the editor of the *Chicago Tribune* and said, `Look, I never talked to this guy in my life. How could he write this falsehood? Would you ask him to retract it or explain it or prove it?'

Never, never, never a reply. Unaccountable.

The political editor of the *Chicago Sun Times*, same thing. Steve Neal. Same thing. Called me all kinds of names. I have never met him, never talked with him.

When you have, and I do not want to say that the people who may be part of such a network would be these columnists. Generally the white press would have at least one apparent African-American columnist to jump on an African-American too in case the African-American hollers too loud and says, `well, these columnists jumping on me are white.' So you have got a page in the *Chicago Tribune*, a raspberry in the *Washington Post*, and all, and that is typical. It is the same kind of columns.

I was on `Cross Fire' on CNN. Some of you may have seen it. And you saw what a time Robert Novak gave me. I am sure if you saw it you could see it was not fair. How much does he earn? Where is he married? Does he not attend church? Has he ever been a member of the Ku Klux Klan? I am not saying that he is. I am not saying that he is married. What are his sexual preferences? I know none of that.

All I am saying is we do not know anything about these powerful bosses or spokesmen or talking heads on television and columnists in the most powerful newspaper of our land. And democracy depends upon a free and fair press.

I held a hearing to try to save the Economic Development Administration that the President has asked to be eliminated. I held a hearing in Pennsylvania, the coal mining area, where because anthracite coal has such high sulfur content people have unemployment, are suffering unemployment in double digits. I held it in Chicago, because there the African-American community suffers unemployment in double digits and have not enjoyed the prosperity that other parts of the country has, that the country in general has enjoyed in the past 8 or 9 years. We need economic development projects in such areas.

I went into Chicago to hold one such hearing, trying to stir up interest in saving EDA, and the press would not even cover it. Not in Chicago.

I will tell you, I have been treated better by the press in Johannesburg, South Africa, than in Chicago, IL.

I sponsored the biggest set-aside in the history of this country, an amendment to the 1986 Defense Authorization Act, that could mean some $8 billion a year to disadvantaged minority-owned businesses. I am very proud of that. It is the largest set-aside of all the others combined.

During this campaign channel 2 in Chicago, the CBS affiliate, a reporter named Mike Flannery insisted right there on television that Gus Savage did not sponsor that legislation.

I said, `Well, wait a minute. Wait a minute. I will give you a Congressional Record. I will get it to you tomorrow. If you are wrong, would you go on your news show tomorrow and admit that you are wrong? And, of course, if I am wrong, go on there and point that out too.'

I sent him the Congressional Record showing, of course, that he was wrong. He never used it. Never another word. Unaccountable. Nothing I can do.

I am the sponsor of legislation for a third Federal building in Chicago, a project costing $153 million and employing some 50,000 people in the construction trades and the spinoff jobs that will result from that—$45 million of that amount in subcontract to small disadvantaged businesses.

On that same television interview show he insisted that I did not do that either. It is easy to ascertain whether I did or not. You have got a Congressional Record. Reporters are certainly familiar with it. Admit that that was a deliberate deceit.

Well, that kind of effort to disinform the electorate is also a danger to our democracy, and to the extent that it relates to activities such as the ones I have described from AIPAC, it makes you wonder are these connected up? In which case the danger would be enhanced.

Look at the strange attacks across this land on African-American leaders. You say, `Oh, well, that one was found guilty, and that one was found guilty.'

I do not mean whether they were guilty or innocent, but the intensity and the frequency with which they are pursued.

Finally, let me say that I hope I have given you enough information already to cause you some concern. We operate in an atmosphere today that is not favorable to civil rights and racial equality. You might call it high-technology racism, the kind of racism that would cause a movie like `Driving Miss Daisy' to be named the best movie of the year. `Driving Miss Daisy.' Because maybe there are those in America who would like to turn back race relations to the old days where blacks did do the driving and Miss Daisy rode in the back.

But those days, my friends, are gone forever. Some of us may have to drive Miss Daisy, but we do not love it. And it does not make a very good movie, for it is insulting to too large a segment of the American population at a time of high-technology racism—`Driving Miss Daisy.'

I wonder how my American Jewish friends would feel if there was a movie about during the Holocaust where some Jewish man who was compelled because of imprisonment or whatever the reasons under the Holocaust to be a chamber maid for some Nazi general, and the movie was about how much he enjoyed that, which of course would not have been true, any more than `Driving Miss Daisy,' how much he enjoyed that, and that movie received an Academy Award. I wonder how they would feel.

That is just how African-Americans in the main also feel. We are losing an understanding of each other, when we need to understand each other more than ever. Because America is losing its competitiveness in world trade. It has become a debtor rather than a creditor nation. And part of the reason is worsening race relations, where the number of male blacks in college is falling down. The number in prison is going up. Unemployment has remained at double digits for the past 10 years. More than 50 percent of black children live in single parent families. The black family is being destroyed to the disadvantage not just of blacks, but of all America.

[Page: H1347]

[TIME: 2040]

When we have a nation that operates in such a way as this high-technology racism that when a black becomes Miss America that the first thing that black feels it is necessary to say is that, `Being black is the least that I am;' if you were Irish, Swedish, Jewish and you happened to win Miss America, how would you feel if the Irish victor got up and said the least thing I am is Irish or Jewish, or the victor said the least thing I am is Swedish? Why does she feel such compulsion? It is because she is trying to survive in this high-technology racist society.

So they create an image of me, a myth, that is no more accurate, no more real than Heathcliff Huxtable.

In the South I understand after World War II—and I will tell you this little bit and I will be through—in the South after World War II they said that a black veteran, and back then in the South often lynch mobs would come after blacks, you see, and a lynch mob came after this black veteran. He still has his M-1, and he was a sharpshooter, shot down 17 of the mob before they got him. And guess what? You would think they would have taken him out and lynched him twice, but no they did not, they did not even arrest him. They did not even put him in jail. Instead they put him in the insane asylum because they wanted it to appear that he was crazy. And that is what they tried to do to many outspoken blacks who said what I have said today, they say he is just crazy, in order to keep you away from him, and try to smear you, but I tell you to check the facts and you will agree with me.

I hope the following column by Vernon Jarrett, from the *Chicago Sun-Times,* and a letter to the editor, of the *Chicago Tribune,* will help you understand my renomination in the recent, controversial primary election:

[FROM THE *CHICAGO SUN-TIMES*, MAR. 29, 1990]

Why Gus Savage Keeps Winning

(BY VERNON JARRETT)

What makes a man like Gus Savage keep running . . . and winning?

'Why would you [black] people want to keep a troublemaker like Gus in office, when you can elect a highly educated young man, a healer like Mel Reynolds?'

'How can you [meaning this columnist] tolerate that man's ranting and raving about racism when there are more moderate voices in your community?'

The above represents a summary of the questions from whites directed to me ever since Rep. Gus Savage was elected to Congress from the 2nd Congressional District.

Savage keeps winning because he has two ingredients that many black voters miss in most of Chicago's 'moderate' black leaders.

I speak from the experience of having participated in two campaigns to unseat Savage, who is in his fifth term.

Here's what I've learned from direct contact with black voters:

Savage's orations don't turn on that many people. They're with him because he 'always has had the guts to speak out,' to express our outrage against common injustices—while moderate blacks, as defined by whites, remain silent.

Gus may be strident, but he's not for sale. Even though black 'moderates' also win elections, their silence and cooperation with known enemies of black political empowerment has been sickening.

Example: In 1955, when a Mississippi mob lynched a teenage Chicagoan named Emmet Till, blacks throughout the nation demanded federal action. Yet Chicago's lone black congressman, William L. 'The Man' Dawson, refused to utter one strong word of protest. Dawson, a 'moderate,' was the late Mayor Richard J. Daley's black lieutenant.

It was a little band of standup crusaders, including Gus Savage and the late union leader Willoughby Abner of the NAACP, who picketed Dawson, the Congress and the White House and later met with Vice President Richard Nixon.

Dawson and Daley attempted to maintain silence by ordering hundreds of black precinct captains to take membership in the NAACP and control future NAACP elections. For years, all prospective candidates for the presidency of the local NAACP had to vow not to criticize the Machine.

Years later, the *Chicago Defender* could describe black members of the City Council as 'the Silent Six.' And shortly before the election of Mayor Harold Washington, it was not uncommon to see black aldermen not only remain silent, but also vote against black interests. On Nov. 30, 1980, it was pathetic watching nine blacks vote for a racist ward map concocted by Mayor Jane Byrne and Ald. Edward Vrdolyak (10th). The actual motion to accept that map was made by a 'moderate' black alderman and committeeman named Wilson Frost (34th), who was a Machine sponsor of Mel Reynolds.

At the same time, blacks are continuously presented Democratic Party slates of candidates who are out to curtail black political empowerment.

'If we are asked to ignore all the faults of our enemies and phony friends, why can't we do the same for an old friend that we know we can trust?' a Savage supporter asked me.

--

More at Stake

Chicago: As one of a handful of whites who supported the re-election of U.S. Rep. Gus Savage, I want to respond to the Tribune's unwarranted attacks on him.

There was much more at stake in this election than a simple race between Gus Savage and Mel Reynolds. The central question was one of self-determination of the mostly black voters in the district and whether they were going to be allowed to choose their own representation or return to the era of plantation politics.

As for your newspaper finding Mel Reynolds so attractive because he was a Rhodes scholar, note that Gus Savage attended law school.

Savage has fought racism all his life. He earned his way into Congress. His opponent has never been active in the black community or held any office. I had never heard of him until he ran for Congress two years ago.

The black community didn't start racial politics, and it is not up to the black community to end racial politics: Kevin Kitchen.

[Page: H1348]

END

# LEGAL COMPLAINT ON CROSSOVER VOTING

UNITED STATES DISTRICT COURT
NORTHERN DISTRICT OF GEORGIA
ATLANTA DIVISION
E. RANDEL T. OSBURN;
LINDA DUBOSE;
BRENDA LOWE CLEMONS;
DOROTHY PERRY;
WENDELL MUHAMMAD;

Petitioners

v.                                                    CASE NO.

CATHY COX, Secretary of State of Georgia;
LINDA LATIMORE, DeKalb County
Elections Supervisor;
LYNN LEDFORD, Gwinnett County
Elections Supervisor;
DENISE MAJETTE, Candidate,
4th US Congressional District,
DEKALB COUNTY, GEORGIA REPUBLICAN PARTY;
GEORGIA REPUBLICAN PARTY;
GEORGIA DEMOCRATIC PARTY;

Defendants

COMPLAINT FOR EQUITABLE RELIEFUNDER THE VOTING RIGHTS ACT AND THE UNITED STATES CONSTITUTION

JURISDICTION AND VENUE

1.

This is an action to enforce the Voting Rights Act of 1965, 42 U.S.C. 1973 and 42 U.S.C. 1988. This action alleges that the crossover voting of the Republicans in the 2002 4th US Congressional District Democratic Primary in Georgia impermissibly diminished and interfered with the voting strength of African American Voters in the District on account of race. This action alleges that the malicious Republican crossover vote violated the First, Fourteenth and Fifteenth Amendments of the United States Constitution and 42 U.S.C. 1983.

2.

Jurisdiction is invoked pursuant to 28 U.S.C. 1331, 1343 and 1367; Plaintiffs' action for declaratory and injunctive relief is authorized by 28 U.S.C. 2201 and 2202; and by Rules 57 and 65, F.R. Civ. P. Venue is proper pursuant to 28 U.S.C. 1391 (b).

3.

Malicious crossover voting occurs when one party invades another party'S primary to sabotage that party's choice of its own nominee for political office. The Republican Party voters crossed over and affected the outcome of the 4th US Congressional District 8/20/2002 Democratic primary.

4.

Incumbent Congresswoman CYNTHIA MCKINNEY and DENISE MAJETTE were the only two Democratic candidates in the August 20, 2002 Democratic Primary.

5.

The date of the official counties' declaration or certification of the result in dispute is August 24, 2002; however, the Secretary of State consolidated the counties' vote totals and certified the results for the 4th District US Congressional District on or about August, 27, 2002.

6.

The Defendants are:

Cathy Cox, Secretary of State, who consolidated the returns and certified the final vote;
Denise Majette, the only other candidate in the Democratic Primary for August 20, 2002;
Linda Latimore, the DeKalb County Elections Supervisor who certified the DeKalb County Elections returns;
Lynn Ledford, the Gwinnett County Elections Supervisor who certified the 4th district returns in Gwinnett County;
The Georgia Democratic Party;
The Republican Party of DeKalb County;
The Georgia Republican Party.

7.

Plaintiffs are E. Randel T. Osburn, Linda Dubose, Brenda Lowe Clemons, Dorothy Perry, Wendell Muhammad, all black democratic voters of the 4th US Congressional District.

COUNT 1

CONSTITUTIONAL VIOLATIONS

8.

Georgia law provides that a political party may hold its own primary to nominate its own candidates for the general election. O.C.G.A. 21-2-150 et seq. (Ex. A) The State Democratic Party has bylaws ensuring the loyalty of those participating in party affairs: "All members, officers, and subdivisions of the State Party, and those seeking to participate in Party Affairs, are subject to this Charter and the State Party Bylaws." Art. I, Sec, I, By laws of the State Democratic Party approved on 8/13/1994. (Ex B)

9.

In the Democratic Primary on August 20, 2002  CYNTHIA MCKINNEY received the majority of democratic votes. (Ex R) Of the overall Democratic vote on 8/20/2002 McKinney won approximately 61% (49,058 and Majette won an estimated 39% (31,112). (Ex. R) In South DeKalb which is majority black and the most heavily democratic area of the district, McKinney won every precinct except one (North Hairston) winning 75% of the South DeKalb vote. The ONLY reason that Congresswoman McKinney lost the election was because of the Republican crossover vote which accounted for over 50% (over 37,500 of her 68,612 votes) of the votes cast for Defendant Majette. Majette had a total of 68,612 votes and McKinney 49,058 votes.(Ex S) Therefore, the result of the election was the selection of a nominee other than the one preferred by a majority of the Democratic voters in the 4th US Congressional District.

10.

Over 37,500 Republican voters were allowed to illegally and unconstitutionally crossover into the Democratic primary election and vote for Defendant Denise Majette. As evidence of the strength of the Republican crossover vote there were 117,670 democratic ballots cast while there were only 5,594 Republican ballots cast in the August 20, 2002 primary. Thus, the Republican crossover votes constituted 32% of the total votes cast in the August 20, 2002 Democratic primary, completely distorting the purpose of the primary. In the 2000 primary in the 4th Congressional District there were 54,861 Democratic ballots cast and 8,689 Republican ballots cast. In 1998 there were 42,648 Democratic primary ballots and 21, 636 Republican ballots. (Ex E) In the 1996 primary there were 62,997 democratic votes and 29,312 Republican votes. (Ex D)

11.

1996 marked the beginning of a trend of high black DeKalb County voter turnout, reflecting the County's demographic changes which also began to effect the County's power relationships. As a result, DeKalb County became the engine for Georgia's statewide democratic vote.

12.

The Georgia and DeKalb Republican Party members conceived a plan to run a candidate in the Democratic primary, funded that candidate, and then encouraged Republican voters to crossover and vote for that candidate. (Ex. F)

13.

Denise Majette was that candidate. Denise Majette regularly met with and sought counsel from Republican party operatives both before and during her candidacy. The Republican backed Majette voted for extreme right wing Republican Alan Keyes in the 2000 Republican presidential primary.(Ex. F) Denise Majette supported Michael Bowers in the 1998

Republican gubernatorial primary that selected the Republican candidate to run against Governor Roy Barnes. (Ex. G) Denise Majette accepted campaign contributions from known Republicans and those known to encourage Republican crossover voting. (Ex. H) Denise Majette maintains many Republican beliefs and positions. (Ex. I)

14.

During the month of August, 2002 former Republican gubernatorial candidate Guy Milner convened at least one meeting of Republican leaders at his home to promote the Republican crossover for Denise Majette. The Republicans believed that they could force McKinney out with a crossover vote, leaving the Democratic party without the one candidate who inspired the party faithful to vote. Such a strategy would also have the effect of diluting black voting strength statewide as the Democratic Party has greatly benefitted from a heavy turnout in the 4th US Congressional District. (Ex. J)

15.

Republican commentators, i.e. Jim Wooten, of the Atlanta Journal-Constitution, openly promoted the crossover. (Ex. K) Majette's own campaign promoted the crossover vote and used it in their polling calculations. Phone banking and mailings targeted the white Republicans for crossover voting. (Ex. M) Mark Davis, a Republican Party operative, with operations based at the DeKalb Republican Party Headquarters, co-founded "goodbyecynthia.com", along with Bubba Head, which promoted the crossover vote. (Exs. N,L) Steve Schultz founded a federal PAC, New Leadership for DeKalb, which funded the website that advocated the Republican crossover vote. (Ex. O) Audrey Morgan, a Republican operative and Denise Majette contributor, circulated a letter promoting the crossover vote. (Ex. P)

16.

Numerous and prominent Republicans contributed to Denise Majette. Bernard Marcus, Bill Dahlberg and Robert Loudermilk contributed to Denise Majette. The Loose Group contributed large donations to the Majette campaign including $5,000 but gave the rest of its $55,000 in donations in Georgia to Republicans. (Ex. Q) The Business Industry Political Action Committee, BIPAC, gave 85% of its donations in the 2002 election cycle to Republican candidates, but managed to give Majette $1,000. (Ex. Q) Audrey Morgan, who authored the pro crossover vote mailing, contributed to the Majette campaign.

17.

The United States Supreme Court found in California Democratic Party v. Jones,530 U.S. 567 (2000) this nation has a tradition of political associations in which citizens band together to promote candidates who espouse their political views. "(T)he First Amendment protects 'the freedom to join together in furtherance of common political beliefs," Tashjian v. Republican Party of Connecticut, 479 U.S. 208, 214 (1986), which 'necessarily presupposes the freedom to identify the people who constitute the association, and to limit the association to those people only.'"Democratic Party of the United States v. Wisconsin ex rel. LaFollette, 450 U.S. 107, 122 (1981), quoted in California Democratic Party v. Jones, 530 U.S. 567,574 (2000). "In no area is the political association's right to exclude more important than in the process of selecting its nominee." Id. "(W)hen a State prescribes an election process that gives a special role to political parties, it ?endorses, adopts and enforces the discrimination against Negroes' that the parties .... bring into the process - so that the parties' discriminatory action becomes state action under the Fifteenth Amendment.'" California Democratic Party v. Jones 530 U.S. at 573. 18.

These Republican crossover votes in the Democratic primary race are unconstitutional and thus illegal: "permitting nonparty members to hijack the party" is unconstitutional. California Democratic Party v. Jones, 530 US 567,584 (2000).

19.

The First and Fourteenth Amendments to the United States Constitution forbid state practices "forcing political parties to associate with those who do not share their beliefs." CaliforniaDemocratic Party v. Jones, 530 U.S. at 585. The scheme employed here unconstitutionally "force[s] political parties to associate with - to have their nominees, and hence their positions, determined by - those who, at best, have refused to affiliate with the party, and, at worst, have expressly affiliated with a rival." California Democratic Party v. Jones, 530 U.S. at 577.

20.

In this case there was an unconstitutional "malicious" crossover as the DeKalb County Republican Party promoted the crossover and expended funds in support thereof and Defendant Majette also openly promoted the Republican crossover into the Democratic Primary. The malicious crossover voting here is the extraordinary exception that the lower court in Democratic Party of California v. Jones, 530 U.S. at 579, indicated would make a difference in deciding whether crossover voting was illegal. California Democratic Party v. Jones, 169 F.3d 646, 656 (9th Cir. 1999).

21.

The malicious crossover vote orchestrated in this case by the Republican Party violates PetitionerS' right of association under the 1st and 14th Amendments to the United States Constitution. "But a single election in which the party nominee is selected by nonparty members could be enough to destroy the party." California Democratic Party v. Jones, 530 U.S. at 579.

22.

The results in the 4th Congressional District are part and parcel of a continuing trend by the Republican Party to interfere with minority voting as further evidenced by the Florida presidential vote in 2000 and the Stoneview, DeKalb County, Georgia, vote in November, 2000.

COUNT 2

VOTING RIGHTS ACT (Section 2)

23.

Becasue of Georgia's documented history of racial discrimination in general and denial of voting rights to black citizens in particular, Georgia is subject to the jurisdiction of the 1965 Voting Rights Act. Indeed, as with most of the other states of the Old Confederacy (Alabama, Missouri, South Carolina, Tennessee, Texas and Virginia) they retain the open primary, which can be used to replicate the infamous outlawed white primary.

24.

Past elections and an analysis of the results in this election, as set out herein and incorporated herein by reference, show that Cynthia McKinney is the candidate favored by black and democratic voters in the 4th US Congressional District in Georgia. (Ex. R)

25.

Racially polarized bloc voting exists in Georgia today and was exhibited in Georgia's 4th US Congressional District Democratic Primary on August 20, 2002. Election results indicate that white voters voted in a bloc. (Exs. C,R)

26.

The result was that the white bloc vote, of both Republicans and Democrats, in the Democratic primary greatly diluted the black democratic vote, rendering it impotent.

27.

The Voting Rights Act has been violated where the "totality of circumstances" reveal that members of protected classes have less opportunity than other citizens to participate in the political process and elect representatives of their choice. Thornburg v. Gingles, 478 U.S. 43, 106 S.Ct. 2752, 2762 (1986).

28.

The malicious crossover has the effect of discriminatorily denying black voters the right to participate in the political process and to elect a democratic congressional candidate of their choice.

29.

Black voters in the 4th US Congressional District in Georgia are politically cohesive as evidenced by the fact that McKinney won all but one South DeKalb precinct with over 74% of the vote in those precincts.

30.

A Democratic primary candidate that is favored by the majority of black and democratic voters in the 4th US Congressional District can be defeated by white republican crossover bloc voting and white democratic bloc voting.

31.

The existing crossover results in the 4th US Congressional District in Georgia has the result of diluting the influence of black voters in electing a candidate of their choice on account of race in violation of Plaintiffs's rights guaranteed by Section 2 of the Voting Rights Act of 1965, as amended, 42 U.S.C. 1973.

32.

The current Georgia statutory scheme, governing primaries, as applied, has the purpose and effect of denying or abridging the right to vote on account of race in violation of Section 2 of the 1965 and 1973 Voting Rights Act: "No ... standard, practice, or procedure shall be imposed or applied by any State or political subdivision to deny or abridge the right of any citizen of the United States to vote on account of race or color."

33.

Plaintiffs have no adequate remedy at law other than this action for declaratory and injunctive relief. Plaintiffs are suffering irreparable injury as a result of the violations complained of herein and that injury will continue unless declared unlawful and enjoined by this Court.

COUNT 3

EQUAL PROTECTION

34.

On August 20, 2002 the State of Georgia conducted the Republican and Democratic Primaries for the 4th US Congressional District to nominate the respective parties' candidates for the November, 2002 General Election.

35.

There is no question that the Republicans held their primary and voted for their candidates without any interference.

36.

However, as set out above and incorporated herein by reference, the Republicans and their operatives, under color of law, conspired to deprive black democratic voters of their right to choose their candidate for the November, 2002 General Election.

37.

"The right to vote is protected in more than the initial allocation of the franchise. Equal protection applies as well to the manner of its exercise." Bush v. Gore, 531 U.S. 98, 104 (2000) 38. "It must be remembered that the ?right of suffrage can be denied by a debasement or dilution of the weight of a citizen's vote just as effectively as by wholly prohibiting the free exercise of the franchise."Gore v. Bush, 531 U.S. at 104, quoting Reynolds v. Sims, 377 U.S. 533, 555 (1964).

39.

Whatever procedures that are adopted by the States must be "consistent with its obligation to avoid arbitrary and disparate treatment of the members of its electorate." Bush v. Gore, 531 U.S. at 105.

40.

"The idea that one group can be granted greater voting strength than another is hostile to the one man, one vote basis of our representative government." Moore v. Ogilvie, 394 U.S. 814,819 (1963) See also Gray v. Sanders, 372 U.S. 368 (1963), The landmark case that was supposed to have killed the Georgia White primary and the County Unit system that led to the undercounting of black votes.

COUNT IV

42 U.S.C. 1983

41.

Plaintiffs hereby incorporate by reference the preceding paragraphs of this complaint.

42.

All Defendants, acting under color of state law, have deprived Plaintiffs of rights, privileges and immunities, secured to them under the Fourteenth Amendment to the U.S. Constitution and 42 U.S.C. 1983.

Wherefore, Plaintiffs request:

A. That this Court enter judgment declaring that malicious crossover voting is unconstitutional in violation of Section 5 of theVoting Rights Act;

B. That this Court enter a permanent injunction against the election results;

C. That this Court enter a permanent injunction against the certification of the vote in the 4th US Congressional District;

D. That the crossover votes be declared unconstitutional and invalid and McKinney declared the winner;

E. That this Court enjoin Defendants from conducting any elections where the use of malicious crossover voting is allowed.

F. To enjoin the November 5, 2002 General Election until this case is resolved;

G. That this Court retain jurisdiction of this case until a voting plan is in place that complies with the requirements of the Voting Rights Act, as amended.

H. That this Court award Plaintiffs their costs and attorneys fees pursuant to U.S.C. 1988.

I. That this Court grant Plaintiffs any further relief which may be necessary and proper.

I would like to add this update concerning Denise Majette:

### Former Georgia Congresswoman
### Denise Majette Faces Disbarment

Former Congresswoman Denise Majette, who once defeated former Congresswoman Cynthia McKinney, is facing disbarment due to Denise Majette "inexcusable" conduct regarding her legal billing practices, according to the *Atlanta Journal Constitution.*

The State of Georgia Bar Association is reportedly recommending that Majette , a private attorney, appear before the State Bar's disciplinary board on Friday if she wants to challenge the recommendation. The disciplinary panel will hear Majette's defense during the Bar's spring meeting at the Ritz Carlton Lodge at Reynolds Plantation.

After the Bar's disciplinary panel has heard Majette's defense, they will make a recommendation to the Georgia Supreme Court, which has the final word on whether an attorney deserves to be disbarred.

A so-called "special master" from the State of Georgia Bar Association is recommending that Majette resign. Special masters are appointed by the State Supreme court for the specific purpose of overseeing evidentiary hearings after a State Bar investigation discovers an ethics violation.

The special master in this case wrote that Majette's actions were both "unfortunate" and "disturbing". According to the special master, Majette has offered no evidence to rebut allegations of a former client as it relates to a disagreement over legal fees. The client accuses Majette of failing to account for fees already paid and submitting fraudulent bills.

Majette is a former Dekalb County State judge who defeated former Congresswoman Cynthia McKinney in a run for Congress in 2002. She resigned after only one term in Congress. In 2004 she mounted a run for Senate and lost.*

They rent you and then they make sure no one else wants to take out a lease when they're done with you.

---

\* See http://www.yourblackworld.net/2013/03/black-news/former-georgia-congresswoman-denise-majette-faces-disbarment/

Made in the USA
San Bernardino, CA
20 January 2018